MUSIC IN AMERICAN LIFE

Volumes in the series Music in American Life
are listed at the end of this book.

Bibliographical Handbook
of American Music

Bibliographical Handbook
of American Music

D. W. KRUMMEL

University of Illinois Press

Urbana and Chicago

Library of Congress Cataloging-in-Publication Data

Krummel, Donald William, 1929–
  Bibliographical handbook of American music / D. W. Krummel.
    p.   cm. — (Music in American life)
  Includes index.
  ISBN 0-252-01450-2 (alk. paper)
  1. Music—United States—Bibliography—Catalogs.   I. Title.
II. Series.
ML120.U5K78   1987   87-20597
780′92′2—dc19   CIP
                                                          MN

For Samuel and Marie-Louise Rosenthal

Contents

Acknowledgments

Those who use bibliographies will readily understand that scholarship without libraries is a contradiction in terms. I am particularly indebted to the Music Library at the University of Illinois, where all but a few of the books described here have been examined. I also owe thanks for checking out unusual titles to colleagues in the music and general library world, literally across the country.

Yeoman service has been provided by my graduate assistants, James Farrington (who was my main consultant on current popular music), Kara Messerly, Elizabeth Weisbrod, and Keith Eiten (who provided valuable help with the sources of band music and pictorial materials), as supported through the Research Board of the University of Illinois. William Shaman indulged me with sage counsel on diverse arcanities discographical, while Richard J. Colwell's expert guidance through the world of music education materials extended into an impressive range of related sources covering current activities and resources, so as to be truly invaluable. Aaron Appelstein's copyediting saved me from a number of blunders (and recognizing here his help may serve as a tribute to all brave copy editors who importune to work with bibliographers). At the University of Illinois Press it was also my privilege to work with Judith McCulloh, who offered support and encouragement in general along with monumental reassurance in matters concerning folk music in particular.

Indeed, the users of bibliographies will further recognize how the odd reference is often at once both the subtlest and the strongest kind of encouragement they can wish for. To numerous other colleagues over the past thirty-some years now — whose intelligence has been passed on in tones ranging from "here is something obscure I'll bet you don't know about and ought to, and now what do you know about that I don't?" on over to "how have you dared to see yourself as competent at all without having the faintest idea that this monument of scholarship even existed?" — I am profoundly grateful.

Urbana, Fall 1986

1

Introduction: American Music and Its Bibliography

American music has emerged as a field of study, beginning slowly at the turn of the twentieth century and growing in its momentum mostly over the past generation. Locally, regionally, and nationally, American music is being performed and noticed, informally, in concerts, and on recordings. Academic survey courses and special instructional programs on American music topics are flourishing. New organizations have been established, special conventions held, journals begun, and books and editions published, devoted to different aspects of American music. Nowhere is the field more readily to be appreciated than in music libraries. Fifty years ago most public and many academic music librarians rather wistfully declined to discard materials—of seemingly little or no value and interesting mostly as a reflection of the local or national past—even at the risk of being labeled pack rats. Today scholars, performers, and general readers are asking to look at those very materials.

Like many fields of study, American music has come to be defined in two ways: either narrowly and zealously or broadly and gregariously. The narrow definitions are prompted mostly by an idealistic search for a truly authentic national expression, whether based on the music of Native Americans, the early New England settlers, or the lower classes, or as a reflection of some melting-pot mixture that captures the quintessence of our society. The broad definitions, in contrast, typically seek to replace the concept of "American music" with one called "music in America," as they address the concerns of lowbrow, middlebrow, and highbrow; of composer, performer, listener, teacher, scholar, and administrator; of those who deal with the historic past and of those who work in the political present. In general, today's growing interest in American music embraces mostly the broad definition. Watchful scholars, however, continue to search for ways to recognize the evidence of a narrow definition, as passionate enthusiasts

1

seek to promote their favorite conceptions of it. Clearly, in any event, the interests are richly diversified.

Despite the flourishing activity, we still have no guide to the literature of the field. Citations must be gleaned from literally hundreds of bibliographical sources of varying degrees of respectability, all laying some claim to legitimacy of purpose and thoughtfulness of conception. The present survey provides a general overview of these reference works.

Inevitably the resulting survey of bibliographical sources will deal not only with documentary evidence but also with scholarly agendas and information networks. Devised in terms of this broad scope, organized through a systematic arrangement (which can be viewed in summary in the table of contents), and critically evaluated through brief introductory essays—as is the plan in the present text—the bibliographical record may help to legitimize the intellectual unity of American music, its coherence and its diffusion, its political objectives, and its conceptual peculiarities. The goal is to promote an awareness of what one might call the "bibliographical infrastructure" of American musical learning.

While the literature can be fitted together in several possible ways, the thought processes of scholars suggest the importance of two classic dichotomies. Instinctively scholars begin by asking when and where. Recognizing time and space—date and place—leads to an analysis of the bibliographical record first chronologically and second geographically (or, the appropriate extension of the latter of these, contextually). The other distinction, less instinctive but no less important, involves the message and the medium. Separating intellectual content from physical form, next, leads to the other major groupings of this study, the third in terms of the subject matter involved, the fourth in terms of the characteristics of the bibliographical medium.

Obviously the four are abstractions, embodied in any given specific instance. A song is characteristic of its historic and geographic community and will be embodied in documents of a certain kind. Historic periods produced their distinctive types of music in particular forms and from different areas; various documents embody different kinds of music from specific times and places. Our bibliography of Confederate musical broadsides fits in all four categories—the period is the Civil War, the area is the South, the genre is the solo song, the medium is the broadside. In other instances the overlap is subtler but nonetheless present. The whole exercise in classification may thus

2

seem redundant—except that those who look for musical documents do, or should, come to think in these terms. Occasionally the "search strategies" in work with American music are productive merely by being eccentric; more often, however, their logical conception works faster and better and provides useful and valid intellectual perspectives along the way.

While physical form is itself one of the basic distinctions in this plan, the major subdivisions need to be suggested at the outset. Four kinds of material make up the historical record of American music: (1) "music" itself, i.e., notated texts, whether printed or in manuscript, that reproduce the symbols read by performers or followed by listeners; (2) literary writings about music, whether books or essays and articles; (3) "ephemera," i.e., miscellaneous printed or manuscript materials, programs, announcements, brochures, pamphlets, and the like; and (4) sound recordings, whether archival or commercial. The first of these is the primary concern of chapters 1–6 and 9–12; the second and third are largely covered in chapter 14; the fourth is the exclusive topic of chapter 15.

Another distinction separates the searches for repertory and for imprints, both broadly defined. A repertory search is here seen as addressing the basic question of discovering the texts in the first place—and not only in terms of the musical medium for performers but also in terms of the subject matter for readers, or the content for listeners. A repertory search typically begins with no particular titles in mind or with a few examples to which more are to be added. ("What exists that I need to know about?") The term *imprints,* on the other hand, suggests a specific concern with printed editions, although it is intended here as applying to physical documents in general, whether manuscript or printed music, writings about music, ephemera, or sound recordings. ("I know that it exists: what more do I need to know in order to find a copy?") All searches ought to end up with "something to lay one's hands on," copies as available from a music store or bookshop, or in a library or archival collection. A repertory search seeks to find the titles in the first place; an imprint search suggests either a willingness to accept any edition devoted to the text in question or an intention to collect all of the editions in search of the most valid or authentic presentation of the text. Chapters 2–5 are devoted essentially to imprints, and only implicitly to repertory. Most of the subsequent chapters focus on repertory, or on imprints in specific discussions as noted.

Expert reference librarians and respected bibliographers necessarily have learned to develop special abilities in using bibliographical rec-

3

ords of one kind in searching for inquiries of another kind. Discographies help to find a song title; lists of critical reviews help to locate a program; folksong guides help to find a variant title of a printed edition. Imprint guides are often scanned in search of repertory. Inevitably the definition of a bibliography itself comes to be extended to include other reference sources—song indexes, publisher's announcements, composer "work lists," and other biographical sources— any of which may be needed to help us be specific about the object for which we are looking. In using the present book for its primary purpose, as a guide to sources, the reader must keep in mind the exact kinds of reference sources under immediate discussion—and often for purposes of considering what other kinds of reference sources may provide the critical evidence that is needed. Any exercise in bibliographical taxonomy is bound to succeed if its categories are rationally defined and thoroughly explained.

Particular attention should be paid to several discussions that typically begin, "Among the lists on this topic are. . . ." The citations that follow are a selection of representative titles intermixed with the especially useful or respected ones. While many topics still await their first bibliography, other topics have been covered many times, often less than definitively. It is simply not possible to list every piano repertory guide, every "works list" in composers' biographies, every publisher's announcement of recent American compositions. Occasionally a single happy bibliography can be cited that covers them all; usually the picture is more complicated. The ideal objective would be to inform the reader of what major bibliographies there are, what supplementary ones there are, how they fit together, and what to do when they do not. The task of spelling out all of this explicitly would be quite overwhelming. Better here to suggest what there is and allow readers to work from there.

Bibliographies and reference lists often appended to prose texts make the latter appear more authoritative and helpful. Even the shabbiest of potboilers will typically end up with some presentation at the end—and often as not these trappings of scholarship prove surprisingly (even disgustingly) useful. There is no shortage of such lists, often imaginatively and admirably conceived. Particularly important are occasional works cited here that are not primarily bibliographies at all, but that include a concise bibliographical essay on sources or are laced with references that make them far superior to the narrowly conceived lists. The gray area of bibliographically useful prose texts is vast; almost necessarily, it is recognized inconsistently in the present book.

Several deviations from conventional bibliographical practice need to be mentioned. Some titles have been cited without the benefit of inspection, as noted by a parenthetical reference to the source. A few introductory prose texts mention authors' names in passing without further particulars: the full citations scarcely belonged in the text, and the person searching for material in the area might find it useful to know about the item. (General biographical sources with a small proportion devoted to American biographies, covered here in chapter 8, are a case in point.) Standard book numbers (ISBN) or, alternatively, periodical numbers (ISSN) or, in their absence, Library of Congress card numbers (LC) are included in the citations, insofar as the entry practices used here will often deviate from cumbersome formulations prescribed in cataloguing practice; and regular rather than inverted name forms have been used in the hope that the text may be read and pondered perhaps even more than it is strategically consulted.

The bibliographical search remains a key process in the growth of our awareness of our country's musical heritage. Whether we are addressing the narrow questions of our American musical identity or the broad range of musical activities and experiences that have taken place in the United States, we need to have recourse to the historical evidence. Above all, seeing how the citations fit together helps us uncover the riches we have and suggests the useful sources we are still missing. It is always stimulating to discover what still needs to be done. Alas, it may also be painfully obvious how much the present compiler has missed in this overview. What started out here as a medium-sized pamphlet is already a small book, and the number of possible addenda (some of limited relevance and usefulness, others likely very important) is probably very great. If readers end up recognizing that there is much more to the field of American music, its literature, and its potential than has previously been appreciated, the purpose of this brief guide will have been fulfilled.

CHRONOLOGICAL PERSPECTIVES

Recognizing a historical context helps both in finding and in understanding music. Often we need nothing more than a broad general time period, such as we can usually infer from the style of the music or from a knowledge of the composer's career. Often we may also know or be able to uncover a precise date of composition, copyright, or printing. Clearly the date, whether approximate or specific, is one of the most important elements in any bibliographical search. The simpler and less arguable the statement, the more we have to go on: a firm date of 1897 is considerably more helpful than a likely date of "around 1900."

Chronology is also a useful starting point for this book, insofar as the present state of our bibliographical record can be meaningfully divided into three periods. Broadly speaking, music published before 1826 may be said to have benefited from two "generations" of scholarship, music from the remainder of the nineteenth century from none, music of the twentieth century from one. For the advanced state of our knowledge of the early period, we are indebted to the legendary Oscar Sonneck, who with Germanic thoroughness saw only one way to proceed: start at the beginning, like any good historical scholar, and expect others to be inspired or compelled by the quality of your good work to continue. Unfortunately, little has been done to continue Sonneck's good work (a fact that may suggest many things, of course, none of which one particularly likes to think about). This notion of "generations" of scholarship seems simplistic, considering that much early music was issued without any explicit publication date at all. It is nonetheless fundamental to our understanding of where we stand today.

The concept of "generations" is also particularly important to those who are scrupulous in bibliographical matters, since important new discoveries still turn up after the third and fourth generations. Bibliographical scholarship is showing in more and more ways that there is rarely such a thing as a true duplicate and that the presence of variants provides us with important historical insights into how music was actually used. Librarians today like to speak of materials as being "under bibliographic control"—a useful planning concept that, for instance, enables us to say that the early period is under good control, the middle period under next to no control, the recent one under fair control. But the term also suggests a finality to our bibliographical record that simply will, or ought, never exist, at least in a dynamic scholarly environment. Finding music from 1765 or 1815, in any event, is today likely to be easier than finding music from 1915; and finding music from 1865 is likely to be hardest of all.

At this point it is necessary to introduce the most disastrous obfuscation of all music bibliography: the term *sheet music*. We all know what it is—more or less. But nobody has ever successfully defined it, since it means different things to different people—to the 1880 parlor organist or the 1930 barroom pianist, for instance, or to today's music merchant, pop combo performer, art-song specialist, opera accompanist, or scholarly hymnologist. As a general rule, the more professional the musicians the less likely they are to use the term, except in a neutral kind of disparagement (instead, they talk about the "music" itself). The term nevertheless may usefully be defined positively, which is to say quantitatively: all music under ten (or six or twenty-five or however many) pages and larger than 9″ by 12″ (or 5″ by 8″ or whatever) is sheet music. Or it may be defined negatively, which is to say subjectively: anything insubstantial that is deemed not worth bothering with can be relegated to the pile called sheet music.

In all truth the decision has been made more often than not in self-defense: by any definition the quantity of American sheet music is stupendous. The present discussions thus involve two kinds of bibliographies: those by scholars who chose to confront the sheet music by bravely excluding it, however inconsistently and often snobbishly; and those by scholars who with equal bravery chose to confront the sheet music by including it, with no view to the artistic quality or historical significance in question and at the risk of being overwhelmed by it.

8

2

Music before 1825

1698–1800

Published music was first issued in the American colonies in 1698, with the ninth edition of the famous Bay Psalm Book, earlier editions having appeared without musical notation. Sacred music — tunebooks as well as sermons with musical references and tutors in the rudiments of music — dominated the music production of the early American press into the last decades of the eighteenth century. Slowly secular music began to appear, words only at first, in books or in newspapers or separately on broadsides; later with the notation printed from wood or metal cuts, movable type, or engraved plates; and finally as engraved sheet music, beginning in the late 1780s and proliferating with the establishment of music shops adjacent to the theaters in the urban centers of Boston, New York, Philadelphia, and Baltimore. The titles in question are covered in two great landmarks of bibliography: Evans and Sonneck-Upton.

The former of these, begun in 1903, is arranged annalistically, year by year up through 1800. Most sheet music is undated, and hence it is automatically excluded — at least from the basic set as compiled by Evans himself and by his early successors. One of the continuing virtues of the set has been the availability of its contents in microform. We have not only the citations but even the books themselves — apart from some of the evasive items that are unlocated or otherwise unavailable, and if perhaps not always the best exemplar as established by later scholarship, at least a copy. The pervasive value of the set is further attested by the supplements and complements — both through the general lists officially recognized as part of the main set itself as cited by Tanselle and through the special music conspectuses by Hixon (1970) and Heard (1975).

Charles Evans. *American Bibliography: A Chronological Dictionary of All*

9

Books, Pamphlets, and Periodical Publications Printed in the United States of America from the Genesis of Printing in 1639 Down to and Including the Year 1820. Vol. 1, 1639–1729. Chicago: Privately printed at the Blakely Press, 1903. LC 3-32909.

—Vol. 2, 1730–50. Chicago: Blakely Press, 1905.

—Vol. 3, 1751–64. Chicago: Blakely Press, 1906.

—Vol. 4, 1765–73. Chicago: Hollister Press, 1907.

—Vol. 5, 1774–78. Chicago: Columbia Press, 1909.

—Vol. 6, 1779–85. Chicago: Columbia Press, 1910.

—Vol. 7, 1786–89. Chicago: Columbia Press, 1912.

—Vol. 8, 1790–92. Chicago: Columbia Press, 1915.

—Vol. 9, 1793–94. Chicago: Columbia Press, 1926.

—Vol. 10, 1795 and 1796/A–M. Chicago: Columbia Press, 1929.

—Vol. 11, 1796/N–Z and 1797. Chicago: Columbia Press, 1931.

—Vol. 12, 1798 and 1799/A–M. Chicago: Columbia Press, 1934.

—Vol. 13, 1799/N–Z and 1800, ed. Clifford K. Shipton. Worcester: American Antiquarian Society, 1955.

—Vol. 14, Index, by Roger Pattrell Bristol. Worcester: American Antiquarian Society, 1959.

[Reprints of the above]. New York: Peter Smith, 1941–59. ISBN 0-8108-0002-0; Metuchen, N.J.: Mini-Print Corp., 1967.

Roger Pattrell Bristol. *Index of Printers, Publishers, and Booksellers Indicated by Charles Evans in His American Bibliography.* Charlottesville: University Press of Virginia, 1961. LC 61-64087.

Clifford K. Shipton and James E. Mooney. *National Index of American Imprints through 1800: The Short-Title Evans.* Worcester: American Antiquarian Society; Barre, Mass.: Barre Publishers, 1969. ISBN 0-8271-6908-6. The entries in Evans are here formulated in cataloguing practices of the day and rearranged in a single alphabet. When one lacks an Evans number or a publication date, this is generally the first place to check in a search of the Evans bibliography.

Roger P. Bristol. *Supplement to Charles Evans' American Bibliography.* Charlottesville: University Press of Virginia, 1970. ISBN 0-8139-0287-8. [A preliminary "checking edition" appeared in 1962.] The index, issued separately (ISBN 0-8139-0037-8), covers authors and titles in one alphabet and printers, publishers, and booksellers in a second.

Additional published addenda and corrigenda are cited in Tanselle, *Guide to the Study of United States Imprints* (1971; 753 below), pp. 1–3. Other later addenda include the lists of "Additions and Corrections to Bristol's Supplement to Evans" that appear in the *Proceedings of the American Antiquarian Society*, 82 (1973), 46–64, with several music titles; 83 (1974), 261–76; and later.   [1.

Donald L. Hixon. *Music in Early America: A Bibliography of Music in Evans.* Metuchen, N.J.: Scarecrow, 1970. ISBN 0-8108-0374-7. A rearrangement of Evans's music entries grouped as (1) main entries for items then available in the microprint edition, (2) main entries for items not then available, and (3–6) name, title, and Evans numerical indexes.   [2.

Priscilla S. Heard. *American Music, 1698–1800: An Annotated Bibliography.* Waco, Tex.: Baylor University Press, 1975. LC 75-14907. Another transcript of the Evans music entries, in three chronological series, for books with musical notation, books about music, and books not in the microprint series.   [3.

Evans's music counterpart is Sonneck, whose 1905 list covers sheet music along with other secular music, or at least the holdings of the major repositories that he could manage to examine. Upton vastly expanded the number of titles in his 1945 revision. Both compilers saw their mandate as one of describing secular music—as their title suggests—and both compilers defined their scope in terms of the particular collections that they could inspect. To be sure, they did not see themselves as limited to particular forms of materials, and thus their citations are mostly for sheet music in the generally recognized sense—music of two to six pages, in large folio format, and arranged for keyboard alone or solo singer accompanied. The compilers also cite occasional broadsides, opera librettos, manuscript copies, and song anthologies, the last of these both as units in their own right and through individual entries for their contents. Furthermore, working from newspaper notices, publishers' addresses, and textual references, Upton, especially, was able to assign conjectural dates to much of the undated sheet music—which dates are picked up in Bristol's 1970 supplement to Evans and thus also in the Shipton-Mooney *Short-Title Evans*, in the Hixon and Heard indexes, and in the microform reprints of the contents. Nonetheless, over half of the entries in Sonneck-Upton, as well as those additional titles picked up by Wolfe, are still outside the purview of the so-called Evans network; the set remains an indispensable source.

O. G. Sonneck. *Bibliography of Early Secular American Music.* Washington: Printed for the author by H. L. McQueen, 1903. LC 5-36554.
————. *A Bibliography of Early Secular American Music (18th Century).* Revised and enlarged by William Treat Upton. Washington: Library of Congress, Music Division, 1945. LC 45-35717. Repr., with a new introduction by Irving Lowens. New York: Da Capo, 1964. ISBN 0-306-70902-3. An alphabetical title listing of about 800 works, supplemented by lists of writings about music, composers, songsters, first lines, patriotic music, and libretti.   [4.

Wolfe, *Secular Music in America* (1964; see 6 below). Appendix 1 (pp. 1001–18, in vol. 3) lists 189 additional eighteenth-century imprints, while app. 2 (pp. 1019–21) reassigns about 140 titles in Sonneck-Upton to the nineteenth century.

Other guides cover the particular genres and forms of eighteenth-century American musical documents, notably among them Anderson on political song texts (1977; 462 below), Britton on published tunebooks and sermons that mention music (1949; 419 below), Rogal (1975; 411 below) on hymnody, Fuld and Davidson (1980) and Keller (1981) on secular manuscripts (464 and 465 below), Lowens on songsters (1976; 463 below), Clark (1974; 267 below) on piano music, Camus (1976; 270 below) on military music sources in general, and Specht (1974; 236 below) on choral music.

1801–25

The first years of the nineteenth century have only recently begun to be covered, through sets that are clearly modeled on the two great eighteenth-century lists. The series started by Shaw and Shoemaker is essentially a continuation of Evans but is based mostly on reports as submitted to the National Union Catalog and as assembled earlier by the WPA Historical Records Survey, not on personal inspection. Again a microform edition of the contents is being made available. Wolfe is basically an extension of Sonneck-Upton, happily with its entries now arranged by composer and with better-conceived indexes. His dating assignments seem to have been largely overlooked by the compilers of the annalistic Shaw-Shoemaker series; in any event, it seems likely that no more than 10 percent of the titles in Wolfe are also to be found, somewhere or other, in Shaw-Shoemaker.

Ralph R. Shaw and Richard H. Shoemaker. *American Bibliography: A Preliminary Checklist for 1801 [–1819].* 19 vols. New York: Scarecrow, 1958–63. LC 58-7809. An alphabetical listing by main entries, with locations or sources.
—*Addenda, List of Sources, Library Symbols* [i.e., vol. 20]. 1965. LC 65-13546.
—*Title Index* [i.e., vol. 21]. 1965. LC 65-22748.
—*Corrections, Author Index* [i.e., vol. 22]. 1966. LC 58-7809.
—*Printers, Publishers and Booksellers Index, Geographical Index,* comp. Frances P. Newton [i.e., vol. 23]. Metuchen, N.J.: Scarecrow, 1983. ISBN 0-8108-1607-5.

A Checklist of American Imprints for 1820 [–1829]. Compiled by Richard H. Shoemaker [later, assisted by Gayle Cooper]. New York; Metuchen, N.J.: Scarecrow, 1964–71. LC 64-11784.
————. *Title Index,* comp. M. Francis Cooper. 1972. ISBN 0-8108-0513-8.
————. *Author Index, Corrections, & Sources,* comp. M. Francis Cooper. 1973. ISBN 0-8108-0567-7.

A Checklist of American Imprints for 1830– . Compiled by Gayle Cooper [later, Scott Bruntjen, Carol Rinderknecht (Bruntjen), and others]. Metuchen, N.J.: Scarecrow, 1972– . LC 64-11784.   [5.

Richard J. Wolfe. *Secular Music in America, 1801–1825: A Bibliography.* New York: New York Public Library, 1964. LC 64-25006. A monumentally valuable listing of over 10,000 titles, with excellent indexes.   [6.

D. W. Krummel. "American Music, 1801–1830, in Shaw-Shoemaker (American Music Bibliography, 5)," *Yearbook for Inter-American Musical Research,* 11 (1975), 168–89.   [7.

There are no specific continuations of the several special genre lists cited above, although the Lowens songster bibliography (1976; see 463 below) extends to 1821, while Richard Crawford's forthcoming successor to Britton's list of sacred music editions will extend through 1810.

3

Music from 1826 to 1900

Music Bibliography

It is still not clear exactly when the U.S. production of published music began to increase by leaps and bounds. However, by the end of the nineteenth century, clearly (1) a great deal of music of all kinds had been published, although (2) we really do not know how much there was, because (3) it is under practically no bibliographical control, in the absence of even a first generation of work on most of it. Herein lies the greatest challenge to America's music bibliographers today. We do know that sheet music began to be deposited more extensively for copyright about 1846. Beginning with the centralization of registration at the Library of Congress in 1870, we have a record of new titles—at least those that were being copyrighted. Unfortunately, many of the depository copies themselves are either lost or dispersed and unrecoverable in the Library of Congress today. Furthermore, a substantial amount of music was never copyrighted and hence will usually appear in undated editions. Occasionally printing variants or manuscripts—never submitted for copyright at all—are our most valuable sources.

Several contemporary bibliographies are worth knowing about for their general coverage of the period. In 1851, for instance, the founding father of American librarianship, Charles Coffin Jewett, made great and impressive plans for a library program at the newly established Smithsonian Institution. Among these was a centralized national bibliography of copyright registrations. His Washington career was, unfortunately, a short and unhappy one, which left us with transcripts of the entries for five years, based on the deposits he received and not on those from the various district courts around the country.

Fortunately most of the manuscript copyright ledger books for the district court registration period before 1871 are preserved, the bulk of them in the Rare Book Room at the Library of Congress, as de-

15

scribed in G. Thomas Tanselle, "Copyright Records and the Bibliographer," *Studies in Bibliography*, 22 (1969), 77–124. The record books from after 1871 are also extant in the Copyright Office. Apart from several transcripts (such as the one prepared for the publisher Leo Feist about 1910), the copyright records are untouched sources for the music bibliographer — obviously indispensable for the period after 1870, likely as well after 1846, when music first began to be registered and deposited in significant quantities.

Jewett's scrupulously formulated entries stand in contrast to those in the other great general music bibliography of the nineteenth century. The massive *Complete Catalogue* of 1871 lists somewhere between 80,000 and 100,000 items of music offered for sale by those major publishers that made up the U.S. Board of Music Trade. In her masterful introduction to the reprint of this catalogue, Dena Epstein explains that the stock of these firms represents the major output of the nation up to this time, thanks to the recent action of several of the major firms (Oliver Ditson in particular) in buying up the small ones. While my own experience suggests that Epstein is correct about the catalogue's completeness, the frugality of its citations and the unconvincing classification scheme and arrangement of its entries all lead one to feel a great need for more.

[Charles Coffin Jewett.] "Appendix to the Librarian's Report: Copyright Publications Deposited prior to 1850 . . . Part II: List of Musical Compositions"; and ". . . for 1850 . . ."; in the *Fifth Annual Report of the Board of Regents* (Washington: Smithsonian Institution, 1851), pp. 223–33 and 286–322. In the government publications "serial set," this is "Senate, Special Session, March 1851: Miscellaneous." In all, 554 music copyright registrations are cited, beginning as early as 1846 but mostly from 1850, mostly from East Coast publishers, arranged by composer with no indexes.   [8.

Complete Catalogue of Sheet Music and Musical Works . . . 1870. New York: U.S. Board of Music Trade, 1871. Repr., with a new introduction by Dena J. Epstein. New York: Da Capo, 1973. ISBN 0-306-71401-9. Page 2 lists the fifty-six categories in the classification scheme, along with the twenty members of the board at this time. A variant presentation of the introduction also appears as "Music Publishing in the Age of Piracy: The Board of Music Trade and Its Catalogue," MLA *Notes*, 31 (1970), 7–29.   [9.

Pre-1900 musical imprints and the repertory they represent are

also cited in profusion through many of the titles discussed in subsequent chapters—local imprint lists in chapter 6 (of which the Harwell and Hoogerwerf Confederate lists and Epstein's Chicago list are
invaluable), secular songs in the chronological overviews in chapter
11, early sacred music in general in chapter 12, source materials in
general in much of chapter 13 and, for collectors' and bibliographers'
purposes, much of chapter 16. Other bibliographies in which the
nineteenth-century emphasis is crucial include Gillespie (1984; 280
below) on piano music, Curtis (1981; 278 below) on organ music,
Toll (1974; 249 below) and Root (1981; 254 below) on dramatic music,
and Janta (1982; 176 below) on Polish music. There are also three
studies specifically devoted to the music of the period:

Willard A. Heaps and Porter W. Heaps. *The Singing Sixties: The Spirit
of Civil War Days Drawn from the Music of the Times.* Norman: University of Oklahoma Press, 1960. LC 60-7739. An extended survey
built around the sentiments expressed in the texts of about 1,500
songs of the period as cited in the index.   [10.

Philip S. Foner. *American Labor Songs of the Nineteenth Century.* Urbana:
University of Illinois Press, 1975. ISBN 0-252-00187-7. A historical
discussion of the genre, with transcriptions of selected words and
music and an index of about 1,000 "Song Titles and First Lines"
(pp. 335–46).   [11.

Pamela Bowden. "Regional Music Publishing of the Civil War Era:
An Analysis and Transcript of the Copyright Entries." Master's
thesis, University of Illinois, Urbana, 1986. A transcript and discussion of 2,541 musical works, published 1860–66 and registered
for copyright in district courts other than those for Boston, New
York, Philadelphia, and Chicago; with title, publisher, and composer
indexes.   [12.

Book-Trade Bibliography

As records of our nation's music publishing output, the two catalogues
mentioned above from the 1850s and 1871 are for better or worse
our successors to Sonneck-Upton and Wolfe. The successors to Evans
and Shaw-Shoemaker are better known but equally unsatisfactory.
Orville Roorbach and James Kelly provide contemporary listings of
the output of the American book trade up to 1871. It is not entirely

clear today when music was considered as coming from the book trade and for what reasons, although the transcripts of the music entries, thanks to the recent music library program at Kent State University, should enable us some day to address this question. The minimal citations in Roorbach and Kelly are also less than we might wish for, but this is rarely a major problem since practically everything they list consists of book-trade publications, which almost always end up in catalogued library collections and thus in the *National Union Catalog: Pre-1956 Imprints* (1968–81; see 452 below).

American book-trade bibliography came to be soundly established in 1871, while the concomitant rise of the American public library led to an increasing concern for cataloguing practices. Inevitably the quality of the citations improved noticeably, as reflected in the weekly listings in *Publishers Weekly* and the cumulations in the *American Catalogue of Books*. The music entries in the *American Catalogue* may be nowhere collected as a group, but the numerous music subject headings testify to a moderately impressive musical activity of the American book trade, mostly of biographies, histories, collected essays, and other literary texts. It should be remembered, however, that even more books about music, and a wide range of other quasi-sheet-music publications came neither from the book nor from the music trade: hymnals and sacred service books issued by churches, songbooks issued by social organizations, instruction books issued by music shops, and important musical texts that appeared incidentally in periodicals and books.

Orville A. Roorbach. *Bibliotheca Americana, 1820–61.* New York: Author, 1852–61. LC 4-8028-31. Repr. New York: Peter Smith, 1939. LC 39-27504. Vol. 1, 1820–51; vol. 2, 1852–55; vol. 3, 1855–58; vol. 4, 1858–60. The music titles are transcribed in the lists below. [13.

Karen Dempsey. "Music and Books about Music in Roorbach's *Bibliotheca Americana.*" Unpublished paper, Kent State University, Department of Library Science, 1972. (Marco 0265) [14.

Mary Jo Kuceyeski. "Music Titles in *Bibliotheca Americana* 1852–61: A Preliminary Checklist." Unpublished paper, Kent State University, Department of Library Science, 1975. (Marco 0823) [15.

James Kelly. *American Catalogue of Books Printed . . . from January 1861 to January 1871.* New York: Wiley, 1866–71. LC 4-8032. Repr. New York: Peter Smith, 1938. LC 38-29060. [16.

David Elsass. "Music in Kelly's *American Catalogue of Books,* 1861–71." M.A. paper, Kent State University, 1972. (Heintze 10; *RILM* 1972:44) [17.

American Catalogue of Books. New York: Publishers Weekly, 1876–1910. LC 1-15566. Repr. New York: Peter Smith, 1941. LC 42-2938. According to the introduction, "The Catalogue aims to include all books . . . published in the United States . . . in print, and for sale . . . July 1, 1876. The exceptions [include] sheet music . . ., the reasons for the exclusion of which were obvious"—also understandably lamentable but nonetheless disappointing. In time the set came to be transformed from a listing of books in print to one of new publications. The thirteen vols. include authors, titles, and subjects, the last sometimes interfiled and sometimes filed separately at the end, as follows: vols. 1–2, 1876; vols. 3–4, through June 1884; vols. 5–6, through June 1890; vols. 7–8, through June 1895; vols. 9–10, through Dec. 1899; vol. 11, through Dec. 1905; vol. 12, through Dec. 1907; vol. 13, through Dec. 1910. [18.

John Weeks Moore. *A Dictionary of Musical Information.* Boston: Ditson, 1876. LC 2-22988. "A List of Modern Musical Works Published in the United States" appears on pp. 187–211, with brief citations of title, author, and often date for about 1,500 books about music, method books, anthologies, songbooks, and hymnals. [19.

Periodical Bibliographies

Nineteenth-century music periodicals are covered in the Wunderlich and the Weichlein lists, also by Davison. Analytical guides to periodical contents include Poole's monumental index, its less heroic but more usable *Nineteenth-Century Readers' Guide,* the sprawling *Early American Periodicals Index,* and the more finely delimited and scholarly 1957 Lowens and 1971 Mussulman indexes.

Charles Wunderlich. "A History and Bibliography of Early American Music Periodicals, 1782–1852." Ph.D. diss., University of Michigan, 1962. A list of titles comprises pp. 304–655. [20.

William J. Weichlein. *A Checklist of American Music Periodicals, 1850–1900.* Detroit: Information Coordinators, 1970. (Detroit Studies in Music Bibliography, 16.) ISBN 0-911772-39-3. An alphabetical list of 309 titles, with chronological and geographical registers. [21.

M. Veronica Davison. "American Music Periodicals, 1853–1899." Ph.D. diss., University of Minnesota, 1973. An annotated list of nearly 300 periodicals, arranged chronologically with varied information on the contents and several useful indexes. [22.

William F. Poole. *Poole's Index to Periodical Literature.* Boston: Norton, 1852. LC 2-9535. Rev. ed., with suppls. Boston: Houghton, 1891–1908. LC 2-9537, suppls. 2-9538, 2-9542, 3-4428, 8-11725. Repr. New York: Peter Smith, 1938. LC 38-32445. The revised ed., which subsumes the 1st, includes music entries accessible through composers' names, through general subject headings like "Music" and "Songs," and through specific headings. The titles below are also helpful. [23.

Marion C. Belland and Jean C. Bacon. *Poole's Index: Date and Volume Key.* Chicago: American Library Association, Association of College and Reference Libraries, 1957. LC 57-7157. A correlation of Poole's numbering plan with the numbers on the periodicals themselves.
[24.

C. Edward Wall. *Cumulative Author Index for Poole's Index to Periodical Literature, 1802–1906.* Ann Arbor: Pierian Press, 1971. ISBN 0-87650-006-8. [25.

Nineteenth-Century Readers' Guide to Periodical Literature, 1890–1899. New York: Wilson, 1944. LC 44-5439. Actually devoted only to the final decade of the century, serving as a continuation of Poole. Music entries are accessible through personal names and subject headings. [26.

Early American Periodicals Index to 1850. New York: Readex Microprint, 1964. LC 65-594. First planned in 1934 by Professor Oscar Cargill at New York University, what came to be known as the "Capital I" index covered some 1,820 periodicals, as listed in *Pamphleteer Monthly,* vol. 1, nos. 7–8 (1940). Nurtured for many years by Professor Nelson Adkins, the card files were eventually filmed and published in eight boxes of microcards. The 650,000 cards are organized in five categories, of which Microcard series E, on 14 cards, is devoted to "Songs" and includes about 8,000 authors, composers, titles (for anonymous works), and first-line entries. The "General Articles" category includes author and subject entries, musical genres, proper names, and other topics among them (cards F 226–50 in the microprint series). Other series cover poetry, book reviews, fiction, and short stories. The *Index* is hardly reassuring in either its scholarship or its convenience of use, but the extent of its coverage inevitably makes it a source one would feel it necessary to consult.   [27.

Irving Lowens. "Writings about Music in the Periodicals of American Transcendentalism," *Journal of the American Musicological Society,* 10 (1957), 71–85. Also in his *Music and Musicians in Early America* (New York: Norton, 1964), pp. 249–63, 311–21. Built around "A Check-List of Writings about Music in the Periodicals of American Transcendentalism (1835–50)," comprising 183 entries in seven journals.   [28.

Joseph A. Mussulman. *Music in the Cultured Generation: A Social History of Music in America, 1870–1900.* Evanston: Northwestern University Press, 1971. ISBN 0-8101-0350-8. Appendixes 1–4 (pp. 200–273) list the music contents of four major American periodicals of the era.   [29.

4

Music since 1900

The twentieth-century bibliography of American music imprints is built around two institutions—the *Catalog of Copyright Entries* (*CCE*), vast and comprehensive, and the *National Union Catalog* (*NUC*), selective but also vast.

The Copyright Catalogues

Newly published music—not all but certainly most of it—is registered for copyright protection, so that the major bibliographical record for the twentieth century will be the *Catalog of Copyright Entries* (or, as it was called before 1906, the *Catalog of Title Entries*), prepared by the Register of Copyrights in the Library of Congress. Publication of the *CCE* is mandated by law, although the publication is chronically underfunded, resulting in less useful a record than is needed. (Admittedly library cataloguers and scholars are never satisfied with what they have: the truth must be conceded, since the future depends on it.) More important for us is to recognize this record for what it is—a bibliography continuing for close to a century, now running cumulatively to over 200,000 pages and citing roughly 2.5 million entries, in a form that for legal purposes aspires to be definitive. For historical purposes the record provides the sole bibliographical citation of well over 2 million of those entries. The bibliographical record has changed its practices over the years, thus requiring a brief history of its policies.

Admittedly, the earliest volumes seem well nigh useless. The weekly registers began to be printed in 1891, although the survival of fewer than five(!) known sets of the issues before 1897 suggests a very small print run, intended mostly to fulfill a legal requirement and little more. The only scholar to survey the lists describes the arrangement at first as "completely haphazard" (this being Joseph W. Rogers, one of the most respected staff members of the Copyright Office itself, on p. 47 of his 1960 book *U.S. National Bibliography and the Copyright Law*). With the weekly issue for July 22–27, 1895 (no. 212), musical compositions began to be arranged alphabetically by proprietor (this being usually the publisher but often the composer). There are no indexes at all, however.

The forty-year history of relatively stable practices began in July 1906, when a separate music section first appeared, designated as "Part 3: Musical Compositions" of the "new series," paginated throughout the year and with its own index at the end of each volume. At first the issues appear weekly, numbered 1–26, for instance, for the second half of 1906. Beginning the next year the numbering continues on a weekly basis, although the issues are cumulated by the month (January, for example, is nos. 1–5, February nos. 6–9, and December nos. 49–52). Beginning in 1911 the numbering is by the month, more or less; the issues are usually numbered 1–12, although for reasons not always obvious many years will also include no. 13 and often even no. 14.

The citations typically give a fairly full title; personal names of composers, arrangers, and lyricists, presumably as they appear on the music; imprint; and the date, entry number, and claimant's name for the copyright registration. The major bibliographical idiosyncrasy, to our eyes, will be the distinction between art music and popular music, necessitating the former to be entered under the name of the composer, the latter under the title. Presumably it reflects the predilections of Oscar Sonneck and later of Carl Engel in the Library of Congress's powerful Music Division, which fell heir to the depository copies (or at least what they saw as the important ones) for purposes of providing library service.

But what exactly is the difference between art and popular music? The anomalies are ever present: on p. 1021 of the 1909 volume, for instance, Rudolph Ganz's *Mélodie*, op. 10, no. 2, is entered under Ganz, while Alexandre Glazunov's *Gavotte* is entered under the title (the latter perhaps because it was being published in an arrangement and with pedagogical connotations in the title statement). Gradually the anomalies were worked out, more or less (or, as some might see it, Gresham's law came to prevail); at least by 1920 one sees almost all title entries, even for works designated as "Sonata" or (occasionally even) "Symphony." Fortunately, all of the injustices were mediated in the indexes, which appear at the end of each issue and are cumulated at the end of each year in one glorious alphabetical sequence of titles, creators' names, and claimants' names that seldom runs to fewer than 500 pages and often approaches 700. The set is really better, and much more impressive, than we have given it credit for being. Admittedly there are problems, occasionally of descriptive detail or of indexing, but mostly having to do with the lamentable dispersal of the copies themselves—through the Music Division collections at the Library of Congress, in some cases by return to the claimant, but pervasively through a general indifference—all of this usually with no record of the dispositions.

The annual production grows—not greatly but somewhat—as the copyright practices evolve. A detailed account of the changing practices is obviously needed; for now several events are relevant and interesting. Through most of the twentieth century, protection has extended for twenty-eight years, plus the option of renewal for twenty-eight more years. This coverage, having been extended from seven plus seven provided for in earlier periods, is today superseded by a period extending fifty years from the death of the creator. While most claimants were and are diligent in depositing copies, no formal depository practices seem ever to have been enforced, except at the time of renewal or in the event of litigation. Music registrations began to be numbered successively in a series prefixed with the letter *C* beginning in 1906 and changed to *E* in 1909. Foreign registrations, admitted beginning in 1891, were recognized through a special *EFo* subseries (later further qualified with an *EF* series, for which one depository copy was permitted rather than the usual two).

Of particular importance was the decision in 1909 that allowed for the registration and protection of unpublished music. (The impact on music publishers was obviously considerable.) Although motion pictures were first provided for as early as 1912, sound recordings were not protected until as recently as 1971. Also worth noting here is the special category for dramatic and "Dramatico-Musical" works (generally class *D*), inasmuch as music publishers often preferred to see operatic and musical comedy editions covered under the law's stronger provisions (music itself being covered by *petit droits,* limited to public performance for profit, dramatic works by *grand droits,* which apply to performances more widely).

A recitation of these events is occasionally useful for bibliographical searching purposes. It also helps to explain the changing quantitative output of the American music publishing industry. The 1907 output of 26,308 registrations, including perhaps 100 dramatico-musical works, grows to 37,862 in 1938, but of these 3,696 are foreign entries and 24,492 unpublished music manuscripts. (In effect, while the annual registration grows, the output of the U.S. music publishers comes to be reduced to less than half.) Full indexing survives the Great

Depression, but beginning in 1939 the annual indexes cover titles only—no composers, lyricists, or claimants. The wartime output burgeons to 63,817 items in 1945 (of which, to be sure, only 10,790 are published U.S. imprints). A crisis is at hand—not in the industry itself (which is, perhaps necessarily, always in a state of crisis) but rather at the Copyright Office.

The 1946 *CCE* is a stopgap solution in four volumes that points to future policies. The first volume is devoted to unpublished music, arranged now by composer (i.e., typically the claimant), with 53,084 titles on 1,414 pages, in typescript—using a variable-spaced typewriter, good for its day but a typewriter nonetheless. The second volume is devoted to the published music, also arranged by composer (and for this material not usually the claimant), with 10,028 U.S. and 3,816 foreign imprints in 699 pages—all of this neatly set in movable type. The third volume is a typescript devoted to renewals, while the fourth volume is a typescript title index to the first two volumes, giving the names of the composers alone for unpublished music and composers with the copyright registration number for the published music.

Since the law required that the registers be published, why not do them right? Instead of producing a cheap and minimally useful list, why not spend a bit more and produce a list that would be usable by publishers, composers, copyright lawyers, and performers as well as by library users in general—in other words, why not create a national record worthy of comparison with the vast German *Deutsche Musik-bibliographie?* The advent of a new series of published copyright registers in 1947 provided the occasion for music librarians, especially in the Library of Congress's Music Division, to argue for proper library cataloguing practices, as implemented under the leadership of the able Virginia Cunningham. The *A* series of the *CCE*, devoted to published music, thus came to consist of a "Name List," with carefully established main entries (frequently from the copyright registration records themselves in the case of names new to the catalogue); minimal description of the physical item; but carefully formulated uniform titles for those entries that lend themselves to collocation in a library catalogue. The name list was complemented with a title index and a claimant index—and, beginning in 1948, even an index by subject headings to provide access to musical mediums and genres. The layout, furthermore, was designed to be reproducible onto cards for interfiling in the Library of Congress's music catalogue, and thus to provide at last some record of the location of copyright depository copies that were being dispersed through the Music Division collections. (Un-

published music was, as before, listed in one alphabetical title sequence.)

Unfortunately the era of impressive copyright records was to last
only for these nine years. While the advent of the current coverage
of the *National Union Catalog* no doubt was part of the reasoning
behind its demise, an even greater problem was the cost of the cataloguing and publication, in a time when music libraries were fewer
and their budgets—and needs and political clout—somewhat smaller
than they are today.

Since 1956 the *CCE* has been thick in its bulk as before but far
more modest both in its coverage and its indexing than any time since
1906. The set's music listings today consist of two parts, each prepared
semiannually. The first is the index, in one alphabet, covering names
and titles associated with each work, the names identifying claimants,
composers, and lyricists, the titles covered by an ample range of
thoughtful cross-references. The second is the numerical listing of
the registrations, by copyright series. A sampling from recent years
suggests these proportions: about 0.4 percent in the *EF* class (foreign,
one copy), 5.1 percent in the *EFo* class (foreign, two copies); 11 percent
in the *EP* class (American published music—now about 30,000 titles
a year); 72.5 percent in the *EU* class (American unpublished music);
and 11 percent in the *R* class (renewals). With about 200,000 items
a year now to consider, it is small wonder that the series has resorted
to microfiche, beginning in 1979 with volume 2 of the fourth series.

The fourth series came into being with the reorganization of the
registers themselves. Since 1978 music has been incorporated into
part 3, along with dramatic works, choreography, pantomime, certain
audiovisual works, and assorted other "Performing Arts." All of this
is fitted into a single alphabetical sequence, with cross-references,
names, and titles interfiled with the entries themselves, so that the-
oretically no indexes should be necessary at all.

How complete is the music *CCE* as a reflection of America's music
publishing output? What is lacking? At the outset two copyright categories must be recognized as part of the picture: some music will be
entered not in the "Music" class but as "Books," presumably when
protection of performance rights was not apparently appropriate, or
among the "Dramatic and Dramatico-Musical Compositions," when
protection of all public performances was possible, and not only the
"public performance for profit" prescribed for music. There are also
the exact reprints—occasionally before 1945 and in considerable
profusion after World War II—issued as a means of meeting a public
demand mostly for German editions of serious music that the original

27

publishers themselves were unable to accommodate. Finally, there is the case of Charles Ives—presumably an uncommon one but nonetheless celebrated—as reported in the Cowells' biography (pp. 121–22). On learning that part of the Fourth Symphony had been copyrighted, Ives expressed his sentiments with customary vigor:

> EVERYBODY who wants a copy is to have one! If anyone wants to copy or reprint these pieces, that's FINE! This music is not to make money but to be known and heard. Why should I interfere with its life by hanging on to some sort of personal legal right in it?

The titles that make up the music *CCE* are summarily cited as follows. In addition, the early cumulations of dramatic registrations are of some interest.

Catalog of Title Entries. Washington: Copyright Office, 1891–1905.

Catalog of Copyright Entries, new series. Washington: Copyright Office, 1906–46. Part 3, Musical compositions. Dramatic compositions are cited in pt. 1, group 3.

Catalog of Copyright Entries, 3d series. Washington: Copyright Office, 1947–56. Part 5-A, published music; pt. 5-B, unpublished music; pt. 14-B, renewal registrations, music; pt. 4, dramas . . . (for which the renewals are in pt. 14-A).

Catalog of Copyright Entries [continuation of the 3d ser.]. Washington: Copyright Office, 1957–83. ISSN 0041-7866. A continuation of the numerical series begun in 1947, with pt. 5 devoted to music as before, but with no. 1 (Jan./June) and no. 2 (July/Dec.) for pt. 5 of each vol., and each of these subdivided into sec. 1 (the indexes discussed above) and sec. 2 (the entries discussed above). Other parts that cover musical materials include pt. 1 for books and pamphlets, pt. 2 for periodicals, pts. 3–4 for "Dramas and Works Prepared for Oral Delivery," pts. 12–13 for motion pictures, and pt. 14 for sound recordings (1978– , covering 1973– ; see 578 below).

Catalog of Copyright Entries, 4th series. Washington: Copyright Office, 1984– . Part 3 is now devoted to the "Performing Arts," including music, while pt. 7 includes the sound recordings.   [30.

Dramatic Compositions Copyrighted in the United States, 1870 to 1916. Washington: Government Printing Office, 1918. An alphabetical title arrangement of about 60,000 texts, with valuable cross-references and a detailed name index.   [31.

Elizabeth K. Dunne and Joseph W. Rogers. "The Catalog of Copyright

Entries" (Study no. 21, Apr. 1960), in *Studies in Copyright: Arthur Fisher Memorial Edition* (South Hackensack, N.J.: Fred B. Rothman; Indianapolis: Bobbs-Merrill, 1963), vol. 1, pp. 451–70. A brief historical survey of the series in general.   [32.

The reference source that is greatly needed now is a merged index to all of the music copyright records. Certainly the day is not far away when an optical scanner could survey the published volumes, at least from 1906 to 1946, giving us machine-readable input for a truly indispensable record of American music. In moments of compromise one would be happy to settle for the published music — a mere million or so titles. In moments of idealism one envisions the record extending backward to pick up the few hundred thousand items since 1870, or even 1826, preferably in terms of a union list of the holdings of major repositories, all of this involving an automated optical disc storage (and preservation) of the copies themselves, tied in to a telefacsimile program for providing access. The vision of the larger scenario makes the smaller 1906–46 conversion seem modest in comparison and inspires one to ask why the communities of music librarians and Americanists seem so frightened to consider a program. Unfortunately, for all the lip service paid to the idea, nobody seems interested in doing anything.

The National Union Catalog

The *CCE* lists all music registered for copyright — a high percentage of which will not end up in any library other than the Library of Congress, if even there. The National Union Catalog records our country's catalogued library collections. One respects its high cataloguing standards, but only for the music that finds its way into catalogued collections. The NUC's history, as part of the history of cataloguing practices at the Library of Congress, is equally long and complicated.

When printed-card distribution practices were set up at the library in 1900, a decision was made to provide description by the regular cataloguing staff. This resulted in printed cards for books about music — however ill-defined. Musical editions, on the other hand, were catalogued in the library's Music Division, at first on handwritten, later on typewritten cards. (The 1913 and 1944 catalogues of the library's pre-1800 books about music, for instance, are mostly assembled from printed cards, in contrast to Sonneck's 1914 libretto catalogue, which was set from his own handwritten cards.) The conspicuous exceptions and anomalies include folksong anthologies, hymnals, and instructional materials.

As a general rule printed cards were prepared (and thus catalogued according to the prevailing standards for printed books) for most items in hardcovers or that otherwise looked like a book or for which orders for cards could be expected from libraries across the country. These items usually appear in the library's 1942–46 published catalogue, and hence they could be cited directly in the monumental *National Union Catalog: Pre-1956 Imprints* (1968–81; see 452 below). In contrast, the vast quantity of the music itself—practically all of what today is in class M, and most in class MT—was catalogued in the Music Division, more pragmatically (i.e., often in a way more scholarly, typically more user-sensitive, but generally more rule-insensitive, and occasionally even rule-contemptuous), and hence was banished from the library's published catalogue.

The reorganization of the library about 1940 and the beginnings of the conception of a published catalogue led at first to an ostensibly more rationalized but probably no more extensive coverage of musical materials through the printed-card program. (This activity of rationalization, however, led to the enhancement of the *Catalog of Copyright Entries* over the period 1949–56, mentioned earlier.) The music catalogued between 1942 and 1953 will thus find its way into the supplements to the Library of Congress catalogue, as well as the *National Union Catalog: Pre-1956 Imprints.* Beginning with the arrival in the library of the late J. M. Coopersmith in 1953, however, sound recordings came to be catalogued. This cataloguing copy, along with that for such selected musical editions as seemed likely to be needed by other libraries for cataloguing purposes, was issued in quarterly printed lists and merged to make up the first *Music and Phonorecords* catalogue for 1953–57. Although published as part of the *National Union Catalog,* this set is devoted exclusively to Library of Congress materials. It is essentially a record, furthermore, not of current imprints but of current cataloguing activity: the few antiquarian books catalogued in any given year, for instance, will be included, along with the numerous manuscripts of major composers added to the library's collections. (The 1958–72 cumulations, for example, and the annual volumes from the early 1980s include cataloguing for a number of Copland and Gershwin holographs from the Library of Congress collections.)

The Library of Congress's anomaly of serving both one institution and all institutions inspired the assembly of the Olmsted catalogue of

1974. This book records the music cataloguing copy for current materials prepared by libraries other than the Library of Congress. The cards were sent to Washington but never edited for inclusion in the *National Union Catalog*. Beginning in 1963 books about music were included in the *NUC*, as reflected in the new title; and starting in 1973 reports from other libraries were included for the first time. The set today remains the librarian's record of American music-publishing activity, intermixing imprints from foreign publishers (both exclusively and jointly with American publishers), along with other current cataloguing copy. The set has appeared semiannually under the imprint of the Library of Congress, with printed cumulations issued by other publishers as follows:

Music and Phonorecords, 1953–57. Ann Arbor: J. W. Edwards, 1958. Volume 27 of the *National Union Catalog*.
Music and Phonorecords, 1958–62. New York: Rowman and Littlefield, 1963. Volumes 51–52 of the *National Union Catalog*. Volume 51 is arranged by personal name and other main entries, while vol. 52 arranges the entries by Library of Congress subject headings.
Music and Phonorecords, 1963–67. 3 vols. Ann Arbor: J. W. Edwards, 1969. Not specified as part of the *National Union Catalog*, and in fact qualified with the statement that they cover "the literature on music and other related materials also included in the *National Union Catalog . . . Books. Subjects*."
Music and Phonorecords, 1968–72. 5 vols. Ann Arbor: J. W. Edwards, 1973. Similarly independent of the *National Union Catalog*. Volumes 4–5 are the subject index.
Music, Books on Music and Sound Recordings [*1973–77*]. 8 vols. Totawa, N.J.: Rowman and Littlefield, 1978. LC 74-640501. Similarly independent of the *National Union Catalog*. Volumes 7–8 are the subject index. Cumulations of the annual vols. (ISSN 0092-2838) are issued by the Library of Congress beginning for 1973 (1974–   ), each in one or two vols. and with a subject index at the end. A seven-vol. merging of the entries for 1978–80 was also issued by the Library of Congress itself in 1983. Based on the cataloguing copy provided by the Library of Congress and seven (or, as of 1985, nine) contributing libraries.   [33.

Elizabeth H. Olmsted. *Music Library Association Catalog of Cards for Printed Music, 1953–1972*. Totowa, N.J.: Rowman and Littlefield, 1974. ISBN 0-87471-474-5. An amalgamation of the music entries submitted to the National Union Catalog from cooperating American libraries, 1956–74, but not otherwise published in that series. The cards were sorted and edited by informal groups attending the MLA's annual conventions. Of the 30,000 titles in the set, perhaps 6,000 consist of U.S. imprints of the period either never acquired by the Library of Congress or not catalogued on printed cards.   [34.

Other Bibliographies

Several other lists serve to record new music publications in general, the second an apparently abortive project that perhaps proved to be a precursor of the third, the last a new work not yet available for examination:

The Musician's Guide (1954–   ; see 48 below). New titles of books about music are typically listed in current directories and yearbooks. (Earlier similar lists include those in the Pierre Key yearbooks, 1925–36, and *The Year in American Music,* 1946–48.) The lists are far from complete, and the criteria for inclusion are not made explicit.

George L. Swanson. *Music Book Guide: 1974.* Boston: Hall, 1974. ISBN 0-8161-6808-3. A listing of 958 titles as part of the Computext Book Guides series, based on Library of Congress citations, largely for books from the years immediately preceding 1974. Essentially a "trial balloon" of sorts for the following title.   [35.

Bibliographic Guide to Music, 1975–   . Boston: Hall, 1976. ISSN 0360-2753. An annual series based on the music cataloguing achievements at the New York Public Library for the year in question. Most imprints come from that year or the one or two preceding, but other cataloguing of retrospective acquisitions is also included. The bibliography is useful primarily for its current information and its access through subject and added entries such as are officially not included in the *National Union Catalog.*   [36.

Thomas P. Lewis. *The Pro/Am Guide to U.S. Books about Music.* White Plains, N.Y.: Pro/Am Music Resources, 1986. ISBN 0-912483-03-2.   [37.

Other bibliographies of twentieth-century American music are, if not numberless, at least pointless to count, all the more so since most of the subsequent chapters will be largely devoted to them, as distinguished by audience, repertory, or medium. Their profusion may disturb some "bibliographical planners" who envision a single unified "national music data base" that would address all of our music information needs. The abundance of bibliographies should be seen rather as evidence of the "fertile chaos" that, for all its shortcomings, will assure a healthy musical future for our country. But what is out there? The current state of affairs—or at least as of the preparation of this handbook—is the subject of chapters 6–17. Chapter 5, which follows immediately, addresses a slightly different objective, that of suggesting the state of affairs tomorrow, if presumably not five years hence.

5

Current Music

"Keeping up-to-date on a continuing basis"—we ignore the redundancy in the statement as we react to the urgency of the need. (In music, talent is essential but knowledge is power.) Special bibliographical projects and services have thus arisen, many of which have now been folded into the mandates of the specialized institutions that have come to flourish in the twentieth century—academic and public libraries; local, state, and federal governmental programs; and formal organizations of scholars and professional musicians. The continued success of the projects and services will obviously depend on effective dialogue between those who make bibliographical citations and those who use them. Admittedly, on close inspection and in retrospect, our various current bibliographical services will be seen to be less complete and less adequate than we might wish—partly because our appetites always grow with use. The better our bibliographical services, the more we need them and expect of them.

This survey of the state of current bibliography separates the sources according to three basic objectives. Current bibliographies tell us what is *new*, what is *available*, or what is *good*. Lists that address one of the three questions usually address implicitly the other two as well: after identifying the basic question and checking its sources, one remembers the other two kinds of sources; but one starts out by asking which of the three is basic.

New Publications

The most extensive listings of new American music publications are the sources discussed in chapter 4. Little more needs to be said about them, other than that they are continuing as noted. One hopes they may long continue. Their coverage, however vast, is still limited to monographic publications and not analytics—that is, to separately

35

published books and music, but not to articles, essays, periodicals, and ephemera or to the individual selections that are collected in musical anthologies. Most readers, now, are interested in content, regardless of the packaging practices of our suppliers. The diversified bibliographical needs of music librarians and library users in general, and of American music specialists, are often better served by the wider range of materials covered in continuing series like the following:

Music Library Association *Notes* (1934–41, irregular; n.s., 1943–   , quarterly). The lists of "Books Recently Published" and "Music Received" have appeared since 1946. The former, recently compiled mostly from the titles catalogued at the Library of Congress, has since 1950 been international in scope, with American titles mostly in the English-language section. (A selection of its scholarly titles was formerly issued as the "Quarterly Booklist" in *Musical Quarterly.*) The music list, as its precise title tells us, describes instead only copies sent in for review, mostly from American publishers, and is classified by genre. In addition, the journal has also from time to time featured lists of other kinds of material currently in demand in music libraries, for instance lists of "Current Catalogues from the Music World" from the 1940s until 1970, resuming in 1977 but for publishers' announcements only; forthcoming books and (in alternate issues) forthcoming reprints on music between 1966 and 1977; and selected popular music irregularly in 1969–70 and regularly from 1973 to 1978.   [38.

Sonneck Society Newsletter (1975–   ; three issues a year and since 1986 entitled *Bulletin*). The lists of "New Publications," which began to appear in 1976, are now often subdivided by genre, i.e., as "Some Recent Books" or "Some Recent Articles and Reviews," listed by journal, mostly for scholarly browsing purposes.   [39.

Institute for Studies in American Music. *Newsletter* (1970–   ; twice a year). New publications and recordings are described, the unusual ones among them with particular diligence and delight.   [40.

ARSC *Journal* (1967–   ; see 573 below). Since 1979 a "Current Bibliography" column has been prepared by Tim Brooks, devoted to "recent English-language articles dealing with recording history," but actually of wider use in its listings of books, discographies, and "labels," i.e., catalogues of record companies.

36

Goldmine (1974–   ). The journal covers rock music records, broadly defined; David Ginsburg's former columns on "The Reference Library," various reviews and listings of current reference services, and "Fadomania" (citing publications, mostly ephemeral) were of particular value to librarians, discographers, and collectors. The journal abandoned or trimmed back its reference features around 1983, although it still contains useful current information for the rock collecting community. Ginsburg's lists, meanwhile, and the strong bibliographical character of the earlier years were taken up in a new journal called *R.P.M.: Record Profile Magazine* (1983–   ). This journal, however, originally projected as a monthly, has loosened its production schedule, thus leaving some question of its very survival—a status that seems to be equally true of another journal covering much the same area, *Record Auction Monthly* (1984–   ).

[41.

Music Educators National Conference, Special Research Interest Groups. *Newsletters* (ca. 1980–   ). Among the various bibliographical features are dissertation lists (see 516–17 below).

"American Composer Update," *Pan Pipes* (1949–   ; see 189 below).

Sheet Music Exchange (1982–   ; see 667 below).

Quite apart from these lists, devoted primarily to new books and musical editions, are the lists devoted to recent periodical articles and other writings about music. Except for a vast and diffuse WPA project for music periodical indexing (its cards now at Northwestern University, having earlier taken space at DePaul University and the Newberry Library), the current indexing of music begins when Florence Kretzschmar (one of the heroines of American music bibliography) left the Detroit Public Library to set up the *Music Index*. Her set remains a public library source in its orientation, pragmatic (i.e., usually minimal) in its subject access—making it less than ideal for complex scholarly inquiries—but popular in its coverage and particularly appropriate for American music studies. While *RILM Abstracts* enjoys the potential for deeper levels of scholarly coverage, the existence of the several other indexes cited below may serve as another reminder that not all specialized literature (not even all of the specialized research literature) is musicological in its orientation.

Music Index. Detroit: Information Services; Information Coordinators,

1949– . LC 50-13627. Selective listing of writings on music in those current periodicals that would be expected in major music library collections. Monthly issues cumulated into annual vols. but usually several years behind, making a comprehensive search painfully time-consuming. Citations appear under the major subject, following a fixed thesaurus (as explained and laid out in the annual *Subject Heading List,* issued separately in the style of the monthly issues), also often under authors. The practices and headings have changed somewhat over the years as the coverage has been extended. A history of the publication would thus be almost as important as putting the whole file into an on-line data base, as well as a prerequisite to the task.　　　　　　　　　　　　[42.

S. Yancey Belknap. *Guide to the Musical Arts: An Analytical Index to Articles and Illustrations, 1953–56.* New York: Scarecrow, 1957. LC 57-6631. Covers about 6,000 articles in fourteen English-language journals, also about 3,000 illustrations, the latter of these a useful feature not found elsewhere.
―――. *Guide to the Performing Arts, 1957–68.* New York, Metuchen, N.J.: Scarecrow, 1960–72. LC 60-7266. Continuation of the above, with about 100,000 entries in the twelve vols., eventually indexing forty-eight journals, the music coverage largely duplicating the *Music Index* but unique in its special coverage of television (in a separate section, 1957–65) and drama.　　　　　　　　　　[43.

Music Article Guide. Philadelphia: Music Article Guide; Information Services, 1966– . "Selected significant signed feature articles in American music periodicals geared exclusively to the special needs of school and college music educators" are covered, including "practical 'how-to' articles for orchestra, choral, and band directors," about 250 in each quarterly issue. Entries are arranged under about 100 subject headings, with cross-references.　　　　[44.

RILM Abstracts. New York, 1967– . An international index of scholarly music books, articles, essays, and reviews, arranged in quarterly classified sections in which folk music appears mostly in class 35: "Ethnomusicology: North America (north of Mexico)," while art music is dispersed. A general index appears as the fourth number each year and is cumulated for on-line access.　　　　[45.

Music Therapy Index: An International Interdisciplinary Index to the Literature of the Psychology, Psychophysiology, Psychophysics, and Sociology of

Music. [Lawrence, Kans.:] National Association for Music Therapy, 1976. Vols. 2 (1978) and 3 (1984) as *Music Psychology Index.* Edited by Charles T. Eagle, Jr., and John Minitier. Dallas: Institute for Therapeutics Research [vols. 2–3]; Phoenix: Oryx Press [vol. 3]. ISSN 0195-5802. Each vol. lists roughly 12,000 entries in one alphabet, drawn from about 400 periodicals, vol. 1 for issues dating 1960–75, vol. 2 for 1976–77, and vol. 3 for 1978–80.   [46.

Recording Industry Index. Cherry Hill, N.J.: National Association of Recording Merchandisers, 1977–   . Citations of writings on commercial, legal, trade, and repertory matters, arranged by broad subjects. The 1977 vol. (published 1978) cites about 4,000 titles, the 1978 vol. (published 1979) about 3,500, the 1979 vol. (published 1980) about 5,000, from about twenty journals each year. The list of journals changes significantly from year to year.   [47.

One step removed from the lists devoted mainly to new musical materials are the general directories to the field of music. The historical lineage begins in the nineteenth century, continues with the Pierre Key directories, 1928–38, and culminates in the title cited below. (A comprehensive and authoritatively prepared bibliography devoted to them, in fact, would be extremely useful in its own right.) Among the typical offerings are lists of new books and current periodicals, as well as other features as noted below:

The Musician's Guide: The Directory of the World of Music. New York: Music Information Service, 1954. 2d ed. 1956. 3d ed. 1957. 4th ed. 1968. LC 54-14954. 5th ed. 1972. ISBN 0-912596-00-7. 6th ed. Chicago: Marquis Who's Who, 1980. ISBN 0-8379-5601-3. 7th ed., retitled *Music Industry Directory.* 1983. ISBN 0-8379-5602-1. Stephen F. Keegan is editor of the 1st ed., John O'Connor of the 3d, Gladys S. Field of the 4th and 5th. A useful range of lists, rarely definitive but reasonably current and extensive, makes this one of the most valuable of all music reference books. The approximate number of entries for and pages on which the lists of music periodicals, recent books on music, and music publishers appear in each of the seven editions are shown below:

Music Periodicals

	1954	1956	1957	1968	1972	1980	1983
Pages	147–52	215–27	640–56	205–43	438–500	111–50	321–43
Titles	100	200	350	700	1,500	1,000	300

The music periodicals section in the 2d ed. is divided into three sections, for U.S. and foreign trade publications and fan magazines, of which the first and third are included in the above total. Later lists omit the third category, materials from which presumably are selectively assimilated into the other two.

New Books about Music

	1954	1956	1957	1968	1972	1980	1983
Pages	[none]	92–94	624–39	162–98	501–76	[none]	[none]
Titles		150	300	400	1,500		

The new book section in the 3d ed. also includes a separate general index, the 4th and 5th eds. a separate title index to this section. The 5th ed. is devoted to the 1967–71 period.

Music Publishers

	1954	1956	1957	1968	1972	1980	1983
Pages	169–94	243–346	34–139	409–596	834–954	581–906	611–75
Firms	1,250	3,000	3,500	5,000	3,500	25,000	1,500

The 2d through 4th eds. contain separate lists for ASCAP, BMI, and SESAC, while the 1st and 5th through 7th eds. are arranged geographically by state and city, with performance rights affiliations indicated in each entry and with separate name indexes. It seems unlikely that the music publishing industry expanded phenomenally in the 1970s and has declined all that greatly since 1980, although the criteria for inclusion and selectivity are not explicit. Indeed, surveying the names in these lists is in itself a highly bemusing exercise in its own right, also an instructive indication of the diversity of music publishing. The presumption that anyone can be a music publisher with a modicum of musical literacy and an affinity to any particular musical repertory—with or without a printing press or business sense—may be sad news to librarians in search of universal bibliographical control, although it is also good news to those who delight in the diversity of musical activity itself. The above lists typically specify "trade and industry" music publishers rather than "music book publishers," who in several eds. are listed separately, for instance on pp. 351–56 of the 7th ed. In addition the 1st and 2d eds. list "Press Clipping Services." Printers, engravers, copyists, and manuscript reproduction specialists are also variously listed in the first five eds.

Other valuable features in many eds., relevant to the purpose of this book, include the various lists of major music libraries and of record companies—both of which, however, are covered more definitively in other specialized lists.   [48.

Beyond these general services, a seemingly endless number of others are devoted to specific topics—sound recordings (as discussed in chapter 15), special repertories, particular favorite composers or performers, localities, audiences, or media. The number of these bibliographical services is constantly changing, and unquestionably expanding, as the few that dissolve (while their sponsoring organizations revise by-laws) are replaced by the many that come together at post-concert socializing. The journals and newsletters that they cover, often their scope and organization, are also continually changing to meet the needs of the members and as persons become available with the imagination and resources needed to get started (easy) and to persevere (difficult). The global village is clearly manifest in the domain of music, for which the muses can rejoice; and rather than developing schemes for keeping the burgeoning activity under control, music administrators, librarians, and information specialists are probably best advised to join in the fun and games.

Music in Print

The availability of musical materials, meanwhile, is a matter that could provoke a tirade, a plea, or a plan for improved music distribution. In recent years our local retail outlets have declined in number and efficiency. Concomitantly, the convenient photocopy, of dubious legality but pernicious impact on music publishers, has become increasingly ubiquitous. It is thus ironic that an ancient dream of comprehensive bibliographies of music in print now seems about to become a reality. The 1871 Board of Music Trade's *Complete Catalogue* (see 9 above) was such a list; thirty years later the Viennese dealer Franz Pazdirek attempted a universal list—and, legend has it, went broke in the process. While the American book trade has been organized for over a century now, the stock of America's music publishers has been a tougher nut to crack. The communities of users have been more widely disparate, and as a result special means have been worked out to enable them to gain access to their preferred repertories. As for the publishers, they have learned to live with this arrangement, providing publicity and controlling their inventories accordingly. Much

41

as musicians and librarians might lament the state of affairs, for many years neither was able to do much about it.

It was not until the 1950s that the band repertory began to be addressed. During the 1960s Margaret Farish heroically proved — doubting librarians and churlish publishers notwithstanding — that in-print lists were possible for string music, dispersed as this repertory was across a wide range of publishers, American and foreign, scholarly and educational, antiquarian and avant-garde. The bibliographical details are not what they might be. Nor should one expect them to be. There is too much music to cite, and it will go out of print and come back into print (almost necessarily at a much higher price). Readers will find the lists less useful than they should be in the absence of detailed citations. Today at least they are being compiled, for use in conjunction with other reference sources as needed. Above all, it should be remembered that the lists below — at least those following the first two titles devoted to book materials — are organized around particular broad repertory categories (thus making their ownership appropriate not only to music stores and libraries but also to performers). In a broad sense the Instrumentalist and Musicdata sets are complementary, insofar as the former grows out of a special sensitivity to and concern for the communities of performers, while the latter benefits from high-speed bibliographic technology and from whatever special access to the publishers may result from an East Coast location.

Books and Miscellaneous Materials about Music

Publishers' Trade List Annual. New York: Bowker, 1873–   . Collected catalogues of major U.S. book publishers, with author and title, and more recently subject indexes issued separately under the title *Books in Print* (1948–   ). Music books issued by the "book trade" are included; generally excluded are not only the music and recordings issued by music publishers and record companies but also the hymnals issued by denominations, the music pamphlets issued by organizations, and many other kinds of "non-booktrade" editions. In addition to the major book-trade firms whose catalogues are reproduced in the main catalogue, the titles available from a number of small publishers are indexed in the special yellow-page section at the front of the first vol. Still others of the small book publishers are listed in the source below.   [49.

AB Bookman's Yearbook. Newark, N.J.: Antiquarian Bookman, 1950–   .
   The miscellaneous announcements of numerous small publishers —

local historical societies, special interest firms, and avocational entrepreneurs—are often most conveniently accessible through the display ads here. Unfortunately there is no subject index to facilitate a search for the occasional music title. American music enthusiasts, like most readers of the *Yearbook* and its counterpart *AB Bookman's Weekly* (1909–   ), are for the most part a curious lot who will consider their time well employed in scanning the delightful range of intellectual work reflected here.   [50.

Single Specialized Lists

Margaret K. Farish. *String Music in Print.* New York: Bowker, 1965. LC 65-14969. *Supplement.* 1968. LC 65-14949. 2d ed. 1973. LC 80-18425. The 1st ed. is a classified list of about 20,000 solo and ensemble editions, with a composer index. (A preliminary version, entitled *Violin Music in Print,* was published by Bowker in 1963.) The supplement adds about 4,500 titles, while the 2d ed. includes "more than 6,000 new" entries, or now about 25,000 in all, by way of cumulating and updating the 1st ed. and the *Supplement.* Reprinted as vol. 6 of the Musicdata "Music in Print Series" (71 below; q.v. for further continuations).   [51.

Joseph Rezits and Gerald Deatsman. *The Pianist's Resource Guide: Piano Music in Print and Literature on the Pianist's Art.* Park Ridge, Ill.: Kjos Pallma, 1974. ISBN 0-910842-04-3. 2d ed. Park Ridge and San Diego: Kjos Pallma, 1978. ISBN 0-8497-7800-X. In the 1974 ed., pt. 1 ("Piano Music in Print," pp. 1–692) consists of a "Composer Index"—actually classified by twenty-six musical mediums and genres, each of these alphabetically by composer—of about 50,000 entries, with a title index. Part 2 ("Literature on the Pianistic Art," pp. 693–932) and subsequent sections are an annotated bibliography of writings about the piano and its pedagogy.   [52.

John Voigt. *Jazz Music in Print.* Winthrop, Mass.: Flat Nine Press, 1975. LC 75-324531. 2d ed. Boston: Hornpipe Music, 1978. LC 78-110189. *Supplement.* 1979. "Jazz is defined as that music played by the Jazz Masters and those musicians directly associated with them. This catalog organizes the music around these people, and not necessarily around those who composed, edited, or published it. . . ." While a less authoritarian approach would have allowed for a title index and better cross-references, the analytic entries for collections are useful, and the book remains the only work in its field.   [53.

W. Patrick Cunningham. *The Music Locator.* Saratoga, Calif.: Resource Publications, 1976. ISBN 0-89390-001-X. *Supplement.* 1978. ISBN 0-89390-004-5. 3d ed. San Jose, Calif.: Resource Publications, 1984. ISBN 0-89390-046-6. A listing of about 13,000 selected editions of music for church service use, arranged systematically with brief codes on availability, character, and medium, with indexes by title and composer. The *Supplement* adds about 7,500 citations not in the 1st ed.; the later eds. have not been compared, although the 3d ed. would appear to be roughly three times the size of the 1st.   [54.

Joseph Rezits. *The Guitarist's Resource Guide: Guitar Music in Print and Books on the Guitar.* San Diego: Kjos Pallma, 1983. ISBN 0-8497-7806-2. Part 1 ("Guitar Music in Print," pp. 15–280) is classified and listed by composer, with a title index. Parts 2–4 (pp. 283–316) are much briefer lists devoted to music in print for the lute, mandolin, and vihuela, respectively, while pt. 5 ("Special Interest Listings," pp. 320–457) picks up ensemble, genre, and occasional repertory. Part 6 (pp. 460–552) is devoted to "Books on the Art of the Guitar."   [55.

Finding List of Vocal Music (1948), *Folio-Dex* (1974–   ), and other analytical indexes of song anthologies in print; also Gargan and Sharma, *Find That Tune* (1984), covering rock anthologies (see 368–79 below).

Phonolog (1948–   ), *Schwann Long-Playing Record Catalog* (1949–   ), and other lists of recordings in print (see 576–79 below).

A number of the evaluative repertory lists, mostly cited in chapter 9, have been compiled with availability as a criterion for inclusion.

Instrumentalist Music Guides

Kenneth Berger. *Band Music Guide: A Listing of Band Music by All Publishers.* Evansville, Ind.: Berger Band Co., 1953. 2d ed. 1954. A listing of about 10,000 band-music editions in print, recognized in the introduction as "but half or less of the total . . . that is available and playable by American instrumentation." Arranged alphabetically by title in four categories: concert music, marches, solos and ensembles, and fanfares. Later eds. were all published in Evanston, Ill., by the Instrumentalist, i.e., 3d ed. (1962), arranged in six categories: band titles, band collections, solos and ensembles, band methods, marching band maneuvers, and fanfares, now including about 12,000 titles, as well as a *Composer Index to Band Music Guide* in a complementary vol.; 4th ed. (1966?); 5th ed. (1970), containing 13,000 titles with the "Composer Index" now in the same vol.; *BM6 Addendum* (1973), supplements the 5th ed., with a six-level grading system; 6th ed., edited by Linda Magee (1975), with additions and deletions but still about 13,000 titles; 7th ed. (1978), with 14,000 titles; 8th ed. (1982), with nearly 16,000 titles.   [56.

R. Winston Morris. *Tuba Music Guide.* Evanston, Ill.: Instrumentalist, 1973. LC 73-79493. An annotated list of about 1,000 entries, in broad categories, each with a separate title index.   [57.

Himie Voxman and Lyle Merriman. *Woodwind Ensemble Music Guide.* Evanston, Ill.: Instrumentalist, 1973. LC 73-87227. Rev. ed. as *Woodwind Music Guide: Ensemble Music in Print.* 1984. A list of about 12,000 entries, classified by medium, without indexes.   [58.

Himie Voxman. *Woodwind Solo and Study Material Music Guide.* Evanston, Ill.: Instrumentalist, 1975. LC 75-22523. Rev. ed. as *Woodwind Music Guide: Solo and Study Material in Print.* 1984. A list of about 16,000 entries, classified by medium, without indexes.   [59.

Paul G. Anderson. *Brass Solo and Study Material Music Guide.* Evanston, Ill.: Instrumentalist, 1976. LC 76-151216. A list of about 7,500 entries, classified by function and medium, with an index of names.   [60.

————. *Brass Ensemble Music Guide.* Evanston, Ill.: Instrumentalist, 1978. A listing of about 8,000 titles, arranged basically by medium, with a general composer index.   [61.

Earl Louder and David R. Corbin, Jr. *Euphonium Music Guide.* Evanston, Ill.: Instrumentalist, 1978. LC 79-301684. An annotated list of about 800 entries, in broad categories, several with separate title indexes.   [62.

Music in Print Series

Thomas R. Nardone, J. H. Nardone, and M. Resnick. *Choral Music in Print—Sacred Choral Music.* Philadelphia: Musicdata, 1974. (Music in Print Series, vol. 1.) ISBN 0-88478-000-7. A listing of about 35,000 full entries under composer, interfiled with brief title references. *1981 Supplement.* ISBN 0-88478-012-0. A listing of about 10,000 additional entries. 2d ed., by Gary S. Eslinger and F. Mark Daugherty. 1985. ISBN 0-88478-017-1.   [63.

———. *Choral Music in Print: 1976 Supplement.* Philadelphia: Musicdata, 1976. ISBN 0-88478-007-4. An interim supplement to the sacred list cited above and the secular list cited below, in two sections with about 20,000 composer entries and title references.   [64.

———. *Choral Music in Print—Secular Choral Music.* Philadelphia: Musicdata, 1974. (Music in Print Series, vol. 2.) ISBN 0-88478-002-3. A listing of about 33,000 entries, following the same plan as the sacred-music set above. *1982 Supplement.* ISBN 0-88478-013-9. A listing of about 8,000 additional titles.   [65.

Thomas R. Nardone. *Organ Music in Print.* Philadelphia: Musicdata, 1975. (Music in Print Series, vol. 3.) ISBN 0-88478-006-6. About 10,000 composer entries and title references in one alphabet.
Walter A. Frankel and Nancy K. Nardone. *Organ Music in Print.* 2d ed. Philadelphia: Musicdata, 1984. ISBN 0-88478-015-5. Expansion of the above, now with about 15,000 entries.   [66.

Thomas R. Nardone. *Classical Vocal Music in Print.* Philadelphia: Musicdata, 1976. (Music in Print Series, vol. 4.) ISBN 0-88478-008-2. About 30,000 composer entries and title references in one alphabet. *1985 Supplement,* ed. Gary S. Eslinger and F. Mark Daugherty. 1986. ISBN 0-88478-018-X.   [67.

Margaret K. Farish. *Orchestral Music in Print.* Philadelphia: Musicdata, 1979. (Music in Print Series, vol. 5.) ISBN 0-88478-010-4. About 43,000 composer entries and title references in one alphabet.
———. *Educational Section of Orchestral Music in Print.* Philadelphia: Musicdata, 1978. ISBN 0-88478-009-0. About 2,000 titles extracted from the above, similarly arranged.
———. *Orchestral Music in Print: 1983 Supplement.* Philadelphia: Musicdata, 1983. ISBN 0-88478-014-7. About 7,000 composer and

title entries, in two sections, one of "Orchestral Music" as a supplement to the basic set, the other of "Educational Orchestral Music" as a supplement to the *Educational Section.*   [68.

―――. *String Music in Print.* 2d ed. (repr. of New York: Bowker, 1973, cited in 51 above). Philadelphia: Musicdata, 1980. (Music in Print Series, vol. 6.) ISBN 0-88478-011-2. *Supplement 1984.* ISBN 0-88478-016-3. About 8,000 additional entries, arranged as above.
                    [69.

Annual *Music in Print* supplements (ISSN 0192-4729) have also appeared since 1979, for cumulation into the separate series above.
                    [70.

American music publishers in the near future will be looking to assemble a collective index to their editions currently in print, for use in music stores and in libraries, comparable to the microfiche set that has already been available in Great Britain for some years now. There are obvious obstacles to an American counterpart. First, no publishers will be happy to see the inadequacies of their inventory control system exposed so conspicuously—as no doubt they would through a collective list. Second, publishers, who at once both love and hate to raise their prices, will also resent the way in which their angst becomes the more public. (Both of these conditions, it should be noted, are equally true of book-trade publishers, who have for many years benefited from their in-print lists.) More serious obstacles are the third and fourth circumstances that characterize American music publishing today—namely, the division of their brethren between the Music Publishers Association, devoted mostly to classical music publishing, and the National Music Publishers Association, devoted mostly to popular music publishing, and the increasing emphasis on performance rights and royalties, coming inevitably at the expense of a concern for the distribution of printed copies. One can add to these a fifth sad truth that some publishers simply do not have adequate inventory records, insofar as they print few copies of particular editions in the first place and are prone to the kind of short institutional memory that often characterizes such highly personalized businesses. A sixth truth is that music publishing goes on everywhere and all the time, as a highly specialized "cottage industry," with nobody knowing about it except the small market of potential purchasers. "Music in Print in the U.S.A.," when it comes to exist, will be less than complete; but users will learn how to find the odd title that is missing as they give thanks for the wealth that is present. Equally true is the prospect that publishers would gain much, considering the gross inadequacies of our information and distribution systems today.

A special kind of availability, meanwhile, accrues to musical works that enjoy performance rights protection. The catalogue holdings of the American Society of Composers, Authors, and Publishers, for instance, are listed in the following:

ASCAP Index of Performed Compositions. New York: ASCAP, 1952. LC 53-2083. 2d ed. 1963. LC 66-50211. 3d ed. 1978. LC 77-95282. The 1st ed. contains a massive listing of about 85,000 compositions, with minimal titles, name of composer or author, and publisher. The expanded 2d ed. registers about 200,000 compositions, and the 3d ed. about 340,000. [71.

Other similar lists include the symphonic catalogues of both ASCAP and BMI (see 261–62 below).

Selective Lists

Recommended titles, for bibliographical purposes, are cited in two ways: as single lists of the endorsed titles, issued once but perhaps with supplements or new editions in mind, and as continuing critical reviewing media, with additional evaluations expected on a continuing basis. The former range from the "basic music libraries," often assembled by official committees, usually published and presumably intended as the basis of library collection development programs, to the recommended repertory lists prepared by respected specialists and professional groups and distributed informally. To my knowledge none of the former is devoted to American music to the exclusion of other music, although some cover music in general (i.e., the National Association of Schools of Music accreditation lists of 1935–57, the 1967 *Basic Music Library,* and Michael Winesanker's booklists of 1977 and 1979; the Baird list for elementary schools [1972; see 530 below], the Clark list for high school libraries in MLA *Notes* in 1969, and the Krummel list for college libraries in *Choice* in 1976; and Pauline Shaw Bayne's Music Library Association committee lists of 1978 and 1983). As for the informal repertory lists, their generally ephemeral nature has meant that they are under absolutely no bibliographical control, notwithstanding the fact that teachers and performers in search of repertory rely heavily on them. Those that are formally published,

often in hard covers (such as the Scarecrow guides and several denominational lists of recommended church music), are included in
the standard book-trade bibliography. In contrast many of the pamphlets (such as those prepared for contests, competitions, clinics, and
other events) are either obsolescent by intention or reevaluated and
updated on the basis of regular response from the individuals who
make use of the lists. Among the best known and most important are
those assembled over the past forty years for the use of music educators, as follows:

Selective Music Lists: Instrumental and Vocal Solos, 1948–1949. Chicago:
National School Band, Orchestra, and Vocal Association, 1948.
*Instrumental Ensembles: Woodwind, Brass, String, Mixed: Graded List of
Recommended Materials.* Chicago: National School Band, Orchestra,
and Vocal Association, 1948.
*Selective Music Lists: Band, Orchestra, String Orchestra, Choral Groups,
1951–52.* Chicago: National School Band, Orchestra, and Vocal
Association, 1951.
————, *1957* [also *1962, 1963, 1964*]. Washington: National Inter-
scholastic Music Activities Commission (an auxiliary of the Music
Educators National Conference, hereinafter abbreviated as MENC).
Materials for Miscellaneous Instrumental Ensembles. Washington: MENC,
1960. LC 60-14971. Prepared by the Committee on Literature and
Interpretation of Music for Instrumental Ensembles.
Bibliography for String Teachers Revised 1964. Washington: MENC, 1964.
LC 67-49283. A report prepared by Albert W. Wassell and Charles
H. Wertman for the MENC Committee on String Instruction in
the Schools.
Contemporary Music: A Suggested List for High Schools and Colleges. Wash-
ington: MENC, 1964. LC 64-23547. Prepared by the Committee
on Contemporary Music.
Selective Music Lists, 1968. Washington: MENC, 1968. LC 68-58545.
Classified lists covering vocal solos, small vocal ensembles, large
choral groups, and junior high choruses.
Selective Music Lists: Band, Orchestra, String Orchestra. Washington:
MENC, 1971. LC 70-176273. Compiled cooperatively with the
College Band Directors National Association, the National Band
Association, and the National School Orchestra Association.
Selective Music Lists: Instrumental Solos, Instrumental Ensembles. Wash-
ington: MENC, 1972. LC 72-75840. Compiled cooperatively with
the American String Teachers Association and the National Asso-
ciation of College Wind and Percussion Instructors.

Selective Music Lists: Vocal Solos, Vocal Ensembles. Vienna, Va.: MENC, 1974. LC 74-81894.

Selective Music Lists, 1978: Full Orchestra, String Orchestra. Reston, Va.: MENC, 1978. LC 78-62207.

Selective Music Lists, 1979: Instrumental Solos and Ensembles. Reston, Va.: MENC, 1979. LC 79-64901. The foreword includes some of this history. [72.

The critical evaluation of new music publications, meanwhile, has a sad and neglected history all its own. Perceptive reviews, whether of musical events themselves or of scores, books, or records, are among the most important of all writings about music. However much one may agree with particular sources, the sentiments and the rhetoric are part of the processes through which the abundant musical life can be understood and enriched. Yet of the tens of thousands of musical works published in the course of any given year, no more than a few hundred can expect to be described and evaluated in print. Among the current journals that include reviews—signed or unsigned, brief or discursive, critical or descriptive, general in tone or directed to particular readers—are the following:

American Choral Review (1958–   ). Occasional reviews of major works.

American Music (1983–   ). Annually about fifty books and twenty recordings are reviewed relating specifically to American music of all kinds.

American Music Teacher (1951–   ). Annually reviews about fifty books and several hundred musical editions of special interest to music teachers.

American Organist (1918–70 and 1979–   ; 1967–78 known as *Music: A.G.O. Magazine*). Annually about twenty-five items are reviewed.

Black Perspective in Music (1973–   ). About fifteen books or musical editions are reviewed every year.

Choral Journal (1959/60–   ). Annually several hundred musical editions, mostly of religious works and grouped by publisher, are briefly covered, along with occasional monographs discussed at greater length.

Church Music (1966–80). Several hundred scores are briefly noted annually, along with occasional books at greater length.

Clarinet (1973–   ). About sixty scores and several recordings and monographs are cited briefly each year.

Clavier (1962–   ). Annually covers about 500 keyboard editions and books.

Down Beat (1934–   ). Reviews several hundred jazz recordings and a few books annually.

Ethnomusicology (1953–   ). Annually covers about 100 books and recordings, and occasionally films.

Fanfare (1977–   ). About 2,000 recordings, mostly classical, are reviewed annually.

High Fidelity/Musical America Edition (1965–   ). About 600 recordings and several dozen books and musical editions are covered each year. Since 1986 *Musical America* has again appeared separately.

Hymn (1949–   ). Covers about forty items a year, including hymnals and sacred song collections, individual songs, and books.

Instrumentalist (1946–   ). Reviews annually about 400 editions.

IAJRC [International Association of Jazz Record Collectors] *Journal* (1968?–   ). About 200 recordings and several dozen books are covered each year.

JEMF [John Edwards Memorial Foundation] *Quarterly* (1965–   ). Several dozen ethnic folk recordings and books are reviewed annually.

Journal of Church Music (1959–   ). Annually covers about ten books and eighty editions of vocal and organ music.

Journal of Research in Music Education (1953–   ). Several pedagogical monographs are covered every year.

Journal of the American Musicological Society (1948–   ). About a dozen items are discussed in scholarly detail.

MLA *Notes* (1943–   ). Annually about seventy-five books and 200 musical editions are reviewed, in addition to the "Index to Record Reviews" (see 575 below).

Music Educators Journal (1914–   ). Annually reviews about a dozen books and describes nearly 200 more in a column, "Book Browsing."

Musical Quarterly (1915–   ). About a dozen books are covered annually. In addition the "Current Chronicle" was long a preeminent reviewing forum for contemporary music.

NATS [National Association of Teachers of Singing] *Journal* (1945–   ; formerly *NATS Bulletin*). Annually covers about 200 titles, also occasional recordings and monographs.

Opera News (1936–   ). Annually reviews over 100 recordings, along with occasional books about opera.

Opera Quarterly (1983–   ). Includes about 150 extensive reviews of books and recordings each year.

Pan Pipes of Sigma Alpha Iota (1908–   ). Annually covers upwards of a dozen books and somewhat more recordings.

Pastoral Music (1976–   ). Reviews about 100 musical editions and several dozen books and hymnals.

Percussive Notes (1962–). Annually covers upwards of a hundred musical editions, also occasional recordings and films.

Piano Quarterly (1952–). About sixty musical editions and occasional recordings and books about music are covered.

Sonneck Society Newsletter (1975–85; and as *Bulletin*, 1986–). Often includes brief notices of books soon to be or just recently issued, in addition to its lists of "New Publications" (see 39 above) and the more considered (and generally later) evaluations in the society's journal, *American Music*.

Soundboard (1974–). Annually reviews several dozen editions of guitar and related music, and somewhat more recordings and occasional books.

Stereo Review (1968–). Upwards of 500 recordings are reviewed annually.

TUBA [Tubists Universal Brotherhood Association] *Journal* (1973–). Covers each year about sixty scores and about a dozen recordings of solo and ensemble music.

Woodwind/Brass and Percussion (1981–85?, merging *Woodwind World*, 1957?– , and *Brass and Percussion*, 1973–). Somewhat under 200 scores and upwards of a dozen recordings are covered annually.

Occasional reviews of American texts and editions may also be found in foreign journals such as *Musical Times* and *Music and Letters*. The totals above are based on an unpublished survey in 1982 by Deborah Pierce; and while these data are updated in several instances, it would be hard to deny that the state of music reviewing in this country is sorely inadequate. A small proportion of these reviews themselves are indexed in sources such as the following:

The Book Review Digest. New York: Wilson, 1905– . Citations of reviews of major books appearing in the major book reviewing sources, thus excluding much specialized music literature.   [73.

An Index to Book Reviews in the Humanities, 1960– . Detroit, [later] Williamston, Mich.: Phillip Thomson, 1960– . An index by authors of books, with no access to reviewers' names or to music as a subject heading.   [74.

Music Index (1949– ; see 42 above). Reviews of new books are cited under the heading "Book Reviews." New music and sound recordings may be covered in other articles but are not cited directly.

Book Review Index. Detroit: Gale, 1965– . A bimonthly index more extensive in coverage than *The Book Review Digest* above, cumulated annually and for 1965–84. Entries are accessible by author and title of the book, with no subject approach to the music coverage as such. [75.

Current Book Review Citations. New York: Wilson, 1976–82. An author index with particulars on source and reviewer, complemented by an abbreviated title index. Popular writings about music are included but are not accessible by subject. [76.

RILM Abstracts (1976– ; see 45 above). Reviews of scholarly materials are included within the main sequence (as designated by a two-letter notation beginning with *r* beneath the entry number, i.e., *ra* for a review of an article, *rb* for a book review, *rm* for a review of a scholarly edition of music) and are accessible in the index under the name of the reviewer and through the item being reviewed.

Arts and Humanities Citation Index. (1977– ; see 568 below)

Several recent bibliographies (most of them composer lists, the subject of chapter 8) cite reviews or quote them in the course of their annotations, and to good effect. The major indexes of record reviews, cited as 582–84 below, are among the major sources for their literature, while the several sources for concert reviews are cited as 487–89 below.

CONTEXTUAL PERSPECTIVES

Chronology is basic to any bibliographical record. In contrast, geography—at least in its narrow and commonly recognized sense and as applicable specifically to American music—often seems either unproductive because it is so little appreciated, or little appreciated because it has been assumed to be so unproductive. It says a good deal about the cultural homogeneity of our country that Connecticut music should be very much like California music, or Minnesota music so much like Florida music—a condition reflected in the writings and in their bibliography, if not necessarily in the music itself.

Geography can be useful, especially as it is broadly recognized as involving not only physical space but also social and communal space. Enlarging "geography" into "context" is justified in a world in which music travels widely and easily; and it is helpful in this presentation, in that two additional dimensions to the bibliographical record thereby can come into consideration. Following the coverage of regional, state, and local bibliographies in chapter 6, at any rate, chapter 7 considers those lists devoted to communities of musicians—Native Americans, blacks, ethnics, and women in particular, these being the most conspicuously recognized of our country's minorities—while chapter 8 is concerned with the sources devoted to musical biography. The logic gets shamefully attenuated; people take up space, but nobody should be proud to propose this argument for including biographical materials as part of a geographical unit. More important, the discussion of biographical sources fits rather comfortably in the overall structure of the book at this point, coming after the imprint lists and before those devoted to mediums and genres and documents as such.

These three chapters thus move away from a discussion of imprints into one focused on repertory. As in the previous discussions the concern is largely with musical editions and texts; but the concern will also be with other forms of documentary evidence, most notably with writings about music and even sound recordings.

55

6

Regional Bibliographies

Geographical identity may be established in any of several ways: first, through the concept of the native composers, of "musical sons and daughters"; second, through indigenous folk music; third, by virtue of the location of a publisher, involving so-called imprint studies; and fourth, through topical references in the music itself—for instance, song titles, textual allusions, settings of dramatic works in a particular location, and festive events for which music was commissioned—as well as through writings about the regional musical activity in general.

The geographical contexts of music deserve more attention than has so far been appreciated. In comparison with the activities of ethnomusicologists working in the Third World and of local historians in Western Europe, work involving the United States, whether for analytical or promotional purposes, fares poorly indeed—and the homogenization of American culture, while far advanced, is still not complete. Among the few books on the topic is George O. Carney's *Sounds of People and Places: Readings in the Geography of Music* (Washington, D.C.: University Press of America, 1979), a beginning effort that concentrates on current popular music. However fascinating the conception behind this book, its "Map 15" on p. 51 should prove particularly saddening, infuriating, in any event perplexing; its simplistic conceptions may persuade others to conceive of the assignment in better detail. In hopes of refining its concepts and in anticipation of more studies in American local music history in general, the bibliographies below should prove particularly useful.

"Musical Sons and Daughters"

The concept of musicians distinctive to a state, city, or region has occasioned several bibliographies of composers born, educated, or active there. Histories of local music and biographical directories of local composers have been prepared, but largely without enough bibliographical facts to be of any more than the most rudimentary of help. (In the absence of a thorough bibliography of the genre, the best lists are probably those on pp. 320–23 of William Phemister's piano concerto bibliography, see 282 below, and on pp. 60–68 of Guy Marco's bibliography, see 757 below.) The exceptions most worthy of being emulated are probably the Eichhorn and Mathis guide, essentially a catalogue of a collection at the University of North Carolina in Greensboro, and the Boston music librarians' project. Extensive activity in local music history was promoted by the National Federation of Music Clubs, through the earlier decades of this century as well as in connection with the 1976 bicentennial celebrations; and while the summary program prepared in connection with this latter effort gives only names of composers and a few of their compositions, hopes run high for lists not yet publicized and files not yet readied for final publication.

National Music Council and National Federation of Music Clubs. *The Bicentennial Parade of American Music, May 7, 1975–December 31, 1976.* A booklet with one page for each state, prepared in conjunction with a series of concerts given at the Kennedy Center, Washington. [77.

Hermene Warlick Eichhorn and Treva Wilkerson Mathis. *North Carolina Composers As Represented in the Holograph Collection of the Library of the Woman's College of the University of North Carolina.* Greensboro: University of North Carolina, 1945. LC 46-14175. Biographical sketches of fifteen composers, with lists of their works (of which about seventy-five items are in the holograph collection, as noted with asterisks) and writings about them. [78.

Nora Dixon [Mrs. Curtis M.] McGee. *Kentucky Composers and Compilers of Folk Music, Native and Adopted.* Frankfort: [Kentucky Federation of Music Clubs,] 1950. LC 51-35498. Biographical sketches of eighty-five composers and arrangers, including lists of their works. [79.

North Carolina Federation of Music Clubs. *North Carolina Musicians: A Selective Handbook.* Chapel Hill: University of North Carolina Library, 1956. (UNC Library Extension Publication, vol. 21, no. 4.) The main section (pp. 5–55) covers fifty-seven "North Carolina Composers," with published compositions and references at the end, and often with unpublished music cited in the biographical (or more often autobiographical) sketches themselves.   [80.

Francis Turgeon Wiggin. *Maine Composers and Their Music: A Biographical Dictionary.* [Rockland:] Maine Federation of Music Clubs, 1959. LC 60-26410. List of about 250 composers, with specific titles, dates, medium, and major concert performances of many works.   [81.

A Catalog of Representative Works by Resident, Living Composers of Illinois. [Carbondale: Southern Illinois University, 1960.] LC 60-9652. Prepared under the supervision of Will Gay Bottje for the Illinois Federation of Music Clubs, the list begins with brief biographies of thirty-two composers, continues with publishers' addresses, and ends with short titles of about 700 works, arranged according to medium.   [82.

Southeastern Composers' League Catalogue. Hattiesburg, Miss., 1962. LC 63-47639.   [83.

Louis Panzeri. *Louisiana Composers.* New Orleans: Louisiana Federation of Music Clubs, 1972. LC 72-188152. Largely biographical, but with a miscellany of added musical and nonmusical compilations, i.e., of bibliographies of Louisiana Negroes in general; collections of and writings on Negro spirituals, work songs, and Louisiana stories; Creole songs in collections; the Acadian folksongs as collected by Harry Oster; books on the Creole and Acadian French languages; and recordings.   [84.

James R. Pebworth. *A Directory of 132 Arkansas Composers.* Fayetteville: University of Arkansas Library, 1979. LC 79-119180. Biographical sketches, with references to other guides and lists of compositions.   [85.

Donna Mendro and Robert Skinner. *A Checklist of Texas Composers.* Dallas: Music Library Association, Texas Chapter, 1980. LC 80-412370. A list of about 800 names, mostly extracted from twenty-five reference books, some standard, others uncommon, as cited on pp. 2–3.   [86.

The Boston Composers Project: A Bibliography of Contemporary Music [in] *Boston Area Music Libraries.* Cambridge, Mass.: MIT Press, 1983. ISBN 0-262-02198-6. A listing of works by about 200 composers (pp. 771–75) now residing in the Boston area or claiming strong roots there, including information on performance resources and availability of published or manuscript texts—as such, a model for what librarians might do by way of promoting the music of local composers.   [87.

Indigenous Folk Music

Alongside the native art-music composers are the indigenous folk-music repertories, typically accessible through title and occasionally subject indexes. The list of regional and state collectors is long, mostly dating from the early and middle decades of this century—Alton Morris for Florida, Charles Neely and David McIntosh for Illinois, Paul Brewster for Indiana, Earl J. Stout for Iowa, Hubert G. Shearin and Harvey Fuson for Kentucky, Edward D. Ives for Maine, Earl Beck and Emelyn Gardner for Michigan, Arthur Palmer Hudson for Mississippi, Henry M. Belden for Missouri, Mary O. Eddy for Ohio, George and Rae Korson and Samuel P. Bayard for Pennsylvania, Reed Smith and Guy Johnson for South Carolina, Mody Boatright and William A. Owens for Texas, Austin and Alta Fife and Lester Hubbard for Utah, Louis Chappell and Arthur Kyle Davis for Virginia, John Harrington Cox for West Virginia, Phillips Barry and Helen Harkness Flanders for New England in general, and John Lomax and Ben Gray Lumpkin for the Rockies in general, as well as in the titles listed below. Their work is typically reflected in archival collections and in published songbooks extracted from these collections. As of today the fullest list of the former is probably the work of Doris J. Dyen in *Resources of American Music History* (see 443 below), accessible under the heading "Folk music collections" (p. 415—about 170 in all); a more convenient brief list of repositories is subsumed in the pamphlet *Folklife and Ethnomusicology Archives and Related Collections in the United States and Canada* (Library of Congress, Folk Archive Reference Aid no. 2, April 1984) and in the Bartis and Fertig *Folklife Sourcebook* (Washington, 1985), pp. 54–124. The published songbooks vary considerably in their scholarly and other bibliographical features; some are anthologies exclusively, while others include anecdotal and source information, of variable levels of scholarship. The first two lists cited below cover the genre; these are followed by citations of several of the most important and respected titles:

Alan Lomax and Sidney Robertson Cowell. *American Folk Song and*

Folk Lore: A Regional Bibliography. New York: Progressive Education Association, 1942. LC 42-12846. An annotated list of about 400 song collections and books, much of it classified by broad geographic and cultural categories (e.g., "The North," "The White South," "The Negro South," and so on). [88.

Haywood, *Bibliography of North American Folklore and Folksong* (1951, 1961; see 307 below). Includes about 6,000 entries in vol. 1 on regional topics, arranged geographically.

Hickerson, "Bibliography of American Folksong" (1974; see 314 below). Includes a valuable geographical summary on pp. 804–9.

Sidney H. Robertson. *Check List of California Songs.* [Berkeley: University of California, 1940.] An index to about 2,500 song texts, first by title (pp. 4–63) and then by first line (pp. 64–114), that appear, mostly without music, in forty-nine songsters as cited on pp. 157–59; and to about 750 song texts, first by title (pp. 115–35) and then by first line (pp. 136–56), that appear as broadsides, as found in the major collections as described on p. 160. Prepared as a WPA project involving the Archive of California Folk Music, of which this is vol. 1 *(Texts in Print)*, intended to be complemented by vol. 2, devoted to the oral tradition (i.e., works sung or known to have been sung in California), which was apparently never published. [89.

Vance Randolph. *Ozark Folksongs.* 4 vols. Columbia: State Historical Society of Missouri, 1946–50. LC 47-1554. Rev. ed., with an introduction by W. K. McNeil. 4 vols. Columbia: University of Missouri Press, 1980. ISBN 0-8262-0297-7/-0298-5/-0299-3/-0300-0. Randolph's notes to the 883 songs (a few of them not in the reprint) are particularly respected, while the indexes at the end of vol. 4 are important for reference use.
———. *Ozark Folksongs.* Urbana: University of Illinois Press, 1982. ISBN 0-252-00815-4. A one-vol. abridgment by Norm Cohen, with additional reference indexes as well. [90.

The Frank C. Brown Collection of North Carolina Folklore. Edited by Newman Ivey White. Durham: Duke University Press, 1952–84. Of the seven vols. in the set, the following are of special musical interest:

—Vol. 2, *Folk Ballads from North Carolina*. Edited by Henry M. Belden and Arthur Palmer Hudson. 1952. LC 52-10967. The 314 titles are broadly classified by source (older and mostly British, native American, North Carolinian), and indexed on pp. 737–47.

—Vol. 3, *Folk Songs from North Carolina*. Edited by Henry M. Belden and Arthur Palmer Hudson. 1952. LC 52-10967. A classified presentation of 658 titles, indexed by informants to vols. 2–3 on pp. 687–703.

—Vol. 4, *The Music of the Ballads*. Edited by Jan Philip Schinhan. 1957. LC 57-8818. A companion to vol. 2, with 25 new titles and further indexes, pp. 403–20.

—Vol. 5, *The Music of the Folk Songs*. Edited by Jan Philip Schinhan. 1962. LC 57-8818. A companion to vol. 3, with 128 new songs and 66 children's game songs, also further indexes, pp. 625–39.

[91.

Bruce A. Rosenberg. *The Folksongs of Virginia: A Checklist of the WPA Holdings, Alderman Library, University of Virginia*. Charlottesville: University Press of Virginia, 1969. ISBN 0-8139-0279-7. A list of 1,604 titles, recorded by twenty informants for the Federal Writers Project, 1938–42. [92.

Ethel Moore and Chauncey O. Moore. *Ballads and Folk Songs of the Southwest: More Than 600 Titles, Melodies, and Texts Collected in Oklahoma*. Norman: University of Oklahoma Press, 1964. LC 64-11329. [93.

Norman Cazden, Herbert Haufrecht, and Norman Studer. *Folk Songs of the Catskills*. Albany: SUNY Press, 1982. ISBN 0-87395-580-3. Discussion and presentation of 178 tunes in a classified arrangement, with title and first-line index on pp. 645–50. [94.

John A. Cuthbert. *West Virginia Folk Music: A Descriptive Guide to Field Recordings in the West Virginia and Regional History Collection*. Morgantown: West Virginia University Press, 1982. ISBN 0-937058-12-2. [95.

Jennifer Post Quinn. *An Index to the Field Recordings in the Flanders Ballad Collection*. Middlebury, Vt.: Middlebury College, 1983. An alphabetical listing of 4,066 titles, indexed by uniform titles, performers, and location. [96.

The list above is devoted to collections in which the emphasis is on the repertory, as accessible through useful title indexes. A separate bibliography of writings about the music may or may not be appended. Bibliographies devoted primarily to writings about the music are cited with the other writings about regional music in the final section of this chapter, among them Ferris for Mississippi (1971; 116 below) and Feintuch for Kentucky (1985; 124 below).

Imprint Lists

Bibliographies of publications emanating from particular states, cities, and areas of the United States are surveyed in section A (pp. 1–67) of the Tanselle guide. Like the chronological lists, these bibliographies will typically include writings about music, often songbooks, hymnals, and instruction books, but rarely any sheet music. There are several important exceptions, however, notable among them the lists for the Confederacy by Harwell and Hoogerwerf. Dena Epstein's study of the Root and Cady firm amounts to a survey of all Chicago music publishing activity before the 1871 fire, with valuable imprint lists.

Tanselle, *Guide to the Study of United States Imprints* (1971; see 753 below). Regional imprint lists are cited in sec. A (1:1–67), book-trade directories in sec. F (1:398–404); see also the writings on particular printers and publishers in sec. G (2:405–762).

The American Imprints Inventory was prepared in the late 1930s under the auspices of the WPA Historical Records Survey. Thirty-six published bibliographies of early regional imprints appeared between 1937 and 1942, as cited individually under the state or city in Tanselle and indexed on pp. 897 and 911; also in Charles F. Heartman, *McMurtrie Imprints* (Hattiesburg, Miss.: Book Farm, 1942; supplement, Biloxi, 1946). Among the few that include significant music citations are the following:

A Check List of Utica, N.Y., Imprints, 1799–1830. Chicago: Historical Records Survey, 1942. (American Imprints Inventory, no. 36.) Repr. New York: Kraus, 1968. Includes a number of Williams and Seward music books. [97.

H. Earle Johnson. *Musical Interludes in Boston, 1795–1830.* New York: Columbia University Press, 1943. LC 43-11010. Repr. New York: AMS Press, 1967. LC 68-18586. Appendixes 1–5 include lists of early Boston music publications and information on Boston publishers, pp. 299–349.   [98.

Richard B. Harwell. "Sheet Music Published in the Confederate States," in his *Confederate Music* (Chapel Hill: University of North Carolina Press, 1950), pp. 101–56.   [99.

————. Music listings in Marjorie Lyle Crandall, *Confederate Imprints: A Check List* (Boston: Boston Athenaeum, 1955). In vol. 2, 693 sheet-music titles are cited on pp. 561–699, while sixteen hymnals are listed on pp. 719–21.   [100.

————. *More Confederate Imprints.* Richmond: Virginia State Library, 1957. LC 57-9084. In vol. 2, thirty-eight sheet-music items are cited on pp. 225–30, and eight hymnals on pp. 250–51.   [101.

Grace I. Showalter. *The Music Books of Ruebush and Kieffer, 1866–1942: A Bibliography.* Richmond: Virginia State Library, 1975.   [102.

Mariol R. Peck. "Music Periodicals in Portland, Oregon, 1879–1925." Master's thesis, University of Oregon, 1980. (Heintze 2027)   [103.

Dena J. Epstein. *Music Publishing in Chicago before 1871.* Detroit: Information Coordinators, 1969. (Detroit Studies in Music Bibliography, 14.) LC 70-019179. About 1,000 Root and Cady imprints are cited on pp. 91–146, with excellent indexes. (Based on a 1943 study; see 707 below.)   [104.

Richard Crawford. "Connecticut Sacred Music Imprints, 1778–1810," MLA *Notes,* 27 (1971), 445–52, 671–79. The first part includes a list of fifty-eight titles, while the second discusses the titles as a reflection on a particularly imaginative musical area.   [105.

Bobbie Pray. "A Piano in Every Parlor," in John W. Ripley, *A Century of Music* (Topeka: Shawnee County Historical Society, 1977; Bulletin no. 54), pp. 19–25, 123–27. Includes a list of 144 sheet-music editions published in Topeka, 1884–1954.   [106.

Paul Richard Powell. "A Study of A. E. Blackmar and Brother, Music

Publishers, of New Orleans, Louisiana, and Augusta, Georgia: With a Check List of Imprints in Louisiana Collections." M.L.S. thesis, Louisiana State University, 1978. About 500 editions are cited in the checklist (pp. 56–108), arranged by title. [107.

Frank W. Hoogerwerf. *Confederate Sheet-Music Imprints.* Brooklyn, N.Y.: Institute for Studies in American Music, 1984. (I.S.A.M. Monographs, 21.) ISBN 0-914678-23-X. A list of about 4,000 items, drawn from primary and secondary sources, with useful indexes. [108.

Bowden, "Regional Music Publishing of the Civil War Era" (1986; see 12 above).

In specialized work with particular editions, it is often worth the trouble, and almost always highly informative, to learn many of the relevant facts about the publishers themselves. The imprint lists are thus usefully complemented by the general studies on historical bibliography and the history of music publishing, as cited in chapter 16.

Meanwhile, how widely was American music published abroad? We know of several examples from the Leipzig firm of Breitkopf & Härtel, for instance, the two sets of quartets, opp. 8 and 9, by Charles Callahan Perkins from the early 1850s, as well as several piano works by Ernst Perabo issued later in the century. Gottschalk bibliographers have turned up Spanish, South American, and French editions. A systematic search of the massive German Hofmeister *Handbuch der musikalischen Literatur* (1831–   ) will probably bring to light even more music by American composers. The European publishing career of Arthur P. Schmidt is probably not unique. Among the few attempts to identify the genre of foreign imprints of American music is a recently announced assemblage of "American Popular Music Issued c. 1900–1940 by Australian Publishers," running to 575 items and consisting mostly of hit tunes. The question of American music issued abroad will always be provocative to pose but impossible to answer comprehensively.

Regional Topics

Topical songs and programmatic instrumental pieces with geographical references have rarely been collected, let alone described and promoted bibliographically (college songbooks being among the exceptions). To find the "Annapolis Quick Step," "I Left My Heart in Wichita," or similar inspirations and sentiments, one must look to those occasional specialized libraries and collections that made conscious decisions to bring out topical concerns. How carefully the decisions were implemented over the years at an institution, of course, may be another matter. "The Missouri Waltz" might be filed as a Missouri topical piece; or it might just as easily be located through its composer (James Royce, also known as J. R. Shannon); or it might be filed under its most celebrated exponent, President Harry S. Truman; or as a waltz or by title (in this instance providing a kind of subject access) or by date alone. Whether through formal classification schemes (for instance, M 1657–58 at the Library of Congress), special card indexes in historical societies and public libraries, or informal categories in large private collections now in institutional collections (among them the Driscoll at the Newberry, the Starr at the Lilly, and the Levy at Johns Hopkins), the search for local references is at best a hit-and-miss affair.

Few published bibliographies trace the songs *about* a particular region. The *Stecheson Classified Song Directory* (1961; 389 below) includes about 1,500 titles with explicit geographical references under the heading "States & Cities, U.S.A." (pp. 421–32), as do several other topical song indexes but in less detail. Among the few separate lists are the following:

James Taylor Dunn. "A Century of Song: Popular Music in Minnesota," *Minnesota History*, 44 (1974), 122–41. A narrative account with numerous references and illustrations.   [109.

Musical Reflections of Alaska's History: A List of Songs & Music in the Alaska Historical Library. Juneau: Alaska Division of State Libraries, 1974. Unannotated list of thirty titles from or referring to Alaska.   [110.

Earl F. Bargainnier. "Tin Pan Alley and Dixie: The South in Popular Song," *Mississippi Quarterly*, 30 (1977), 527–64. Descriptive essay, followed by a list of "300 Songs about the South: 1895–1955" (pp. 546–64), extracted from standard bibliographical reference works cited here mostly in chap. 11.   [111.

Finally, the following are among the few lists of writings about music of particular states, cities, or regions in general or that include a modest section on the history of music in the area. Several will be seen to be not "true bibliographies" at all but rather exhibition catalogues (such as the 1983 one from New Orleans or Brubaker's 1985 Chicago book) or promotional publications that resort extensively to visual materials. They are thereby perhaps all the more valuable, as they call attention to the variety of ephemera and other miscellanea that needs to be preserved.

Edna Reinbach. *Music and Musicians in Kansas.* Topeka: Kansas Historical Society, 1930. LC 30-30188. The "Bibliography" (pp. 49–51) lists about forty titles, many concerning the history of the "John Brown" song.   [112.

Leroy Schlinkert. *Subject Bibliography of Wisconsin History.* Madison: State Historical Society of Wisconsin, 1947. LC 48-5744. Thirteen music entries are cited on p. 156.   [113.

Frank James Gillis. "Minnesota Music in the Nineteenth Century: A Guide to Sources and Resources." M.A. thesis, University of Minnesota, 1958. (Heintze 15)   [114.

"Chicago: A Musical Accompaniment," *Chicago History,* vol. 8, no. 12 (Summer 1969), pp. 353–74. Discussion of the collections at the Chicago Historical Society.   [115.

William R. Ferris. *Mississippi Black Folklore: A Research Bibliography and Discography.* Hattiesburg: University and College Press of Mississippi, Southern Station, 1971. ISBN 0-87805-026-4. Includes bibliography (pp. 7–48), discography (pp. 49–58), and other reference indexes.   [116.

Ernst C. Krohn. *Missouri's Music.* New York: Da Capo, 1971. ISBN 0-306-70932-5. An anthology of the author's writings, 1923–66, including studies of *The Missouri Harmony* and other essays of bibliographical interest.   [117.

Frederick Freedman. "Music in Ohio: A Preliminary Bibliography." [Cleveland, 1974.] An unannotated list of 226 titles, distributed for a Midwest Chapter meeting of the American Musicological Society, Iowa City, Apr. 26–28, 1974.   [118.

Annie Figueroa Thompson. *An Annotated Bibliography of Writings about*

Music in Puerto Rico. Ann Arbor: Music Library Association, 1975. (MLA Index Series, 12.) ISBN 0-914954-02-4. A list of 304 titles, alphabetically by author with a subject index. [119.

Margaret Long Crouch. "An Annotated Bibliography and Commentary concerning Mission Music of Alta California from 1769–1834," *Current Musicology,* 22 (1976), 88–99. A listing of approximately fifty published writings about and collections of the music, followed by an inventory of some fifty contemporary manuscripts. [120.

Ralston Crawford. *Music in the Street: Photographs of New Orleans, an Exhibition Sponsored by the Historic New Orleans Collection, the William Ransom Hogan Jazz Archive of Tulane University, April 13–July 22, 1983.* New Orleans: Historic New Orleans Collection, 1983. ISBN 0-917860-14-4. [121.

[Neil Bunker and Louise Goldberg.] *Rochester's Music: Its Beginnings* [and] *Rochester's Music: 1860–1900.* Rochester, N.Y.: Eastman School of Music, 1984. Catalogues of two exhibits, mostly of sheet music, celebrating the city's sesquicentennial. [122.

Robert L. Brubaker. *Making Music Chicago Style.* Chicago: Chicago Historical Society, 1985. LC 85-070022. Catalogue of an exhibition, Feb. 16–Oct. 27, 1985, broad in scope and with superb annotations and illustrations. (See also the 1969 music issue of *Chicago History,* 115 above.) [123.

Burt Feintuch. *Kentucky Folkmusic: An Annotated Bibliography.* Lexington: University Press of Kentucky, 1985. ISBN 0-8131-1556-6. A list of 709 titles, including musical anthologies as well as books, articles, and reference sources on the topic, broadly classified with subject and author indexes. [124.

"The Music of Indiana: A Brief Bibliography," *Resound* (Indiana University, Archives of Traditional Music), Fall 1985, pp. 5–6. Twenty-nine titles. [125.

Bryan C. Stoneburner. *Hawaiian Music: An Annotated Bibliography.* Westport, Conn.: Greenwood, 1986. ISBN 0-313-25340-4. A list of 564 writings about Hawaiian music of all varieties, with a glossary. [126.

7

Group Bibliographies

Bibliographies often serve to identify, describe, and ultimately rationalize and promote the music of particular groups of persons. The four most conspicuous of these—Native Americans, blacks, ethnic immigrants, and women—are the subject of this chapter. The guides in question may emphasize either the musicians or their audience—that is, they may be, broadly speaking, either biographical or ethnological in their considerations, whether of women, blacks, or other ethnic, cultural, or linguistic groups. Their varying concerns for repertory, musical editions, or writings about music should also be noted. Their definitions of scope must be understood if we are to evaluate them and appreciate their usefulness and limitations. One may be bothered if one wishes, for instance, by the inclusion or exclusion of Puerto Ricans in the black music lists or of Carlos/Carla Baker in the women's music bibliographies or by vestiges of territorial imperatives in the nationalistic lists. The larger and redeeming value of the works in question, however, lies in their concern for the wide range of musical activities involving those groups that come together as social units and make music as they celebrate their commonalities.

The bibliographies cited and discussed below are not the only ones relevant to their fields. References to black, Native American, and other ethnic and national musical traditions dealing exclusively with folk music and other popular forms (jazz as the most conspicuous case in point) are treated mostly in chapter 10, and in the discographies cited in chapter 15. Other materials relevant to their topics turn up elsewhere, often as noted, or in sources not mentioned explicitly (i.e., in the historical record of American music cited in chapters 2–6) and no doubt in still other bibliographies that have escaped the present purview. The range of presentations suggests something of the character of the literature in question. One general list may be cited at the outset:

"Source Materials in the Music of American Indians, Blacks and Chicanos," *Music Library Association Newsletter,* no. 14 (Sept.-Oct. 1973). Includes Alex J. Chavez, "Recommended Sources for Commercially Available Discs and Field Tape Collections of Chicano Music" (grouped around seventeen sources); Charlotte Heth, "Select Bibliography of American Indian Music" (about sixty works); Portia K. Maultsby, "Sources of Films, Video-Tapes, Dissertations, and Field Recordings for Afro-American Music" (twenty-three sources); and Gertrude Rivers Robinson, "Resources for Afro-American Music" (about twenty-five titles).   [127.

Native American Music

The specialized bibliography devoted to American Indian music conveys the distinctive character of high seriousness. Scholars are usually the intended audience, and thus the compilers typically have taken some pains to evaluate the literature, in hopes of perspectives useful for the cause of future research based on that literature. Addressing a general public audience seems beside the point; at their most strident the political messages are usually but subtle overtones. Thus, while the citations themselves come to be redundant between the lists cited below, the conceptual framework is rich in its historical changes. Most of the titles are writings about music; musical works are accessible through passing references or in the archival citations mentioned.

Helen Heffron Roberts. *Ancient Hawaiian Music.* Honolulu: Bishop Museum, 1926. LC 27-13067. Repr. New York: Dover, 1967. LC 67-18240. An extended survey of sources of all kinds, including a bibliography of 187 titles (pp. 391–97).   [128.

George Herzog. *Research in Primitive and Folk Music in the United States: A Survey.* Washington: American Council of Learned Societies, 1936. (Bulletin no. 24.) LC 36-59. Nearly 400 titles are cited at the ends of sections, i.e., on pp. 33–36, 39–41, and 78–93.   [129.

Charles Haywood. *A Bibliography of North American Folklore and Folksong.* New York: Greenberg, 1951. LC 51-1941. 2d ed. New York: Dover, 1961. LC 62-3483. Section 2 (pp. 749–1159—which constitutes all of vol. 2 in the 1961 ed.) is entitled "The American Indians North of Mexico" and includes about 10,000 titles, classified by cultural context, with annotations. The 2d ed. is essentially a photographic reproduction of the 1st, reportedly with corrections, and with an expanded index, which now covers entries for particular tribes.   [130.

Joe Hickerson. "Annotated Bibliography of North American Indian Music North of Mexico." M.A. thesis, Indiana University, 1961. LC 72-290048. An alphabetical list of about 1,000 titles, with indexes by topic and region.   [131.

Beverly Cavanagh. "Annotated Bibliography: Eskimo Music," *Ethnomusicology*, 16 (1972), 479–87. Selective list of extensive discussions, with relevant general works on Eskimo culture.   [132.

Anna Lee Stensland. *Literature by and about the American Indian: An Annotated Bibliography.* Urbana, Ill.: National Council of Teachers of English, 1973. ISBN 0-8141-4203-7. 2d ed. 1979. ISBN 0-8141-2984-6. Includes a section on "Music, Arts, and Crafts," mostly for children's and general rather than scholarly use. The sixteen titles in the 1st ed. are not entirely subsumed within the fifty-three in the 2d ed., which is grouped for class levels.   [133.

A Selective Bibliography of Ceremonies, Dances, Music & Songs of the American Indian from Books in the Library of Gregory Javitch, with an Annotated List of Indian Dances. Montreal: Osiris, 1974. LC 75-301810. An elegant limited ed. (of 20 and 280 copies) of an impressive private collection catalogue, valuable for its scholarly annotations in general, particularly of those texts from the sixteenth to the nineteenth century that mention Indian arts in passing.   [134.

Charlotte J. Frisbie. *Music and Dance Research of Southwestern United States Indians: Past Trends, Present Activities, and Suggestions for Future Research.* Detroit: Information Coordinators, 1977. (Detroit Studies in Music Bibliography, 36.) ISBN 0-911772-86-3. An extended survey of the scholarship, as reflected in roughly 600 writings cited on pp. 67–109.   [135.

David McAllester. "North American Native Music," in Elizabeth May, *Musics of Many Cultures* (Berkeley and Los Angeles: University of California Press, 1980). The brief bibliography (pp. 328–31) provides useful entry into materials in media particularly appropriate to the subject, notably recordings and films.   [136.

Arlene B. Hirschfelder, Mary Gloyne Byler, and Michael A. Dorris. *Guide to Research on North American Indians.* Chicago: American Library Association, 1983. ISBN 0-8389-0353-3. Chapter 22 ("Music and Dance," pp. 243–46) comments on fourteen major research studies and seven bibliographies. [137.

Marsha Maguire. *American Indian and Eskimo Music: A Selected Bibliography through 1981.* Washington: Library of Congress, 1983. (LC Folk Archive Reference Aid, 1.) ISSN 0736-4911. An alphabetical list of about 500 titles, without annotations. [138.

Black Music

In contrast to the bibliography of Native American music, that of black music is generally less scholarly, more frequently overtly political in its promotional objectives, and often devoted to musical texts themselves if not always to writings about music. Except in the narrow areas announced in their titles, the lists below are all largely superseded by the recent de Lerma, Skowronski, and Floyd-Reisser compilations — the second of these the most extensive but the other two more thoughtfully conceived. The 1971 collection of essays should also be singled out for the beginning search, since it will be particularly useful for its suggestions of how black music fits into its various larger cultural contexts.

Monroe Nathan Work. *Bibliography of the Negro in Africa and America.* New York: Wilson, 1928. LC 28-17150. Repr. New York: Octagon, 1965. LC 65-28242. A landmark list of 17,000 selected books, pamphlets, and periodical articles, classified by subject with a "Music" section (pp. 433–51) containing 500 titles, including interesting early materials on jazz. [139.

Index to Negro Spirituals. Cleveland: Cleveland Public Library, 1937. LC 44-3922. A title index to thirty-one standard published anthologies. [140.

Index to Selected Periodicals Received in the Hallie Q. Brown Memorial Library, 1950–59. Boston: Hall, 1961– . Prepared at Central State University in Wilberforce, Ohio, the list combines author and subject entries, the latter based on Library of Congress subject headings. The set is continued by the *Index to Periodical Articles by and about Negroes* in vols. covering 1960–70, 1971, and 1972. The annual continuations beginning in 1973 now are entitled *Index to Periodical Articles by and about Blacks* (ISSN 0161-8245). Several dozen music entries appear in each annual issue under subjects and proper names.   [141.

Earle H. West. *A Bibliography of Doctoral Research on the Negro, 1933–1966.* Ann Arbor: University Microfilms, 1969. ISBN 0-8357-0638-9. Thirteen music dissertations are listed in the original set, none further in the 1967–69 supplement.   [142.

Marguerite Martha Lawrenz. *Bibliography and Index of Negro Music.* Detroit: Board of Education, 1968. LC 70-39471. Citations of 75 books on Negro music in general; 51 books, articles, and dissertations on jazz; 89 periodical articles; and about 200 citations of biographies, references in general sources, and a few periodical articles. For general readers.   [143.

Richard Colvig. "Black Music," *Choice,* 6 (1969), 479–87. A list of seventy-one titles, selectively annotated, arranged topically, and not limited to the United States.   [144.

Dominique-René de Lerma. *The Black-American Musical Heritage: A Preliminary Bibliography.* Kent, Ohio: Kent State University, 1969. (Music Library Association, Midwest Chapter, Explorations in Music Librarianship, 3.) An alphabetical listing of about 600 books, articles, and anthologies, with a subject index.   [145.

Betty Jo Irvine and Jane Ann McCabe. *Fine Arts and the Black American* [and] *Music and the Black American.* Bloomington: Indiana University Libraries, Focus Black America, 1969. LC 71-9220. McCabe's music section covers general music sources, by way of complementing the fine arts section by Irvine.   [146.

James Sjolund and Warren Burton. *The American Negro: A Selected Bibliography of Materials Including Children's Books, Reference Books, Collections and Anthologies, Recordings, Films and Filmstrips.* Olympia, Wash.: State Supt. of Public Instruction, 1969. (Music of Minority Groups, 1.) LC 70-627891. A list of about 120 titles.   [147.

[Egon Kraus.] "Bibliographie: Jazz — Blues — Worksong — Spiritual—Gospelsong," *Musik und Bildung,* vol. 2, no. 6 (1970), pp.

290–92; vol. 5 (Apr. 1973), pp. 198–202. The latter cites 210 books and articles, including many German titles and early translations of English-language texts. [148.

James M. McPherson, Laurence B. Holland, James M. Banner, Jr., Nancy J. Weiss, and Michael D. Bell. *Blacks in America: Bibliographical Essays.* Garden City, N.Y.: Doubleday, 1971. LC 70-164723. Music topics are covered on pp. 14–15 and 286–93, or elsewhere as available through subject entries in the index. The main value lies in the placement of music in its classified context. [149.

"New Music (1970–72)," *Black Perspective in Music,* 1 (1973), 97–100. A list of first performances and publication information on art music (including film scores and films on black subjects) by black composers, continued occasionally, usually in the first or second issues of subsequent vols. [150.

Harry A. Ploski, Otto J. Lindenmeyer, and Ernest Kaiser. *Reference Library of Black America.* New York: Bellwether Publishing Co., Afro-American Press, 1971. LC 74-151239. An expansion of the *Negro Almanac* into five vols., of which vol. 3 covers "The Black Entertainer in the Performing Arts" and "The Jazz Scene." [151.

"Selected Resources for Black Studies in Music," *Music Educators Journal,* vol. 58, no. 3 (Nov. 1971), pp. 56, 111–17. Contains 110 entries. [152.

James A. Standifer and Barbara Reeder. *Source Book of African and Afro-American Materials for Music Educators.* Washington: MENC, 1972. LC 72-77987. A report generated by the Contemporary Music Project, covering about 500 works in various media, with extensive guidance on classroom experiences. [153.

Jonathan J. Stanley. "A Critical and Annotated Bibliography of Negro Minstrelsy in America." M.A. thesis, University of Maryland, 1972. ("Almost every aspect of the subject is covered. The organization is in three parts: a critical essay evaluating sources about minstrelsy and describing minstrel collections; a bibliographical listing of minstrel show books, anthologies, jokebooks, music books, and catalogued collections of several libraries; and an annotated bibliographical listing of sources about minstrelsy. Also lists an additional

26 theses which touch on the subject of minstrelsy."—Heintze
35)   [154.

Dominique-René de Lerma. *A Name List of Black Composers*. Minneapolis:
AAMOA Press, 1973. (Afro-American Music Opportunities Association, Resource Papers, 2.) LC 78-40669. Not strictly a bibliography
but rather a valuable list of 1,700 name versions, "in general harmony
with the guidelines of" AACR-1 practices.   [155.

James P. Johnson. *Bibliographic Guide to the Study of Afro-American Music*.
Washington: Howard University Libraries, 1973. LC 75-6473. A brief
"pathfinder" with about 500 titles of general writings.   [156.

Ora Williams. *American Black Women in the Arts and Social Sciences: A
Bibliographic Survey*. Metuchen, N.J.: Scarecrow, 1973. ISBN 0-8108-
0615-0. Rev. ed. 1978. ISBN 0-8108-1096-4. The 1973 ed. includes
a good introduction on black music in general, as well as sketches
of seventy musicians on pp. 95–124, with about 450 bibliographical
references to scores and recordings. The 1978 ed. omits the introduction but covers seventy-nine musicians on pp. 102–35. Both are
based on "A Bibliography of Works Written by American Black
Women," *CLA Journal*, 14–15 (Mar. 1972), 354–77, in which music
is covered briefly on p. 361.   [157.

Dominique-René de Lerma. "Black Music: A Bibliographic Essay,"
Library Trends, 23 (1975), 517–32. Commentary on the various
genres of the literature, as reflected in somewhat over 100 of the
most important writings.   [158.

William J. Jones. "Music Materials for Instructional Use from the
Ethnic American Art Slide Library of the University of South Al-
abama," *College Music Symposium*, vol. 17, no. 1 (Spring 1977), pp.
102–19. Inventory of a collection devoted to "musical subject matter in visual art works by native American artists," arranged by
ethnic groups.   [159.

John F. Szwed and Roger D. Abrahams. *Afro-American Folk Culture:
An Annotated Bibliography of Materials from North, Central, and South
America and the West Indies*. Philadelphia: Institute for the Study of
Human Issues, 1978. (American Folklore Society, Bibliographical
and Special Series, no. 31.) ISBN 0-915980-80-0. The arrangement

is geographical, with about 300 music titles accessible through music entries and cross-references in the index. [160.

Meadows, *Theses and Dissertations on Black American Music* (1980; see 504 below).

Mary Mace Spradling. *In Black and White: A Guide to Magazine Articles, Newspaper Articles, and Books concerning More Than 15,000 Black Individuals and Groups.* Detroit: Gale, 1980. ISBN 0-8103-0438-4. The section on musicians (pp. 1180–96) in the occupational index includes about 3,200 personal names, with a separate bibliography on pp. 1267–82. [161.

Camille C. Taylor and William Ballinger. *A List of Black Derived Music and Black Related Music Materials Submitted by Music Companies and Individuals.* New York: MENC, National Black Music Caucus, 1980. Catalogue of several thousand items exhibited at the MENC convention, Miami Beach, Apr. 9–12, 1980. [162.

Dominique-René de Lerma. *Bibliography of Black Music.* Westport, Conn.: Greenwood, 1981–84. ISSN 0272-0264. Volume 1 (*Reference Materials,* 1981) includes about 2,500 bibliographies, discographies, and other lists. Volumes 2 (*Afro-American Idioms,* 1981), 3 (*Geographical Studies,* 1982), and 4 (*Theory, Education, and Related Studies,* 1984) each include approximately 6,000 entries. The lack of general indexes, made more difficult by the renumbered entry series, limits the usefulness of what otherwise is the most extensive, if largely unannotated bibliography in the field. [163.

JoAnn Skowronski. *Black Music in America: A Bibliography.* Metuchen, N.J.: Scarecrow, 1981. ISBN 0-8108-1443-9. A list of 14,319 entries, without annotations. The first 12,079 are arranged under the names of "Selected Musicians and Singers" (the difference between the two, however conspicuous, being here essentially irrelevant). The 2,146 "General References" are arranged by decade and are followed by 94 resource guides. An author index is included. [164.

Alice Tischler. *Fifteen Black American Composers: A Bibliography of Their Works.* Detroit: Information Coordinators, 1981. (Detroit Studies in Music Bibliography, 45.) ISBN 0-89990-003-8. A list of about

76

500 titles on major contemporary composers of classical music.
[165.

Richard Newman. *Black Access: A Bibliography of Afro-American Bibliographies.* Westport, Conn.: Greenwood, 1984. ISBN 0-313-23282-2. Several dozen music entries are accessible in the subject index at the back of the book, under proper names, "Music," and other topical headings. [166.

Samuel A. Floyd and Marsha J. Reisser. *Black Music in the United States: An Annotated Bibliography of Selected Reference and Research Materials.* Millwood, N.Y.: Kraus International, 1983. ISBN 0-527-30164-7. A selection of 413 of the most important works, with title, name, and subject indexes, particularly valuable for its thoughtful annotations and for the contexts suggested by its classified arrangement. [167.

Other black music bibliographies covering specific genres cited elsewhere include Brown (1976; 269 below), Phillips (1977; 272 below), and Hildreth (1978; 276 below) on keyboard music; Everett (1978; 273 below) on band music; de Lerma (1972; 235 below) on choral music; Hatch (1970; 248 below) on black dramatic works and Sampson (1980; 253 below) on blackface shows—all in chapter 9; Garcia (1974; 428 below), White (1975; 430 below), and Jackson (1979; 435 below) on church music in chapter 12; and Godrich and Dixon (1963; 604 below) and de Lerma (1973; 607 below) as discographies in chapter 15. Ferris's Mississippi folklore list (1971; 116 above) and Panzeri's Louisiana list (1979; 84 above) are cited in chapter 6, along with other regional lists in which black music is often identified.

Music of Immigrant Ethnic Communities

The following bibliographies will predictably range from impressive, scholarly publications to fiercely chauvinistic ones, along with some that are both and a few that are neither. More important is that each provides access to citations listed nowhere else, at least among the works discussed in this book, as well as cumulative perspectives on little-recognized dimensions of American music. The two 1983 Clio titles serve to place the literature about music in the general context of American studies.

Giovanni Ermenegildo Schiavo. *Italian-American History.* New York: Vigo Press, 1947. LC 48-779. Repr. New York: Arno, 1975. ISBN 0-405-06418-7. This vol. comprises the three music "books" of a projected set of fifteen such books on various topics. The "Dictionary of Musical Biography" (pp. 217–470) covers nearly 1,000 names, with many uncommon bibliographical references, while the bibliography (pp. 471–76) is in fact generally less interesting, since most of its 100 titles are neither unusual nor Italian in any of their significant particulars.   [168.

Albert Weisser. *Bibliography of Publications and Other Resources on Jewish Music.* New York: National Jewish Welfare Board, 1969. LC 70-3537. A revised and enlarged ed. of Joseph Yasser's *Bibliography of Books and Articles on Jewish Music* (New York: National Jewish Music Council, 1955, a rev. ed. of earlier lists dating back to 1946–47). American topics are included but not specially collected as a unit or in the indexes—as is true of the 1955 Yasser text as well as of such other Jewish music sources as Alfred Sendrey's *Bibliography of Jewish Music* (New York: Columbia University Press, 1951), A. W. Binder's and Leah Jaffa's *Bibliography of Jewish Instrumental Music* (New York: National Jewish Music Council, 1956), Annabelle B. Sonkin's *Jewish Folk-Song Resources* (New York: National Jewish Music Council, 1957), and Lewis Appleton's *Bibliography of Jewish Vocal Music* (New York: National Jewish Music Council, 1968).   [169.

Jorge A. Huerta. *A Bibliography of Chicano and Mexican Dance, Drama, and Music.* Oxnard, Calif.: Colegio Quetzalcoatl, 1972. While the few titles directly pertinent to the present bibliography are on pp. 58–59, they are evasive ones and reflect a context for which Huerta's work provides a valuable backdrop.   [170.

Don Heinrich Tolzmann. *German-Americana: A Bibliography.* Metuchen, N.J.: Scarecrow, 1975. ISBN 0-8108-0784-X. Cites 128 writings about music in the music section on pp. 267–74.   [171.

Esther Jerabek. *Czechs and Slovaks in North America: A Bibliography.* New York: Czechoslovak Society of Arts and Sciences in America; Chicago: Czechoslovak National Council of America, 1976. LC 77-155955. The music section (entries 3400–3686) on pp. 170–83 includes 225 monographs and 62 articles, many of them standard references to Moravian writings, but also a goodly number of folk-song books and nationalistic works by Czech composers working in

America—both the famous and the little known—as well as writings on music, much of it in Czech. [172.

Michael Heisley. *An Annotated Bibliography of Chicano Folklore from the Southwestern United States, III: Singing, Dancing, and Musicmaking Traditions.* Los Angeles: University of California, 1977. (*RILM* 1978:5705) [173.

John Donald Robb. *Hispanic Folk Music of New Mexico and the Southwest: A Self-Portrait of a People.* Norman: University of Oklahoma Press, 1980. ISBN 0-8061-1492-4. About 550 songs discussed in the text are accessible through the indexes (pp. 875–91). [174.

Chicano Periodicals Index, 1976–78. Edited by Richard Chabrán and Francisco Garcia. Boston: Hall, 1981. ISBN 0-8161-0363-1. An index to selected journals, 1967–78, in which several dozen entries are accessible under headings beginning "Music."
Chicano Periodicals Index, 1979–81. Edited by Francisco Garcia-Ayvens and Richard Chabrán. 1983. ISBN 0-8161-0393-3. [175.

Aleksander Janta. *A History of Nineteenth Century American-Polish Music.* New York: Kosciusko Foundation, 1982. LC 84-107566. A list of several hundred titles of works by twenty-seven Polish composers in America and of works on Polish subjects. The detailed citations and extensive background notes are particularly useful. This text, published after the author's death, supersedes his "Early XIX Century American-Polish Music," *Polish Review,* 6 (1961), 73–105; 10 (1965), 59–63. [176.

David L. Brye. *European Immigration and Ethnicity in the United States and Canada.* Santa Barbara, Calif.: ABC-Clio, 1983. ISBN 0-87436-258-X. About thirty citations from the *America: History and Life* data base (see 552 below) are indexed under "Music," while about fifteen more music titles appear under other entries. [177.

Neil L. Shumsky and Timothy Crimmins. *Urban America: A Historical Bibliography.* Santa Barbara, Calif.: ABC-Clio, 1983. ISBN 0-87436-038-2. Also selected from the *America: History and Life* data base (see 552 below). The section "Leisure, Entertainment, and Recreation" (pp. 60–64) includes about ten entries, that entitled "Artistic and Intellectual Life" (pp. 66–73) about twenty-five, while about twenty others are accessible through related subject headings. [178.

Irene Heskes. *The Resource Book of Jewish Music: A Bibliographical and Topical Guide to the Book and Journal Literature and Program Materials.* Westport, Conn.: Greenwood, 1985. ISBN 0-313-23251-2. The American materials from among the 1,220 entries in this book are best accessible not through the classification scheme but through subjects in the "Topical Index" (pp. 281–302). [179.

Of special value in this study are the ethnic recording activities reflected in the 1982 Library of Congress symposium (617 below) and Richard Spottswood's research (beginning with 603 below).

Women in American Music

Writings on America's women musicians may be located in biographical studies that cover American music in general, as, for instance, the works surveyed in chapter 8; or in women in music, as, for instance, in Hixon and Hennessee (1975) or Stern (1978); or in sources on American women, like the Hinding guides (1972, 1979); or, most precisely of all, in the following:

Mu Phi Epsilon, Composers and Authors. N.p., 1954, with supplements 1956, 1958, and 1960. New eds. 1962, 1972. A list of (in 1972) about 10,000 works by about 1,500 members of the national music fraternity, here arranged by medium. [180.

Mrs. Edward C. Mead. *Catalog of the Composer's Library.* [Cincinnati: Delta Omicron, 1977.] A listing of about 1,500 works by members, maintained in the collection at the Cincinnati Public Library.
[181.

JoAnn Skowronski. *Women in American Music: A Bibliography.* Metuchen, N.J.: Scarecrow, 1978. ISBN 0-8108-1109-X. A list of 1,305 entries, mostly annotated, arranged by broad period classes, with a name index. [182.

Adrienne Fried Block and Carol Neuls-Bates. *Women in American Music, a Bibliography of Music and Literature.* Westport, Conn.: Greenwood, 1979. ISBN 0-313-21410-7. A list of 5,024 annotated citations, in a systematic arrangement by genre and period, with a detailed author-subject index. Entries 1–47 further cover the bibliographical record of published and library-specific lists on women in American music.   [183.

Cynthia E. Harrison. *Women in American History: A Bibliography.* Santa Barbara, Calif.: ABC-Clio, 1979. ISBN 0-87436-260-1. Extracted from the *America: History and Life* data base (see 552 below), the set includes a subject index that brings out about forty music references in each vol., the first devoted to chronological periods, the second containing a section on "Images of Women in Art, Literature, and Folklore" (pp. 155–61).   [184.

Judith Lang Zaimont and Karen Famera. *Contemporary Concert Music by Women: A Directory of the Composers and Their Works.* Westport, Conn.: Greenwood, 1981. ISBN 0-313-22921-X. Brief biographies of seventy-two composers, with portraits and autograph facsimiles, followed by a list of about 2,000 titles, arranged by genre or medium.   [185.

Other bibliographies describe the work of women as members of other groups, e.g., Williams (1973; see 157 above) in the black music list above.

8

Personal Bibliographies

Biographies themselves often provide our best access to the bibliography of writings by and about particular composers and other musicians. Admittedly, the lists—especially in popularized biographies—will often consist of highly selective writings about the person and minimal work lists of their compositions or literary texts, along with discographies of ancient and unobtainable recordings.

Collective Bio-Bibliography

The major sources, the most useful and important of them cited by Jackson, range from the venerable Reis books through the useful Claghorn and Anderson. It is almost inevitable that these books, like the biographies themselves, should include useful bibliographical information, if nothing more than musical titles. The reference works that follow are either bibliographical in a narrow sense of the term—they include scrupulously formulated citations of physical documents—or important to mention for bibliographical reasons noted.

Richard Jackson. *United States Music: Sources of Bibliography and Collective Biography.* Brooklyn, N.Y.: Institute for Studies in American Music, 1973. (I.S.A.M. Monographs, 1.) ISBN 0-914678-00-0. Covers ninety major reference sources, with annotations at once both delightfully opinionated and highly authoritative. The biographical sources, dispersed through the list, will often cite the names of the composers who are covered and whose names are included in the index at the end.   [186.

W. S. B. Matthews. *A Hundred Years of Music in America.* Chicago: Howe, 1889. LC 6-32339. Repr. New York: AMS Press, 1970. LC

73-135725. Includes titles of musical works throughout, perhaps most useful being those in chaps. 20 ("Composers of Salon and Chamber Music," pp. 636–71) and 21 ("Dramatic, Orchestral, and Oratorio Composers," pp. 672–702). A "Supplementary Dictionary of American Musicians" follows (pp. 703–15). [187.

Bio-Bibliographical Index of Musicians in the United States of America since Colonial Times. Washington, 1941. LC 41-13993. 2d ed. Washington: Pan American Union, Music Section, 1956. LC 57-4. Repr. New York: AMS Press, 1970. ISBN 0-404-08075-7. Repr. St. Clair Shores, Mich.: Scholarly Press, 1972. ISBN 0-403-01362-3. A vast and invaluable index to personal names cited in the major writings about American music, prepared (under the supervision of Keyes Porter, 1936–39, and Leonard Ellinwood, 1940) by the District of Columbia Historical Records Survey, Division of Community Service Programs, under the auspices of the Board of Commissioners of the District of Columbia, the Pan American Union, and the Library of Congress. The "2d ed." is a reprint with several corrections and added death dates. The "Bibliography" (pp. xvii–xxii) lists the sixty-six titles indexed along with twelve supplementary titles, these constituting the generally recognized corpus of American musical scholarship at the time. [188.

Pan Pipes of Sigma Alpha Iota. The annual "American Composer Update" (formerly entitled "Amer-Allegro") sections have appeared since 1949 in the winter issues, providing a valuable chronicle of the activities of contemporary composers, about 200 of them in the latest issue, with information on new works, first performances, commissions, and awards. [189.

Sheila Keats. "Reference Articles on American Composers: An Index," *Juilliard Review,* vol. 1, no. 3 (1954), pp. 21–34. A list of 118 titles about fifty-six composers. [190.

Compositores de America: Datos biograficos y catalogos de sur obras / Composers of the Americas: Biographical Data and Catalogs of Their Works. Washington: Pan American Union, 1955–72. Annual listings of from three to several dozen selected major composers, 306 in all, of whom close to half are from the United States. An invaluable series, praiseworthy for the inclusion of features such as photographs and manuscript music facsimiles. [191.

John Edmunds and Gordon Boelzner. *Some Twentieth Century American Composers: A Selective Bibliography.* New York: New York Public Library, 1959–60. LC 59-15435. Based on the texts in the *Bulletin of the New York Public Library,* 63 (1959), 341–54, 404–23; and 64 (1960), 361–76. Lists of writings about the music of thirty-two major composers and of their literary output. [192.

Composium: A Quarterly Index of Contemporary Compositions. Los Angeles: Crystal Record Co. (later Sedro Woolley, Wash.: Crystal Musicworks), 1971–83; cumulated annually as *Directory of New Music.* For major American composers—about 70 in the first annual vol., growing to about 500 in the last—summary biographies followed by brief citations of new works with minimal information on availability, along with an index by medium at the end. [193.

Claudia D. Johnson and Vernon E. Johnson. *Nineteenth-Century Theatrical Memoirs.* Westport, Conn.: Greenwood, 1982. ISBN 0-313-23644-5. A listing of 427 British and American titles, in which several dozen references to operatic and other musical careers are accessible through personal names and through headings like music, opera, or orchestra in the index. [194.

Andrew Farkas. *Opera and Concert Singers: An Annotated International Bibliography of Books and Pamphlets.* New York: Garland, 1985. ISBN 0-8240-9001-2. A list of 1,840 monographs, published and unpublished, covering individually or collectively 796 operatic and art-song performers, of which roughly 20 percent were born in the United States and 30 percent more performed extensively in the United States. The introduction is particularly praiseworthy. (The bibliography by Robert Cowden, covering much the same area, devotes a smaller proportion to American singers.) [195.

Other collective biographical sources cited elsewhere include the lists of regional "musical sons and daughters" (pp. 57–60); the lists of ethnic and women composers in the preceding chapter; folksong and jazz bibliographies that approach the repertory through the singers (such as Lawless in 1965, 311 below, and Kinkle in 1974, 345 below); dictionaries of sacred music composers (notably Metcalf in 1925, 416 below, and Knippers in 1937, 422 below); and performer discographies (pp. 203–4 below).

Individual Bio-Bibliography

Composer bibliographies range from brief (but often authoritative) work lists in general music dictionaries to single volumes now incorporated into special publishers' series (of which those from Greenwood and Garland are by now the best established, those by Pro/Am Music Resources perhaps the more imaginatively useful). Rather than attempt to reconstruct this vast bibliographical record of America's musical bio-bibliography, the present discussion will suggest what can happen when compilers are not limited by constraints of ideology (as in the vanity and authorized biographies) and space (as in many tightly packed encyclopedia articles). Given freedom to consider alternatives, bio-bibliographers have often come up with special features—a nice array of them, as discussed below, each of which may or may not be appropriate to the music, the life, and the editions of the composer in question, or of other composers who may be the subject of future studies.

Certainly the prime requisite, following the established practice of the monumental thematic catalogues of major composers, should be a listing of the music itself—not only the titles but also the editions (if not all of them, at least the first and the authoritative ones), together with the location of those not generally available or still in manuscript. Beyond this the detail and the precision of the data are perhaps best determined by the catalogue of the composer in question. Stephen Foster was much republished in his lifetime, and thus his editions are likely to contain both potential textual variants and useful evidence of the spreading popularity of his songs. Under the circumstances the details of scholarly descriptive bibliography are much in order—as in the succession of lists by Whittlesey and Fuld. Whether this level of detail is needed in studies of MacDowell may be more open to question.

Thematic incipits may be useful for composers whose works are easy to confuse or are most identifiable through the musical content itself—as reflected in the bibliographies devoted to Gilbert and Krogmann, where such conditions may or may not be present. Certainly for composers significant for their pedagogical works, a grading of the repertory is in order—as in the older Krogmann list. Other composers who wrote short pieces mostly available in anthologies and songbooks, hymnals and tunebooks, and other such collections justify analytical indexes, as with Lowell Mason. Extensive unpublished material serves to justify particulars on the manuscripts themselves (as for Fry and Gottschalk) or on the circumstances of first performance (as for Sousa or Griffes). Illustrations often convey the character of the original documents and, implicitly, of the conditions under which the composer worked (as in Nathan's Billings book). For those composers who recorded their own or others' works or for folk and popular music, a discography is called for. For a composer like Irving Berlin who spanned the eras dominated by sheet music and recordings, one must agree (whatever one might think of Jay's title) that a recitation of song titles covering both is perhaps about all that is needed. The Hovhaness inventory of opus numbers performs a service of special importance to this prolific composer. As for the John Cage volume, it is especially appropriate to the present discussion both for its imaginativeness and for its conventionality. (While one should grieve to think that a Cage bibliography might be anything other than imaginative, it is nonetheless reassuring to know that conventional bibliographies are not entirely on the wrong track.)

Doyle's Gottschalk bibliography is the landmark example of a proliferating bibliographical genre that attempts to do everything, as it describes not only published editions and manuscripts but also music and literary texts by the composer, the *Nachlass* of personalia, writings about the composer (even some brief references that seem hardly significant enough to be worth citing), commercial and archival sound recordings, and perhaps even performances and reviews. For some composers it has seemed more sensible, or more feasible, to divide such a daunting task into parts, to allow each part better to speak for itself. Anderson's 1977 book describes the writings about Griffes, for instance, her 1983 book the music by the composer. Manion lists the writings about, Saylor the literary writings by, and Lichtenwanger the music of Henry Cowell.

For all their impressiveness and usefulness, composer bibliographies—perhaps more so than other bibliographies—inevitably ask the larger question (and the better and more useful the bibliographies, the louder they ask): Why? Or to be more specific: Having gone to all the trouble, why doesn't the compiler finish the job with a proper biography or at least a "life and works" job based on the documents or—perhaps most appropriate of all—an engaging study like Bierley's Sousa? Posing such a question may seem churlish. Perhaps such sentiments are merely telling us that the music of America is by its nature not as "composerly" as that of Europe—not all the world's musical *Kleinmeister* lived in eighteenth-century Vienna. Or perhaps the bio-bibliography, more than any other genre of music bibliography, makes it painfully apparent that composers cry out for the advocacies of listening and criticism rather than of compiling.

The list below, arranged by the musician's name, is limited to the works mentioned in the previous discussion.

Dave Jay. *The Irving Berlin Songography, 1907–1966.* New Rochelle, N.Y.: Arlington House, 1969. ISBN 0-87000-998-2. A chronological list of songs, with minimal information on sources, well laid out for the early years but difficult to follow in the later years, and unfortunately with no indexes at all.   [196.

Hans Nathan. *William Billings: Data and Documents.* Detroit: Information Coordinators, 1976. ISBN 0-911772-67-7. A scholarly overview of the original documents with numerous contemporary illustrations.   [197.

John Cage. New York: Henmar Press, 1962. LC 66-32674. Essentially a catalogue, imaginatively presented for reference access.   [198.

Bruce Saylor. *The Writings of Henry Cowell: A Descriptive Bibliography.* Brooklyn, N.Y.: Institute for Studies in American Music, 1977. (I.S.A.M. Monographs, 7.) ISBN 0-914678-07-8. While not strictly speaking a "descriptive bibliography" at all, the list is valuable for its annotations of Cowell's three books, 197 articles and reviews, and thirty-seven other literary texts, lacking only several unpublished manuscripts and Cowell's notes for Ethnic Folkways recordings. Like many other scrupulous scholarly studies, this book has the unfortunate flaw of not being indexed.   [199.

Martha L. Manion. *Writings about Henry Cowell: An Annotated Bibliography.* Brooklyn, N.Y.: Institute for Studies in American Music, 1982. (I.S.A.M. Monographs, 16.) ISBN 0-914678-17-5. An extensively annotated list of 1,359 biographical and general texts, accounts, reviews of performances and descriptive texts, and record reviews—each of these four groups arranged chronologically to reflect in detail Cowell's changing reputation.   [200.

William Lichtenwanger. *The Music of Henry Cowell: A Descriptive Catalog.* Brooklyn, N.Y.: Institute for Studies in American Music, 1986. (I.S.A.M. Monographs, 23.) ISBN 0-914678-26-4.   [201.

Walter R. Whittlesey and Oscar G. Sonneck. *Catalogue of the First Editions of Stephen C. Foster (1826–1864).* Washington: Government Printing Office, 1915. LC 14-30011. Repr. New York: Da Capo,

1971. ISBN 0-306-70162-6. A detailed descriptive bibliography of the first editions at the Library of Congress, whether certain (i.e., as copyright depository copies) or conjectural on the basis of collateral information. See further Nelson F. Adkins, "A Note on the Bibliography of Stephen C. Foster," *Notes and Queries,* 163 (1932), 331–32.   [202.

James J. Fuld. *A Pictorial Bibliography of the First Editions of Stephen C. Foster.* Philadelphia: Musical Americana, 1957. LC 56-10746. A "photo-bibliography," useful for identifying the "points" that establish first editions, largely updating the Whittlesey-Sonneck study above.   [203.

William Treat Upton. *The Musical Works of William Henry Fry in the Collections of the Library Company of Philadelphia.* Philadelphia: Free Library of Philadelphia, 1946. A listing of forty-five holographs along with other manuscripts and printed editions. The list is reprinted in Upton's biography *William Henry Fry: American Journalist and Composer-Critic* (New York: Crowell, 1954), pp. 305–23. [204.

Katherine E. Longyear. "Henry F. Gilbert: His Life and Works." Ph.D. diss., Eastman School of Music, 1968. LC 71-42570. Includes a thematic catalogue.   [205.

John G. Doyle. *Louis Moreau Gottschalk, 1829–1869: A Bibliographical Study and Catalog of Works.* Detroit: Information Coordinators, 1982. (Bibliographies in American Music, 7.) ISBN 0-89990-015-1. Included are a painfully exhaustive alphabetical list of 742 writings of "Literature and Modern Performances" (pp. 17–161); an overview of the contemporary "Newspapers and Periodicals," domestic and foreign, in which Gottschalk was reviewed (pp. 163–82); a "Collections" section listing sixty repositories of source material (pp. 183–214); a "Manuscripts" section with brief citations of seventy-seven extant holographs (pp. 215–51); an alphabetical "Catalog of Gottschalk's Compositions" with 161 titles (pp. 253–332); a classified list of fifty-eight "Modern Editions" (pp. 333–43); and a list of sixty "Recordings" (pp. 345–61).   [206.

Donna K. Anderson. *Charles T. Griffes: An Annotated Bibliography-Discography.* Detroit: Information Coordinators, 1977. ISBN 0-911772-87-1. A list of 525 writings about Griffes, with a chronology of the published music, discography, and list of first performances.   [207.

————. *The Works of Charles T. Griffes: A Descriptive Catalogue*. Ann Arbor: UMI Research Press, 1983. ISBN 0-8357-1419-5. A catalogue of the composer's music. [208.

Richard Howard. *The Works of Alan Hovhaness: A Catalog, Opus 1–Opus 360*. White Plains, N.Y.: Pro/Am Music Resources, 1985. ISBN 0-912483-00-8. A numerical list, with condensed information on the named subdivisions and performance medium, supported by a classified index by medium. [209.

Thematic Catalogue of Musical Compositions by C. W. Krogmann. Boston: B. F. Wood, 1913. Includes thematic incipits for 175 piano works, grades 1A–3C. [210.

Oscar G. Sonneck. *Catalogue of First Editions of Edward MacDowell (1861–1908)*. Washington: Government Printing Office, 1917. Repr. New York: Da Capo, 1971. ISBN 0-306-70161-8. A descriptive bibliography of the first editions, established or conjectural, at the Library of Congress. [211.

Henry L. Mason. *Hymn-Tunes of Lowell Mason: A Bibliography*. Cambridge: Harvard University Press, 1944. LC 44-5358. Includes fourteen lists that provide different perspectives on Mason's output, consisting of both individual hymns and anthologies (hymnals and songbooks). [212.

Paul E. Bierley. *The Works of John Philip Sousa*. Columbus, Ohio: Integrity Press, 1984. ISBN 0-918048-04-4. Mainly a classified list arranged by genre (operettas, marches, other works, arrangements, and transcriptions), with historical background on the works, often lengthy and typically engaging, followed by brief specifics on the manuscripts, publications, and copyrights. Essentially a re-packaging of the author's *John Philip Sousa: A Descriptive Catalog of His Works* (Urbana: University of Illinois Press, 1973; ISBN 0-252-00297-0), with a chronology and general index. In its attractive graphic appearance and conception, a model bio-bibliography, the only possible reservations being that the entries in each section might better have been listed chronologically than alphabetically and that the editions might have been cited more fully. [213.

Other Musical Personalia

Other bibliographies record the musical tastes of famous people (as with Jefferson and Lanier); suggest their fame as reflected in songs about them (e.g., Lincoln); establish the bibliographical record of collected criticism (as with the Huneker and Rosenfeld lists); or document the fame of poets and other literati as reflected in settings of their texts (e.g., Poe). The poetical settings of major American authors are also reported in the great set begun by Jacob Blanck.

A. W. Kelley. "Music and Literature in the American Romantic Movement: A Study of the Knowledge of, Use of, and Ideas Relating to Music in Emerson, Hawthorne, Longfellow, Poe, Thoreau, Lowell, Whitman, and Lanier." Ph.D. diss., University of North Carolina, 1929. (*Amerigrove*, passim) [214.

Jacob Nathaniel Blanck et al. *Bibliography of American Literature.* Compiled for the Bibliographical Society of America. New Haven: Yale University Press, 1955– . Bibliographically scrupulous citations of significant early editions by major American literary figures. The music coverage is described in Blanck's "Sheet Music in *BAL,*" MLA *Notes,* n.s., 21 (1964), 337–39, as well as in vol. 1, pp. xxi–xxii. Musical material in early vols. is interfiled within the main sequence, as for the fifteen entries of songs set to poetry by William Cullen Bryant or the several settings under Thomas Dunn English or Joyce Kilmer. Later vols. separate the sheet music into its own section, as with the 31 settings of eleven different poems by Sidney Lanier and the roughly 260 settings of ninety-five titles by Henry Wadsworth Longfellow. For John Howard Payne, the early libretti and musical editions of *Clari; or, The Maid of Milan* and "Home Sweet Home" appear in sec. 1, while the early reprints are listed in sec. 2. Other music entries involve occasional religious poetry in hymnals, essays on musical topics, and dramatic texts set to music. [215.

Michael Hovland. *Musical Settings of American Poetry: A Bibliography.* Westport, Conn.: Greenwood, 1986. ISBN 0-313-22938-4. A listing of about 2,400 poems by ninety-nine authors, identifying about 5,800 published musical settings. Separate indexes cover the roughly 2,100 composers involved and the titles both of the original poems and the musical settings. [216.

91

Joseph Lawren. "James Gibbons Huneker: A Bibliography," in Benjamin De Casseres, *James Gibbons Huneker* (New York: Lawren, 1925), pp. 41–62. A listing of Huneker's twenty-two books, with useful contents lists, and over 100 contributions on music and other topics. [217.

Helen Cripe. *Thomas Jefferson and Music.* Charlottesville: University Press of Virginia, 1974. ISBN 0-8139-0504-4. Jefferson's collecting activity is discussed on pp. 77–87. Appendix 1 (pp. 97–104) is a transcript of Jefferson's music catalogue of 1783, while app. 2 (pp. 105–28) lists the extant copies at the University of Virginia. [218.

Philip Graham and Frieda C. Thies. "Bibliography," in *The Centennial Edition of the Works of Sidney Lanier* (Baltimore: Johns Hopkins University Press, 1945), vol. 6, pp. 377–412. "Section E: Musical Compositions" (pp. 389–90) cites the ten extant works, summarizes the evidence of twelve more works that do not survive, and describes the extant fragments. [219.

Louis A. Warren. *Lincoln Sheet-Music Check List.* Fort Wayne, Ind.: Lincolniana Publishers, 1940. LC 41-14701. An alphabetical list of 329 titles, 1859–1940, with an author index. [220.

May Garrettson Evans. *Music and Edgar Allan Poe: A Bibliographical Study.* Baltimore: Johns Hopkins University Press, 1939. LC 39-32446. An alphabetical composer list of about 230 settings with detailed annotations. [221.

Charles L. P. Silet. *The Writings of Paul Rosenfeld: An Annotated Bibliography.* New York: Garland, 1981. ISBN 0-8240-9532-4. A list of twenty-one books by Rosenfeld; 406 published articles, reviews, and letters; archival holdings of major libraries; and 249 writings about the early twentieth-century critic and proponent of contemporary art music. [222.

Kenneth P. Neilson. *The World of Walt Whitman Music: A Bibliographical Study.* Hollis, N.Y.: Author, 1963. LC 62-21031. [223.

MUSICAL MEDIUMS AND GENRES

The next four chapters are devoted to the lists that cover particular kinds of music. Bibliographical theory and bibliographical practice meet—which of course is to say that they converge awkwardly—in music classification. Broad categorization may be both convenient and convincing—serious versus popular, secular versus sacred, vocal versus instrumental. Often, however, further specifics are needed, to require hymns to be usefully separated from psalms and anthems, city folk music from rural folk music, parlor songs from ballads, blues from rock (not to mention rockabilly and rhythm and blues), opera from operetta (not to mention musicals, musical comedies, and musical shows), band from orchestra music, and serious from popular chamber music (i.e., string quartets from jazz combos, however ignoring jazz string quartets). As refinement enters the picture the broad categories begin to look anything but convenient and convincing.

The practice of "pigeonholing" comes both naturally and necessarily for the "insiders" of music—performers, listeners, and others involved in repertory for actual musical events. Rather than search through the universe of learning, they (and after all they are the heart of the music world) want lists that serve their essential requirements. "Give us what we need, and forget the rest." For "outsiders," on the other hand, more comfortable with objective criteria and more inclined to look around for context instead of to the center for immediacy—bibliographers, librarians, and scholars, as well as merchants, managers, and other administrators—the pigeonholing is more likely to seem peripheral and secondary. At once both canonic and impressionistic, the dichotomies of music are as useful and as solid as we want them to be. The distinctions are, in other words, political in the broad and honorable sense of the term.

It is often useful to distinguish on theoretical grounds between musical mediums and musical genres. Musical mediums are performance resources—voices, instruments, and combinations of these. (In this book the anglicized plural *mediums* is used for performance presentation, as distinguished from the latinized plural *media,* used for documentary presentation, especially for the "audiovisual media" of films and sound recordings.) Musical genres, in contrast, are particular forms and kinds of music (operettas, hymns, jazz, symphonies, acid rock, parlor songs), incorporating both character (what the music is supposed to be and do) and terminology (what the work is called). In theory the distinction between mediums and genres makes rather elegant sense; in practice the two are always intermixed, leaving us to wonder why we bothered with this particular distinction in the first place.

In addition to mediums, character, and genre names, other complications enter into consideration. Basic aesthetic and sociological dichotomies are important in separating classical from vernacular music, serious from popular, commercial from noncommercial. Admittedly the neater the categories the more prone they are to collapse— usually to everyone's advantage. The entertainment industry of the 1930s, for instance, found it profitable fun to force the question: Are you "with it" (in your relaxed and enjoyable love of the popular music of nice people), or are you a stuffy and villainous lover of old-fashioned classical music, in need of a good dose of "real relaxation?" The entertainment market of the 1980s is much less silly—more honest and more complicated, in fact much like that of the bibliographer and librarian. Often no less suspect, to be sure, are the self-conscious musical androgynes, experiments ranging from rock symphonies to string quartets performed on musical combs, occasionally successful but more often producing effects that run from bewildering provocativeness to disastrous insincerity.

Under the circumstances music classifiers of all kinds—both those who work formally in libraries or in preparing classified lists and all of us as we make informal day-to-day distinctions—can generally be excused for a cynical candor. In truth most art music is conspicuously inartistic; most vernacular music is created for rather than of and by the people; most concert music is rarely heard in a concert hall; much serious music is rather comical and much comic song quite sobering; most aspiring popular music is never very popular with anybody; and most commercial music is not very profitable to anybody in contrast to those noncommercial works that occasionally prove to be spectacularly lucrative.

Distinctions are thus probably best made as quickly and painlessly as possible—sonatas are always serious and blues vernacular, violins are always classical and saxophones popular, university music presses always noncommercial and Tin Pan Alley commercial—midst much justifiable outrage at results that may be convenient but are anything but convincing. In the meantime classifiers will no doubt do best as they are allowed to reflect realities more than theories; and they live in profound hopes that the users of their work will be thoughtful enough to consider as many of the alternatives as possible.

Such a tortuous prologue is necessary to the four chapters that follow, ostensibly concerned with physical documents but in fact concerned with the repertories of particular musicians. Musical texts and editions are the major interest. Writings about the music in question are covered in passing, as noted, and extensively in chapter 10, but usually more thoroughly in the lists discussed in chapter 14, while the appropriate specialized discographies are found mostly in chapter 15. The musical audiences, it should be further noted, will bear a slightly different focus in each of the four chapters. The quintessential musicians for chapter 9 (concert music) are professional performers in search of repertory; for chapter 10 (vernacular music) they are amateur enthusiasts, least of all the professionals who either know where to get what they need or write it themselves. For chapters 11 (popular song) and 12 (sacred music), we are probably dealing with the widest range of audiences, from grateful passive listeners to scholars in nonmusic fields, but once again perhaps least of all with performers themselves.

9

Concert Music

American operas, symphonies, and chamber music need to be distinguished from — what? Popular music? Folk music? When one compares the lists cited in this chapter with those in the next, it becomes obvious that different materials are involved. In the absence of any more intellectually intricate and operationally consistent definition, concert (or serious or art) music is perhaps best defined here on the most profound and simplistic of bibliographical terms. It is that music from those repertories best known, or at least most appropriately known, through the name of a composer. Band music and film music are included (even when most of us have trouble associating composers with particular marches or movies), while jazz and pop tunes are treated elsewhere (even when most of us know who wrote "Stardust" or "Maple Leaf Rag").

The music considered in this chapter typically aspires to large forms, and it is usually conceived for concert audiences. Its essence is the world of operas and symphonies, of chamber music and a wide range of recital literatures. Compromises will often make for some of the most interesting and best music of all. Repertories are often at their best, in fact, as they fit into intermediary domains between pure art and pure commerce. Italian opera and Gilbert and Sullivan, Sousa marches and Gunther Schuller jazz, Victor Herbert operettas and Frank Loesser musicals, and Virgil Thomson film scores and Stan Kenton big band music come to mind. The compromised repertories at times descend into music that not only sells well but insults the buyer in the process, or rise to ennoble the listeners by making fools of them. Ultimately the genres themselves need to stand as the units of bibliographical study: quality is irrelevant.

What is true of the literature itself should be true of the bibliographies as well. Some of the lists are austere in their limitations and valuable for that; others are broadly based and equally valuable; still others are flawed for being neither austere nor broadly based. The

97

polyglot character of our musical environment should serve to remind us once again that bibliographies, such as those listed below, function best when they are directed to clearly defined users. The peripheries are so numerous and diverse as to preclude any comprehensive commentary on each of them here; and brief hints of an evaluation in the annotations below suggest which of the peripheries have been considered. Compilers of a list intended for serious woodwind ensembles, for instance, would want to think seriously—depending on the performers they hope will use and respect their list—before including (1) arrangements of marches from the colonial and federal periods, (2) arrangements of Broadway hits from the 1930s, (3) high-school band simplifications, or (4) original American salon music in a Viennese style. Indeed it is a sign of a rich musical pluralism that performers should be able to be so choosy—and should have published bibliographies to call on in their choosiness.

The promotional function of bibliographies is obvious in lists like those discussed below. Citation is a means of recommending and publicizing, as much as a newspaper or television advertisement— merely of a different kind and for a different type of audience.

General Sources

Several valuable bibliographies have addressed the totality of the world of art music, irrespective of genre or medium. Most of these lists reflect the promotional activities of organizations, in varying ways resulting from the efforts of committed supporters and compilers.

Martha Caroline Galt. *Know Your American Music: A Handbook.* Augusta, Maine: Kennebec Journal Print Shop, 1943. LC 44-30737. 2d printing. Ithaca, N.Y.: National Federation of Music Clubs, 1945. LC 47-6589. A promotional pamphlet for the cause of American music of all kinds, built around a classified listing of about 1,500 available editions. [224.

Library of American Music Scores. [Washington: U.S. Office of War Information, 1945?] LC 49-57091. (*Pre-1956 NUC*, vol. 621, p. 560; a 1950 supplement is also said to have been prepared.) [225.

Angelo Eagon. *Catalog of Published Concert Music by American Composers.* Washington: U.S. Information Service, 1964. Rev. ed. Metuchen, N.J.: Scarecrow, 1969. ISBN 0-8108-0175-2. *First Supplement.* 1971.

ISBN 0-8108-0387-9. *Second Supplement.* 1974. ISBN 0-8108-0728-9. Classified by medium, with author and composer indexes.
[226.

Music of the Last Forty Years Not Yet Established in the Repertoire. Cambridge: Harvard University, Fromm Music Foundation, [1975]. A list of the works submitted in response to a questionnaire from the foundation, with brief citations of about 1,800 compositions, more than half of them by American composers.
[227.

"Selective List of American Music for the Bicentennial Celebration," *Music Educators Journal,* vol. 61, no. 8 (1975), pp. 54–61 (choral music); vol. 61, no. 9 (1975), pp. 48–52 (band music); vol. 62, no. 2 (1975), pp. 66–72 (orchestral music); and vol. 62, no. 6 (1976), pp. 55–63 (operatic music).
[228.

American Music before 1865 in Print and on Records: A Biblio-Discography. Brooklyn, N.Y.: Institute for Studies in American Music, 1976. (I.S.A.M. Monographs, 6.) ISBN 0-914678-05-1. Includes 199 performing editions.
[229.

Richard E. Jackson. *U.S. Bicentennial Music, I.* Brooklyn, N.Y.: Institute for Studies in American Music, 1976. (I.S.A.M. Special Publication, 1.) ISBN 0-914678-06-X. Lists about 500 editions of early American music published 1970–76, when forthcoming festivities were clearly in mind.
[230.

Margaret Jory and Leslie Hinkle. *The New Music Repertoire Directory.* New York: American Music Center, Chamber Music America, 1982. A list of about 150 contemporary works, with brief information on performance resources and availability.
[231.

Cumulatively serving the same purpose are the various American Music Center catalogues cited later in this chapter, e.g., *Choral and Vocal Works* (Finell, 1975; 238 below), *Chamber Music* (Famera, 1978; 274 below), *Music for Orchestra, Band, and Large Ensemble* (1982; 279 below), *Opera and Music Theater Works* (Richmond, 1983; 255 below); and *Keyboard Music* (in preparation). Other catalogues devoted to particular repertories—potentially mixing both vocal and instrumental music—include the following:

Carol Melby. *Computer Music Compositions of the United States.* N.p. 1976.

LC 78-305572. A list of about 200 works by ninety-one composers, with data on the character of the materials and their availability, "compiled for the First International Conference on Computer Music, October 28–31, 1976, Massachusetts Institute of Technology."   [232.

Vocal Music

Among the specialized bibliographies of American vocal music, early choral music is cited in the Specht bicentennial list, while contemporary choral music is described in the recent Lust list. Art song (to the extent that it can be separated from popular song, as discussed in chapter 8) is the subject of the historical surveys of Upton and Yerbury and the Carman list.

William Treat Upton. *Art-Song in America*. Boston: Ditson, 1930. LC 30-33445. *Supplement*. 1938. About 250 composers, covered in the index, are discussed in terms of about twice that number of individual titles.   [233.

Grace Yerbury. *Song in America, from Early Times to about 1850*. Metuchen, N.J.: Scarecrow, 1971. ISBN 0-8108-0382-8. Citations of about 1,000 published editions of works of a wide variety, arranged by groups on pp. 87–100, 138–54, 180–95, 221–39, and 270–87.   [234.

Dominique-René de Lerma. "A Selective List of Choral Music by Black Composers." *Choral Journal*, vol. 12, no. 8 (Apr. 1972), pp. 5–6. Cites fifty-eight titles by forty-three composers, annotated for performers.   [235.

R. John Specht. *Early American Vocal Music in Modern Editions*. Albany: New York State American Revolution Bicentennial Commission, 1974. A list of about 100 titles of choral (i.e., excluding solo vocal) works.   [236.

Judith Elaine Carman et al. *Art-Song in the United States: An Annotated Bibliography*. New York: National Association of Teachers of Singing, 1976. LC 77-150078. *Supplement*. 1978. LC 80-117465. An annotated list of about 2,500 titles, alphabetically arranged by composer and title, with subject and name indexes.   [237.

Judith G. Finell. *Catalog of Choral and Vocal Works.* New York: American Music Center, 1975. ISBN 0-916052-02-8. An alphabetical composer list of about 4,500 titles.   [238.

Anthony Peter Thein. "American Art Songs for Tenor, Baritone, and Bass Voices from 1850–1920." Ph.D. diss., University of Minnesota, 1978. (*RILM* 1978:4569)   [239.

Patricia D. Lust. *American Vocal Chamber Music, 1945–1980: An Annotated Bibliography.* Westport, Conn.: Greenwood, 1985. ISBN 0-313-24599-1. Marred by errors but strong in its enlightened annotations of some 544 works, mostly from the avant-garde repertories.   [240.

Thurston J. Dox. *American Oratorios and Cantatas: A Catalog of Works Written in the United States from Colonial Times to 1985.* Metuchen, N.J.: Scarecrow, 1986. ISBN 0-8108-1861-2. A listing of 3,455 works (439 oratorios, 2,841 choral cantatas, 114 ensemble cantatas, and 61 choral theater works) with particulars on availability and resources, occasional descriptive annotations (based mostly on the composer's words for recent works, or critical reviews for numerous works from earlier periods, many of which are unfortunately not extant). Indexes cover titles, authors, and close to 100 subjects.
                                                                [241.

The texts above are devoted primarily to music itself. Among the useful bibliographical works that address the literature, the following includes a variety of specially designed lists and bibliographies:

American Choral Foundation. *Research Memorandum* (1959–   ; the latest is no. 137, for Oct. 1984). Includes numerous repertory lists, title indexes, and bibliographies of analytical writings, of special value to choral conductors.   [242.

Major works of dramatic music are covered by a different group of sources, as suggested below. The Central Opera Service has assumed special responsibility for promoting the cause of American opera. Of peripheral emphasis but intriguing fascination is the Johnson list of operas set in or otherwise involving the Western Hemisphere. In addition titles of particular selections from larger productions are covered in the sources listed on pp. 137–39 below; and these will often be useful for the titles of the larger productions as well, particularly for the musicals and light works.

John Towers. *Dictionary-Catalogue of Operas and Operettas Which Have Been Performed on the Public Stage.* Morgantown, W.Va.: Acme Publishing Co., 1910. LC 10-16640. Repr. New York: Da Capo, 1967. LC 67-25996. A list of about 25,000(!) titles, international in scope and with minimal information in tabular form. Scanning the third column, for nationality, will turn up many American works not recorded elsewhere, but for which further particulars can often be derived from the composer index (pp. 691–881).   [243.

Dramatic Compositions Copyrighted . . . , 1870–1916 (1918; see 31 above). A listing of copyright registrations.

Julius Mattfeld. "A Hundred Years of Grand Opera in New York, 1825–1925," *Bulletin of the New York Public Library,* 29 (1925), 695–702, 778–814, and 873–914. The first part provides a general introduction and a list of about fifty writings on the topic. The second consists of a detailed history of opera in New York, and letters *A–D* of the list of about 450 operas performed. The third completes the alphabet and concludes with a chronological conspectus.   [244.

H. Earle Johnson. *Operas on American Subjects.* New York: Coleman-Ross, 1964. LC 64-17352. Alphabetical list of about 350 operas—many by European composers—with descriptive notes on the American setting, followed by detailed indexes.   [245.

Paul C. Sherr. "Bibliography: Libretti of American Musical Productions of the 1930s," *Bulletin of the New York Public Library,* 70 (1966), 318–24. A list of eighty-nine titles, citing specific copies of the libretti in seven major collections.   [246.

"Directory of American Contemporary Operas," *Central Opera Service Bulletin,* vol. 10, no. 2 (1967), pp. 3–59. A list of about 1,000 titles.   [247.

James V. Hatch. *Black Image on the American Stage: A Bibliography of Plays and Musicals, 1770–1970.* New York: DBS (i.e., Drama Book Specialists) Publications, 1970. LC 72-115695. A list of about 1,800 titles, grouped chronologically (pre-nineteenth century, nineteenth

century, and by decade in the twentieth century), with indexes by
title and author on pp. 123–60.   [248.

Robert C. Toll. *Blacking Up: The Minstrel Show in Nineteenth-Century
America.* New York: Oxford University Press, 1974. LC 74-83992.
"Minstrel Primary Sources"—including the names of the major
library collections, about 140 short titles of "Jokebooks and Songbooks," about 150 "Farces, Playlets, and Burlesques," and about
150 other titles—are listed on pp. 285–302.   [249.

Cameron Northouse. *Twentieth Century Opera in England and the United
States.* Boston: Hall, 1976. ISBN 0-8161-7896-8. A brief list of 1,612
operas, chronologically by the year of first performance, and 941
additional operas for which performance information was lacking.
Supplementary lists are devoted to 400 "Operas Based on Literary
Works," with names of composer and brief references to the source,
and 540 "Published Operas," arranged by composer. The cumbersome plan becomes quite workable, thanks to a useful general
index, making this a valuable source of basic information on obscure
works.   [250.

Arthur Schoep and Brenda Lualdi. *The National Opera Association
Catalog of Contemporary American Operas.* New York: National Opera
Association, 1976. A loose-leaf index of seventy-five operas, with
synopses and particulars on the performance resources.   [251.

*The National Endowment for the Arts Composer/Librettist Program Collec-
tion.* New York: American Music Center, [1979]. LC 79-114655. A
list of about 280 names, with brief biographical data and citations
of the somewhat over 350 works commissioned by the program,
complemented by an index of titles and genres.   [252.

Henry T. Sampson. *Blacks in Blackface: A Source Book on Early Black
Musical Shows.* Metuchen, N.J.: Scarecrow, 1980. ISBN 0-8108-1318-
1. Chapter 5 (pp. 131–327) lists about 500 "Black Musical Comedy
Shows, 1900–1940," with extensive particulars on performances
(plots, cast lists, photographs), while app. B ("A Partial List of Black
Musical Shows, 1900–1940," pp. 457–515) arranges the titles
chronologically.   [253.

Deane L. Root. *American Popular Stage Music: 1860–1880.* Ann Arbor:
UMI Research Press, 1981. ISBN 0-83571-174-9. Appendix A

("Popular Stage Music Works," pp. 219–44) lists about 250 productions, mostly 1860–80, with information on extant textual materials.   [254.

Eero Richmond. *Opera and Music Theater Works.* Vol. 4 of the *Catalog of the American Music Center Library.* New York: American Music Center, 1983. ISBN 0-916052-06-0. A composer list of about 350 titles, with information on first performance, required resources, and availability, and with indexes for librettist, duration, author sources, and subject.   [255.

Richard Chigley Lynch. *Musicals! A Directory of Musical Properties Available for Production.* Chicago: American Library Association, 1984. ISBN 0-8389-0404-1. A list of about 400 shows, with information on scores, resources, licensing agents, and other data relevant to production.   [256.

The discussion above has concentrated on major works, and mostly on serious ones at that — operas rather than operettas, revues, musical comedies, and Hollywood musicals. Analytical indexes to the songs are discussed in chapter 11, especially on pp. 137–39. As for a bibliographical guide to writings about American dramatic music — contemporary accounts, related materials, and modern studies — these are discussed in several of the above works, notably Mattfeld, Toll, Sampson, and Root, as well as in the following:

Stanley Green. *Encyclopaedia of the Musical Theatre.* New York: Dodd, Mead, 1976. ISBN 0-396-07221-6. Includes annotated lists of productions, as well as about sixty-five reference titles and a discography of original cast productions.   [257.

Julian Mates. *America's Musical Stage: Two Hundred Years of Musical Theatre.* Westport, Conn.: Greenwood, 1985. ISBN 0-313-23948-7. The brief "Bibliographical Essay" (pp. 225–31) provides a useful entrance into the secondary literature.   [258.

Instrumental Music

In addition to the various titles cited above, the bibliographical record includes the organ music lists by Curtis and Kratzenstein and the piano music lists of Arlton and Gillespie. Landsman concentrates on violin music, Weerts on wind and percussion music. The contemporary publications of band literature are impressively covered by Berger, the beginning of the historical record by Camus. For orchestral music in general, the ASCAP and BMI volumes are valuable, as well as the catalogues of libraries like the Fleisher collection in Philadelphia.

The Edwin A. Fleisher Collection . . . : A Descriptive Catalogue. Philadelphia: Free Library of Philadelphia, 1933–45. LC 33-4966. *Supplementary List, 1945–55.* 1956. Rev. ed. 1965. LC 65-29889. *Cumulative Catalog, 1929–1977.* Boston: Hall, 1979. ISBN 0-8161-7942-5. An alphabetical composer list of about 12,000 titles, with a rather complex classified index. While the collection itself is international in scope, its copying program has been famous for providing performance parts for an impressive array of works by lesser-known early American composers. [259.

List of Orchestral Works Recommended by WPA Music Project Conductors, 1941. Washington: WPA, 1941. LC 42-992. List of about 250 titles, some published but many then available only through state project libraries and other repositories. [260.

ASCAP Symphonic Catalog. New York: ASCAP, 1959. LC 63-4992. *Supplement.* 1966. LC 67-4434 [which, with the 1st ed., comprises the 2d ed.]. Rev. 3d ed. New York: Bowker, 1977. ISBN 0-8352-0910-5. According to its preface the 3d ed. contains roughly 26,000 titles, of which 10,000 are to be found in the 1st ed. and 7,000 more in the supplement. These are arranged in one composer-title alphabet, with no indexes. [261.

Broadcast Music, Inc. *Symphonic Catalogue.* New York: BMI, 1963. LC 64-55150. Rev. ed. 1971. LC 72-91521. *Supplement.* 1978. LC 81-133842. The 1971 ed. contains somewhat over 10,000 titles, arranged alphabetically by composer and title, without indexes. [262.

Richard K. Weerts. *Original Manuscript Music for Wind and Percussion Instruments.* Washington: MENC, 1964. Rev. ed. 1973. LC 73-76728. A classified list of about 400 titles, subdivided by composer, without indexes. Based on earlier lists in the NACWAPI *Bulletin*, ca. 1960–63, some compiled by Paul J. Wallace. [263.

Jerome Landsman. "An Annotated Catalogue of American Violin

Sonatas, Suites, and Works of Similar Character, 1947–1961." Ph.D. diss., University of Southern California, 1966. Also published as *An Annotated Catalogue of American Violin Music Composed between 1947–1961.* Urbana, Ill.: American String Teachers Association, 1968. LC 68-3123. An alphabetical composer list of over 200 titles, with useful annotations.   [264.

Dean K. Arlton. "American Piano Sonatas of the Twentieth-Century: Selective Analyses and Annotated Index." Ph.D. diss., Columbia University, 1968. LC 70-87510.   [265.

Ronald McCreery. "A Preliminary Catalog of Violoncello Concert Music by American Composers." M.S. thesis, Kent State University, 1972. (*RILM* 1972:52)   [266.

Williams, "The Times As Reflected in the Victor Black Label Recordings" (1972–76; see 606 below). Includes important perspectives on the repertory and the editions, as reflected in recordings in the author's collection.

J. Bunker Clark. "The Renaissance of Early American Keyboard Music: A Bibliographic Review," *Current Musicology,* 18 (1974), 127–32. An evaluative survey of modern editions of keyboard music first published between 1787 and 1830.   [267.

Sollinger, *String Class Publications* (1974; see 531 below).

John Celentano and Creech Reynolds. *A Catalogue of Contemporary American Chamber Music.* N.p.: American String Teachers Association, 1975. A highly selective list of about 250 works, arranged by composer and with data on medium, availability, and occasionally other details.   [268.

Ernest James Brown. "An Annotated Bibliography of Selected Solo Music Written for the Piano by Black Composers." D.M.A. diss., University of Maryland, 1976. A list of about 200 works by twenty-seven black composers, intermixing art music and ragtime. [269.

Raoul F. Camus. *Military Music of the American Revolution.* Chapel Hill: University of North Carolina Press, 1976. ISBN 0-8078-1263-3. Appendixes B, C, and E are devoted to about eighty early published fife tutors, drum manuals, and band collections, of which nearly half are American imprints. [270.

Terry S. Hill. "A Comprehensive Analysis of Selective Orchestra Music Lists Published in the United States for Educational Purposes between 1962 and 1975." M.A. thesis, Brigham Young University, 1977. (*RILM* 1977:166) [271.

Linda Nell Phillips. "Piano Music by Black Composers: A Computer Based Bibliography." D.M.A. diss., Ohio State University, 1977.
[272.

Thomas Gregory Everett. "A Selected List of Concert Band Music by Black American Composers," *Black Perspective in Music*, 6 (1978), 143–50. [273.

Karen M. Famera. *Chamber Music*. Vol. 2 of the *Catalog of the American Music Center Library*. New York: American Music Center, 1978. ISBN 0-916052-04-4. Citations for 3,161 works according to medium, annotated for use by performers, with composer index. [274.

Acton Eric Ostling, Jr. "An Evaluation of Compositions for Wind Band according to Specific Criteria of Serious Artistic Merit." Ph.D. diss., University of Iowa, 1978. LC 78-22438. Appendix E (pp. 245–370) consists of "Bibliographic and Classified Listings" of about 380 editions, cited in two groups—a large general list and a smaller one for "Symphonic Marches"—followed by an index by genre. (The list is selective, based on recommendations by recognized major band conductors, who were instructed to follow ten "Criteria for Judgment" as specified in app. C, pp. 236–41.) Appendix F arranges the titles in terms of level of difficulty assigned in five major selective lists. Also of bibliographical value is the overview of published selective lists of wind-band music on pp. 201–10.
[275.

John Wesley Hildreth. "Keyboard Works of Selected Black Composers." Ph.D. diss., Northwestern University, 1978. Seven composers are covered, with work lists and references on pp. 406–97. [276.

Marilou Kratzenstein. *Survey of Organ Literature and Editions*. Ames: Iowa State University Press, 1980. ISBN 0-8138-1050-7. "The

United States" (pp. 178–203) includes a selective list of several hundred titles by about 100 composers, individually and in twelve anthologies. [277.

Prudence B. Curtis. "American Organ Music North of Philadelphia before 1860: Selected Problems and an Annotated Bibliography." Ph.D. diss., Manhattan School of Music, 1981. [278.

Catalog of the American Music Center Library. Vol. 3, *Music for Orchestra, Band, and Large Ensemble.* New York: American Music Center, 1982. ISBN 0-916052-05-2. A dictionary catalogue of over 2,300 works, with entries for composers, titles, mediums and genres, and authors of relevant literary texts. [279.

John Gillespie and Anna Gillespie. *A Bibliography of Nineteenth-Century American Piano Music.* Westport, Conn.: Greenwood, 1984. ISBN 0-313-24097-3. A list of about 2,000 editions by about 250 composers. Since most of these are known only in contemporary editions, the references to specific copies are invaluable. The supplementary lists at the end (notably app. D, "Select Reference Sources") also provide a useful access to the literature about the editions in the main list itself. [280.

Nancy R. Ping-Robbins. *The Piano Trio in the Twentieth Century: A Partially Annotated Bibliography.* Raleigh, N.C.: Regan Press, 1984. LC 83-62831. A list of about 1,000 works, some with annotations describing the music or the composer. [281.

William Phemister. *American Piano Concertos: A Bibliography.* Detroit: Information Coordinators, 1985. (Bibliographies in American Music, 9.) ISBN 0-89990-026-7. A listing of about 1,000 works, with brief but well-chosen bibliographical details and useful quotations from contemporary reviews. [282.

In addition to the lists above, primarily devoted to the music itself, the following bibliographies are devoted to writings about the music:

Kenneth Berger. *Band Bibliography: A Bibliography of Books regarding Bands and Bandsmen, plus Selected Articles from Periodicals.* Evansville, Ind.: Berger Band, 1955. LC 56-23796. A classified list of about 300 writings, complementing the *Band Music Guide* (1953–   ; see 56 above), which lists editions currently in print. [283.

Frank J. Cipolla. "Annotated Guide for the Study and Performance of Nineteenth-Century Band Music in the United States," *Journal of Band Research,* 14 (1978), 22–40.   [284.

―――. "Dissertations [on] Bands and Band Music" (1979–80; see 503 below).

Film Music

Marks provides the best overview of a field that has not developed as much as one might suspect. The guides cited here cover either or both of two things, as noted below: the film music itself, and most typically its existence rather than its manifestation in extant copies of the films or as performance materials (an example being the venerable McCarty list), or the writings about the music (of which Wescott is likely to remain the major source for many years). Hollywood musicals are further covered in chapter 11.

Clifford McCarty. *Film Composers in America: A Checklist of Their Work.* Glendale, Calif.: Valentine, 1953. LC 53-10345. Repr., with a foreword by Lawrence Morton. New York: Da Capo, 1972. ISBN 0-306-70495-1. A listing of film scores by about 150 composers, arranged by year under each name, with an index to the roughly 2,500 films in question.   [285.

American Film Institute. *Catalog of Motion Pictures Produced in the United States.* New York: Bowker, 1971– . ISBN 0-8352-0440-5. The massive set is designed to include several series, of which F (feature films) and S (short films) most conspicuously concern music. Each of these two is subdivided by decades, and thus far two publications have appeared, each in two vols.: F2 (*Feature Films, 1921–30,* ed. Kenneth W. Munden, 1971), and F6 (*Feature Films, 1961–70,* ed. Richard P. Krasfur, 1976). The first vol. of each set consists of title entries for roughly 6,000 films, in which summary particulars on the music will typically appear in the second paragraph. The second vol. consists of indexes, mostly of personal names, including composers and arrangers of the film score and songs, also singers and occasionally other performers. The subject indexes also include topics and genres, e.g., "music stores," "musical revues," and "musicians." The 1960s set further includes a "Literary and Dramatic

Source Index," in which several films based on operas are cited under the name of the composer. [286.

James L. Limbacher. *Film Music: From Violins to Video.* Metuchen, N.J.: Scarecrow, 1974. ISBN 0-8108-0651-7. 2d ed. as *Keeping Score: Film Music, 1972–1979.* Metuchen, N.J.: Scarecrow, 1981. ISBN 0-8108-1390-4. The 1st ed. includes an anthology of about fifty short essays on film music, by various authors, pp. 13–188, as well as lists superseded by those in the 2d ed. The latter, while expanded, is missing the essays included in the 1st ed. and is limited to lists of "Film Titles and Dates" (pp. 8–78), a chronological list, 1908–79, of "Films and Their Composers/Adapters" (pp. 79–217), "Composers and Their Films" (pp. 218–333), and a discography of "Recorded Musical Scores" (pp. 334–510). [287.

W. Sharples. "A Selected and Annotated Bibliography of Books and Articles on Music in the Cinema," *Cinema Journal*, vol. 17, no. 2 (1978), pp. 36–67. [288.

Martin Marks. "Film Music: The Material, Literature, and Present State of Research," MLA *Notes*, 36 (1979), 282–325. [289.

Steven D. Wescott. *A Comprehensive Bibliography of Music for Film and Television.* Detroit: Information Coordinators, 1985. (Detroit Studies in Music Bibliography, 54.) ISBN 0-89990-027-5. A vast annotated list of 6,340 titles, classified in terms of history, composers, aesthetics, special topics, and research, with cross-references and indexes. Somewhat over half of the entries are American in source or content. Of particular importance here is the last group of sections (pp. 368–82), which lists bibliographical and other reference sources. However invaluable and extensive, the set is still usefully complemented by a list of about 500 titles prepared by Gillian B. Anderson, mostly as extracted from Richard Dyer MacCann and Edward D. Perry, *The New Film Index* (New York: Dutton, 1975), and from the *Arts and Humanities Citation Index*. [290.

In bibliographical work with specific American musical works, meanwhile, it is often useful to know the related circumstances of performance history. Among the works that can be called on are the following:

Henry C. Lahee. *Annals of Music in America: A Chronological Record of Significant Musical Events, from 1640 to the Present Day, with Comments on the Various Periods into Which the Work Is Divided.* Boston: Marshall Jones, 1922. LC 23-76. Repr. New York: AMS Press, 1969. LC 78-97889. A chronicle, 1640–1921, with detailed index. [291.

Julius Mattfeld. *A Handbook of American Operatic Premieres.* Detroit: Information Coordinators, 1963. (Detroit Studies in Music Bibliography, 5.) LC 64-55003. [292.

H. Earle Johnson. *First Performances in America to 1800: Works with Orchestra.* Detroit: Information Coordinators, 1979. (College Music Society, Bibliographies in American Music, 4.) ISBN 0-911772-94-4. [293.

10

Vernacular Music

The concept of "vernacular" musics—of styles, practices, and repertories that emanate anonymously from their societies, preferably in ways that are unobtrusive and expressive of the essence of those societies—is basic to the established discipline of ethnomusicology and profoundly relevant to the long-awaited study of the sociology of music. As particular repertories may need to be isolated—for instance, in decisions over where to search for specific texts in a library—the essential difference between art and folk music becomes particularly capricious and bothersome. For bibliographical purposes the ancient joke of a definition—"folk music is music that was written by nobody"—proves to be oddly useful. The problem is not that such a criterion lacks profundity but rather that it lacks sensitivity. Vernacular music inevitably overlaps with almost every kind of nonvernacular music, particularly in the context of musical commerce, much as the vernacular traditions are affected, contaminated and enriched, and historically altered by the nonvernacular traditions. Defining the genres is in itself often an exercise in truculence and militancy. Such being the case, one way to express oneself in a useful way, short of singing or playing, and without appearing too precious and doctrinaire, seems to be to compile bibliographies. The fundamental problems of definition never go away; but the results, as we shall also see, are often surprisingly delightful (as bibliographies go) and useful.

Readers should be alerted to an amazing range of different definitions of scope. Books with obvious-sounding titles often range into marvelous peripheries. Popular music may or may not include jazz; folksong may or may not include parlor music; blues may or may not include rock; country music may or may not include ragtime. A few such definitions are the result of ignorance; a few are deliberate, based on ideological considerations (too rarely, however, spelled out in the introduction); while a few are based on hopes of selling more copies of a book, with curious results indeed. Some names seem virtually universal in their concern: Duke Ellington comes to mind. But it should not surprise the reader to see Gershwin and Scott Joplin recognized among the acid-rock stars, Bob Dylan as a logical successor to Louis Armstrong, Elvis a bop hero, Ella Fitzgerald joining the ranks of country and western, and the Beatles inserted almost everywhere. (A bit hyperbolic, perhaps—but not much.)

The basic context of folk music, meanwhile, is as part of oral rather than written tradition. To the extent that its varied essences can and should be captured at all, this is typically best done through sound recordings rather than notation. Most of the bibliographical objects themselves thus consist of sound recordings—such as are treated (albeit rather summarily) in chapter 15—or writings about music, but rarely do they consist of musical editions. Writings about music are the primary emphasis of this chapter; those several bibliographies that cover or include musical editions or texts are listed on pages 120–21 and 124–25 below or are otherwise noted in annotations of particular titles.

Folk and Popular Music in General

Here as nowhere else in this study do we appear to have too many books, all attempting to do much the same thing. Each is slightly different and fills a slightly different place in the total picture—which place may or may not be useful. Horn purports to cover the total spectrum of American music, although his special strength lies in his coverage of the less common sources of American folk and pop. In contrast, Booth's catholic definition of scope makes for a list that overlaps with the present book perhaps more than any other title listed here. All of these titles emphasize the writings about folk music, although many include song anthologies, either intermixed or in a separate section.

Annabel Morris Buchanan. *American Folk Music.* Ithaca, N.Y.: National Federation of Music Clubs, 1939. LC 40-14592. A classified list of about 1,000 titles, including writings about folk music, but mostly anthologies and concert arrangements. [294.

Joseph C. Hickerson, Neil V. Rosenberg, and Frank J. Gillis. "Current Bibliography and Discography," in *Ethnomusicology* (1970–). A regular feature through which specialists keep up-to-date. [295.

David Horn. *The Literature of American Music*. Exeter [England]: American Arts Documentation Center, University Library, 1972. 2d ed. as *The Literature of American Music in Books and Folk Music Collections: A Fully Annotated Bibliography*. Metuchen, N.J.: Scarecrow, 1977. ISBN 0-8108-0996-6. The 1st ed. cites 518 titles in the Exeter University Library, while the 2d includes 1,388 writings "in books and folk music collections." The title of the book may suggest a comprehensive coverage of all aspects of American music, and indeed there is a bit of everything in the list; but the coverage of folk and popular music topics reflects a knowledge of the field and turns up useful out-of-the-way titles, whereas the general coverage is unconvincing and erratic in contrast.   [296.

David Tudor [with Nancy Tudor or other associate compilers]. *Popular Music Periodicals Index, 1973–76*. Metuchen, N.J.: Scarecrow, 1974–77. ISSN 0095-4101. Originally devoted to a complete indexing of forty-seven English-language periodicals in full and nineteen more selectively, the set in subsequent annual eds.—later involving Andrew D. Armitage and Linda Biesenthal as collaborators— came to cover more titles in full and fewer selectively. Indexes, by subject and author but not by title, cover major articles but not news items, unsigned notes, and the less significant of the editorial pieces. A supplementary "list of books on popular music published recently and generally favorably reviewed" began to appear in 1974.   [297.

Kinkle, *Complete Encyclopedia of Popular Music and Jazz* (1974, esp. vol. 4; see 345 below).

Abstracts of Popular Culture: A Quarterly Publication of International Popular Phenomena. Edited by Ray B. Browne. Bowling Green, Ohio: Bowling Green University Popular Press, 1976–82. Author lists, with detailed annotations, the music content accessible through the subject "Music" or through more specific headings in the indexes at the end of each of the six parts. Volume 1, covering 1976–77, is in four parts and includes 11,646 entries. Volume 2, covering 1978, is in two parts, which were issued together and include 2,970 entries. Volume 3, extending to 1982, is also in two parts issued together and includes 2,347 entries. Of these entries only perhaps 10 percent are specifically on music, but a goodly proportion of these appear to be titles not covered elsewhere.   [298.

115

Larry N. Landrum. *American Popular Culture: A Guide to Information Sources.* Detroit: Gale, 1982. ISBN 0-8103-4260-3. The music section (pp. 165–94) includes 193 items, supplemented by entries elsewhere as accessible through the subject index (esp. pp. 422–23) and name index. The first sections of the book (pp. 1–32) also provide useful bibliographical context. [299.

Don B. Wilmeth. *Variety Entertainment and Outdoor Amusements: A Reference Guide.* Westport, Conn.: Greenwood, 1982. ISBN 0-313-21455-7. Among the twelve categories—each with a historical summary, survey of the sources, and selective bibliographical list—are 7 ("The Minstrel Show"; pp. 118–29, with 82 titles), and 10 ("The Musical Review and Early Musical Theater"; pp. 165–84, with 158 titles), each of which picks up what would appear to be some obscure journal articles and dissertations. [300.

Mark W. Booth. *American Popular Music: A Reference Guide.* Westport, Conn.: Greenwood, 1983. ISBN 0-313-21305-4. A useful perspective on the field, containing about 250 general titles on pp. 30–41; 100 on pre-twentieth-century music on pp. 50–54; 200 on the music of the early twentieth-century mass media on pp. 76–84; 100 on black popular music on pp. 97–100; 250 on ragtime and jazz on pp. 126–36; 150 on country and folk music on pp. 149–53; and about 250 on rock on pp. 174–83. Each of the discussions is preceded by a general introduction to the literature with commentary on its types and major exemplars. [301.

B. Lee Cooper. *The Popular Music Handbook: A Resource Guide for Teachers, Librarians, and Media Specialists.* Littleton, Colo.: Libraries Unlimited, 1984. ISBN 0-87287-393-5. Features sections on "Popular Music in the Classroom" (pp. 3–62); "Printed Resources on Popular Music" (pp. 65–247), including about 3,000 entries for bibliographies and related works; "Discographies" (pp. 251–310), with about 800 titles; and other features mostly for nonspecialist use. This text complements, and for present bibliographical purposes largely supersedes, the author's *Images of American Society in Popular Music: A Guide to Reflective Teaching* (Chicago: Nelson-Hall, 1982; ISBN 0-88229-514-4), which, however, includes a few titles in the "Selected Bibliography" (pp. 235–64) that I have not located in the 1984 book, as well as some potentially useful contexts for the numerous bibliographical references in the notes at the ends of chapters. Also largely subsumed is the author's essay "Examining

116

a Decade of Rock Bibliographies, 1970–1979," *JEMF Quarterly,* 17 (1981), 95–101.   [302.

Arthur Frank Wertheim. *American Popular Culture: A Historical Bibliography.* Santa Barbara, Calif.: ABC-Clio, 1984. ISBN 0-87436-049-8. Extracts from the *America: History and Life* data base (see 552 below), 1973–80, including abstracts, and probably most useful for entries in specialized nonmusic journals (e.g., *Southern Quarterly, Marine Corps Gazette*). The music section (pp. 20–29) lists 149 entries; others appear under related headings (e.g., Broadway, radio, film, folk music) and are accessible through the indexes.   [303.

Traditional Music

While Horn and Booth in particular cover American traditional music, for this material it is generally preferable to call on works compiled from within the older and more rigorous intellectual tradition of American folk-music scholarship, stretching back to the work of Cecil Sharp and Maud Karpeles, and extending into the contemporary field of ethnomusicology. General works are cited immediately below, followed by the specialized titles.

Julius Mattfeld. "The Folk Music of the Western Hemisphere: A List of References in the New York Public Library," *Bulletin of the New York Public Library,* 28 (Nov./Dec. 1924), 799–830, 864–89. Repr., with additions. New York: New York Public Library, 1925. Repr. of the 1925 book. New York: Arno, 1980. ISBN 0-405-13335-9.
                                                                          [304.

Mellinger Edward Henry. *A Bibliography for the Study of American Folk-Songs with Many Titles of Folk-Songs (and Titles That Have to Do with Folk-Songs) from Other Lands.* [London: Mitre Press, 1937.] LC 37-21469. An alphabetical author list, unannotated and without indexes, of about 2,500 titles, including some relatively obscure articles and anthologies.   [305.

G. Malcolm Laws, Jr. *Native American Balladry: A Descriptive Study and a Bibliographical Syllabus.* Philadelphia: American Folklore Society, 1950. LC 51-1319. Rev. ed. 1964. (Bibliographical and Special Series, 1.) LC 64-17007. Appendix 1 (". . . A Bibliographical Syllabus," pp. 113–256, in the rev. ed.) details the sources for 256 songs, followed by three additional appendixes on questionable texts. [306.

Charles Haywood. *A Bibliography of North American Folklore and Folksong.* New York: Greenberg, 1951. LC 51-1941. 2d ed. New York: Dover, 1961. LC 62-3483. A monumental annotated guide to over 25,000 writings, classified in two basic sections, each subdivided. The first covers "The American People North of Mexico, Including Canada" (i.e., the music and folklore of the settlers), with about 4,000 general works, 6,000 writings on regional topics, 4,000 on ethnic materials, 1,500 occupational, and another 1,500 miscellaneous. The second section (which comprises vol. 2 in the 1961 ed.) is devoted to "The American Indians North of Mexico" and includes about 10,000 titles. The 2d ed. corrects some of the statements (i.e., the title of vol. 2 now reads "Including the Eskimos"), but the usefully ex-panded index (pp. 1293–1301), with a supplement for composers, arrangers, and performers, is clearly the important feature in the new ed., along with the occasional corrections. A supplementary vol., several times referred to and much to be welcomed, has ap-parently not been issued. [307.

G. Malcolm Laws, Jr. *American Balladry from British Broadsides: A Guide for Students and Collectors of Traditional Song.* Philadelphia: American Folklore Society, 1957. (Bibliographical and Special Series, 8.) LC 57-12600. Appendix 1 (". . . a Bibliographical Syllabus," pp. 123–293) details the sources for 290 songs. [308.

D. K. Wilgus. *Anglo-American Folksong Scholarship since 1898.* New Brunswick: Rutgers University Press, 1959. ISBN 0-8135-0310-8. Essentially a historiography of the methodology, with highly selec-tive but valuable bibliographical features on pp. 365–427. [309.

Linnell Gentry. *A History and Encyclopedia of Country, Western, and Gospel Music.* Nashville: McQuiddy Press, 1961. LC 61-1461. Repr. St. Clair Shores, Mich.: Scholarly Press, 1972. ISBN 0-403-01358-5. 2d ed. Nashville: Clairmont Press, 1969. LC 70-7208. The 2d ed. includes about 600 "Biographies of Country, Western, and Gospel Singers, Musicians, Comediennes, and Comedians" (pp. 358–598, up from 334 in the 1st ed., pp. 176–351), with selected titles of the repertory associated with them. Several features in the 1st ed. are deleted in the 2d, however, and neither one has an index.
[310.

118

Ray M. Lawless. *Folksingers and Folkways in America.* New York: Duell, Sloan and Pearce, 1965. LC 65-21677. Includes a list of ballad and folksong anthologies (pp. 271–430), a checklist of 844 favorite folksongs drawn from forty collections (pp. 451–84), and about 700 recordings, 1948–58 (pp. 485–630). [311.

Gillis and Merriam, *Ethnomusicology and Folk Music . . . Dissertations and Theses* (1966; see 505 below).

Bill C. Malone. *Country Music, U.S.A.* Austin: University of Texas Press, 1968. LC 68-66367. Rev. ed. 1985. ISBN 0-292-71095-X. The "Bibliographical Essays" in the 2d ed. (pp. 417–509), one for each of the eleven chapters, provide an invaluable overview of the source materials of all kinds. About 1,300 song titles are indexed on pp. 547–62. [312.

Egon Kraus. "Bibliographie: Schlager und Beat, Tanz- und Unterhaltungsmusik," *Musik und Bildung,* 4 (Apr. 1972), 202–4. (*RILM* 1972:74) [313.

Joseph C. Hickerson. "A Bibliography of American Folksong in the English Language," in Duncan Emerich, *American Folk Poetry: An Anthology* (Boston: Little, Brown, 1974), pp. 776–815. A selective list classified by topics. Particularly useful are the entries by genres (pp. 775–802), fitted to the structure of Emerich's text, and the geographical overview (pp. 804–9). [314.

Dundes, *Folklore Theses and Dissertations* (1976; see 506 below).

Larry Sandberg and Dick Weissman. *The Folk Music Sourcebook.* New York: Alfred A. Knopf, 1976. ISBN 0-394-49684-1. A series of overviews of several dozen of the major traditions, with bibliographical and discographic references. [315.

Cathleen Flanagan and John Flanagan. *American Folklore: A Bibliography, 1950–1974.* Metuchen, N.J.: Scarecrow, 1977. ISBN 0-8108-1073-5. The section "Ballads and Songs" (pp. 90–162) cites just under 700 titles, often with brief annotations. [316.

Library of Congress. Various publications—from or about the variously named Archive of Folk Song, Archive of American Folklore, and most recently the Archive of Folk Culture, and variously located in the Music Division and most recently in the American Folklife Center—include *A Bibliography of Publications Relating to the Archive of Folk Song* (latest updating in 1978); *An Inventory of the Bibliographies and Other References and Finding Aids* (latest updating in Aug. 1984); and the *LC Folk Archive Reference Aid* series (June 1983–   ). [317.

Bibliographies devoted to writings about folk music in particular regions and states are covered in chapter 6 and include the lists by Ferris covering Mississippi (1971; 116 above) and by Feintuch on Kentucky (1985; 121 above).

The above bibliographies are devoted primarily to writings about folk music. Several repertory lists are indispensable for bibliographical purposes, usually through their source annotations. As noted, they are either indexes to the repertory or major scholarly presentations of the repertory itself:

Folk Music: A Catalog of Folk Songs, Ballads, Dances, Instrumental Pieces, and Folk Tales of the United States and Latin America on Phonograph Records. Washington: Library of Congress, 1964. LC 58-60095. Earlier lists of the recordings appeared in 1948, 1953, and 1959, and while further lists have been issued, the one from 1964 is of continuing importance for its detailed coverage and geographical indexes. [318.

Check-List of Recorded Songs in the English Language in the Archive of American Folk Song to July, 1940. Washington: Library of Congress, 1942. LC 42-15513. Volumes 1–2, alphabetical list, of about 10,000 titles, A–K and L–Z. Volume 3, geographical index, subdivided by state and city or area. Repr. in 1 vol. New York: Arno, 1971. ISBN 0-405-03420-2. Updatings of the list are in card files. [319.

Tristam P. Coffin. *The British Traditional Ballad in North America.* Philadelphia: American Folklore Society, 1950. (Bibliographical and Special Series, 2.) LC 51-1318. Rev. ed., with a supplement by Roger deV. Renwick. Austin: University of Texas Press, 1977. ISBN 0-292-70719-3. [320.

Bertrand Harris Bronson. *The Traditional Tunes of the Child Ballads, with Their Texts, according to the Extant Records of Great Britain and America.* Princeton: Princeton University Press, 1959. LC 57-5468.

120

The definitive scholarly presentation of the authentic canon of 299 ballads, as uncovered by Francis James Child and later studied in their Appalachian context by Cecil Sharp and Maud Karpeles. Indexes and bibliographical features are in vol. 4, pp. 517–76.

[321.

Folk music is also included in many of the general song repertory indexes cited in chapter 11, Brunnings (1981; 376 below) perhaps most conspicuously.

Jazz

The literature is inevitably interwoven with that of black music in general, as discussed on pp. 72–77 above. The historical lineage of jazz bibliographies begins with Ganfield, continues with Reisner and with Merriam and Benford (still the most extensive list), and continues with Kennington and Read and, for a more limited repertory, with Hoffman. The several German bibliographies may be particularly valuable for foreign-language materials, weaker for the American side of the Atlantic; they still offer the most impressive and ongoing coverage of the field, for all their limitations, e.g., Carl Gregor's exclusion of most articles and poor indexing, Ruecker's concern exclusively with current periodical literature, and Hefele's minimal citations.

Work, *Bibliography of the Negro* (1928; see 139 above). The music listings on pp. 344–51 constitute what is probably the earliest functional bibliography of jazz.

Jane Ganfield. *Books and Periodical Articles on Jazz in America from 1926–1932.* New York: Columbia University, Graduate School of Library Service, 1933. An annotated list of forty-seven titles, subsumed in the bibliographies below. [322.

Robert George Reisner. *The Literature of Jazz: A Selective Bibliography.* New York: New York Public Library, 1955. LC 55-287. Also issued in the *Bulletin of the New York Public Library,* 58 (1954), 126–50, 186–97, 242–54. 2d ed. 1959. An alphabetical author list of close to 2,000 selected titles, arranged in four categories — "Books" (pp. 9–25), "Background Books" (pp. 27–30), "Selective List of Magazine References" (pp. 31–59), and "Magazines Devoted Wholly or Principally to Jazz" (pp. 61–63) — with no further subject access.

This is "primarily a check list and not a subject list," with a few nonjazz articles in sec. 3 and foreign-language titles.   [323.

Alan P. Merriam and Robert J. Benford. *A Bibliography of Jazz*. Philadelphia: American Folklore Society, 1954. LC 55-1225. Repr. New York: Kraus, 1970. ISBN 0-527-00128-2. A "non-selective" list, with "no claim to completeness," containing 3,324 entries issued before 1951, followed by a list of 113 jazz magazines. The subject index at the end lists entry numbers according to thirty-two broad categories, with further entries for names.   [324.

Carl Gregor, Herzog von Mecklenburg. *International Jazz Bibliography: Jazz Books from 1919 to 1968*. Strasbourg: Heitz, 1969. (Sammlung musikwissenschaftlicher Abhandlungen, 49.) LC 71-92004. An alphabetical list of 1,526 titles, with series, personal, national, and subject indexes, followed by 36 supplementary titles.
————. *1970 Supplement to the International Bibliography (IJB)*. Graz: Universal Edition, 1971. (Issued with the *International Drum & Percussion Bibliography* as Beiträge zur Jazzforschung/Studies in Jazz Research, 3.) Citations for 429 additional titles, in seventeen broad categories in the basic edition.
————. *1971/72/73 Supplement to International Jazz Bibliography (IJB) & Selective Bibliography of Some Background Literature & Bibliography of Two Subjects Previously Excluded*. Graz: Universal Edition, 1975. (Beiträge zur Jazzforschung/Studies in Jazz Research, 6.) ISBN 3-7024-0075-3. Part A contains 1,394 additions to the categories previously included. Part B contains an additional 338 entries on poetry and fiction dealing with jazz and 12 entries for cartoons and drawings. (See also the 1983 list below.)   [325.

Kraus. "Bibliographie," *Musik und Bildung* (1970; see 148 above).

Donald Kennington. *The Literature of Jazz: A Critical Guide*. London: Library Association, 1970; Chicago: American Library Association, 1971. ISBN 0-85365-074-8, 0-8389-0102-6. 2d ed., with Danny L. Read. London: Library Association; Chicago: American Library Association, 1980. ISBN 0-85365-663-0, 0-8389-0313-4. A highly selective list addressing a narrow, if rigorous and well-defended, definition of jazz, with useful section commentaries and entry annotations. The 2d ed. runs to almost twice as many pages with about 1,000 entries, over twice as many as in the 1st ed. But whereas the older text included some major periodical articles and foreign texts by major critics, the latter one excludes all periodical articles and foreign texts except in translations. The indexes are also reconceived, mostly (if not always) for the better.   [326.

Thomas G. Everett. "An Annotated List of English-Language Jazz Periodicals," *Journal of Jazz Studies*, vol. 3, no. 2 (Spring 1976), pp. 47–57; addenda in vol. 4, no. 1 (Fall 1976), pp. 110–11; vol. 4, no. 2 (Spring/Summer 1977), pp. 94–97; and vol. 5, no. 2 (Spring 1979), pp. 99–103. (*RILM* 1978:1448; 1979:5379)   [327.

Norbert Ruecker and Christa Reggentin-Scheidt. *Jazz Index: Quarterly Bibliography of Jazz Literature in Periodicals and Collections.* Frankfurt: Norbert Ruecker, 1977– . ISSN 0344-5399. A bilingual English-German list, including record, book, concert, and festival reviews along with journal articles. The lists of "unconventional" and "hard-to-get" literature include books privately printed or from small publishers, often difficult to obtain or to verify further. "Blues" coverage begins in vol. 2 in a separate section.   [328.

Bernhard Hefele. *Jazz-Bibliographie.* Munich: K. G. Saur, 1981. ISBN 3-598-10205-4. A list of over 6,600 books, articles, and periodical titles through 1979, on jazz broadly defined, including blues, spirituals, and gospel music. "The bibliography is non-evaluative and subjective only in respect of the 28 subject groups the author has chosen," subsuming much from the above titles (with some curious American gaps) but also introducing many European titles, most of them German. Through his broad definition of jazz, Hefele admits some curious titles but also includes some interesting peripheries. The "Bibliographien" section (pp. 27–34) cites 132 sources, some of them typescripts, others general works, most of them not included in the present work.   [329.

Eddie S. Meadows. *Jazz Reference and Research Materials: A Bibliography.* New York: Garland, 1981. ISBN 0-8240-9463-8. A highly selective list of 2,563 titles, covering first the literature in general and by major genres—each section subdivided by books, articles, and theses and dissertations—and second the reference sources of various kinds. The indexes are weak; and apart from some masters' theses not conveniently cited elsewhere, the coverage is much like that in other established bibliographies.   [330.

Carl Gregor, Herzog von Mecklenburg, and Norbert Ruecker. *Inter-*

national Bibliography of Jazz Books. Vol. 1, *1921–1949.* Baden-Baden: Valentin Koerner, 1983. (Sammlung musikwissenschaftlicher Abhandlungen, 67.) ISBN 3-87320-567-X. A revision and expansion of 557 titles from the *Internationale Jazz Bibliographie,* reconceived as "a new basic work in its own right" (p. 7), listed alphabetically with indexes, to be followed by separate vols. devoted to the succeeding decades. [331.

The specialized bibliographical record devoted specifically to ragtime includes sections of two recent major works:

David A. Jasen and Trebor Tichenor. *Rags and Ragtime: A Musical History.* New York: Seabury Press, 1978. ISBN 0-8164-9342-1. A respected historical survey of the genre, built around biographical sketches of fifty major composers, with citations and commentary on about 1,000 major works. [332.

John Edward Hasse. *Ragtime: Its History, Composers, and Music.* New York: Schirmer, 1985. ISBN 0-02-871650-7. Essays by several authors, supplemented by several bibliographies of titles, anthologies, and writings about ragtime, a discography, and other reference lists (pp. 305–400). [333.

Among the few specialized lists of musical editions of jazz are Voigt's *Jazz Music in Print* (1978–79; see 53 above), along with the following titles:

Reese Markewich. *Bibliography of Jazz and Pop Tunes Sharing the Chord Progressions of Other Compositions.* Riverdale, N.Y.: Markewich, 1970. LC 70-104899. Groupings according to harmonic sequence for somewhat over 300 published or recorded works, with publishers' addresses. Potentially a useful guide to the jazz practitioner most particularly but also to the jazz critic, although the lack of cross-references limits its utility. [334.

————. *The Definitive Bibliography of Harmonically Sophisticated Tonal Music.* Riverdale, N.Y.: Markewich, 1970. LC 77-104898. A companion vol. to the above, a selective and somewhat subjective listing of about 400 works—mostly jazz, a few classical, also some pop tunes, most of them usable as jazz vehicles, next to no rock—that "move relentlessly from one key center to another," challenging "keen eared performers" to "develop [their] harmonic ability" (p. 1).   [335.

Taft, *Blues Lyric Poetry* (1983; see 391 below).

Rock and Other Current Popular Music

Among the titles cited in section 1 of this chapter, both Horn and Booth show a special affinity for the current scene. The works below are especially valuable not only for the recent titles that they pick up but also for their presentation from the special vantage of the community itself: their organization, access structure, and commentary are necessarily those of "insiders."

Lana Stanley. *Folk-Rock: A Bibliography on Music of the 'Sixties.* San Jose, Calif.: San Jose State College Library, 1970. LC 70-74762. A list of about 1,500 titles, drawn from standard sources and not annotated or indexed, the first third of them under the general heading "Popular Music," the next third on several of the varieties, and the last third on particular major performers.   [336.

Hugo A. Keesing. "Annotated Bibliography of Pop/Rock Music," *Popular Culture Methods,* 3 (1976), 4–22. A list of 322 citations.
                                                                    [337.

Joseph C. Hickerson. "Rhythm and Blues: A Bibliography of Books," *Sonneck Society Newsletter,* vol. 6, no. 1 (Spring 1980), pp. 7–8. A brief listing of forty-two titles.   [338.

Frank Hoffmann. *The Literature of Rock, 1954–1978.* Metuchen, N.J.: Scarecrow, 1981. ISBN 0-8108-1371-8. A distinctive conception of this book is its classification scheme based on subject headings. The twenty categories and fifty-two additional subcategories are often well conceived and generally helpful but also frequently debatable, the index at the end notwithstanding. The great strength of the book is still its wide coverage, including analytic entries for Stambler's *Encyclopedia of Pop, Rock, and Soul* (1975).
Frank Hoffmann and B. Lee Cooper. *The Literature of Rock, II: 1979–1983, with Additional Material for the Period 1954–1978.* 1986.

125

ISBN 0-8108-1821-3. A two-vol. expansion (and improvement) of the above. [339.

Paul Taylor. *Popular Music since 1955: A Critical Guide to the Literature.* London: Mansell, 1985. ISBN 0-7201-1727-5. The scope is narrowly defined to include recent pop and rock, excluding folk music and jazz. English-language titles, arranged by genre—most impressively in the "Lives and Works" section, pp. 176–436)—with excellent access through indexes. [340.

Eric Tamm. "Materials for Rock Research," *Cum Notis Variorum* (University of California Music Library, Berkeley), 90 (Mar. 1985), 3–6; 91 (Apr. 1985), 7–8; 92 (May 1985), 19–21; 93 (June 1985), 15–16. An annotated list of 146 titles—"a relatively modest quantity of materials"—for purposes of "efficiently representing the various approaches." The ten classified sections have introductions suggesting work yet to be done. Useful for its frequent insights, occasional errors notwithstanding. [341.

Of all the areas of popular music, rock stands as the one that least demands to be read about, through writings such as those cited in the lists above, but rather to be listened to, on sound recordings as cited in chapter 15. For the musical editions themselves, the following title will be useful:

Gargan and Sharma, *Find That Tune: Rock, Folk-Rock, Disco, and Soul in Collections* (1984; see 378 below).

Finally, to the extent that labor and protest songs are within the purview of folk music, attention should be called to the lists by Denisoff (1970; see 394 below), Foner (1975; see 11 above), and Dunaway (1977; see 395 below).

11

Popular Song

America's song literature is profuse and, in general, kindly remembered. Its survival is tenuous, and its immense quantity poorly cited bibliographically. Music reference librarians thus learn to look for particular titles, not only in sheet music but also in songbooks, opera and oratorio scores, and a variety of anthologies. The present chapter is devoted primarily to the guides that they call on (the writings about the songs being discussed elsewhere, notably in chapters 9, 10, 12, 14, and 15).

Those who search for songs learn that the information they work from always needs to be evaluated both for what it precisely says and for what it confuses and misses. For instance, the title one starts with may be incomplete, translated, or garbled. It may be a chorus line ("Glory Hallelujah!"), a first line ("Mine eyes have seen the glory"), a part of a larger work ("Hail, hail, the gang's all here," these words being different from those with which the tune started out), or a nickname ("Swanee River"). Furthermore, memorable music is memorable in different ways, to different people, at different times and in ways that prefer textual archetypes to precise bibliographical statements. Obviously the search for songs will rely on experience and imagination—not to mention a rich network of cross-references, whether in books, side indexes, or available expert consultants. Keywords in context can be of some help, but more often success depends on persistence, inspiration, knowledgeable friends, and good fortune.

Many song inquiries are less precise than we should wish for; but they also likely contain more information than we may at first realize. The structural syntax and speech rhythm of a statement, for instance, will often identify a nickname, chorus line, or punch line. A beginning music reference librarian is also well advised to browse through Mattfeld's *Variety Music Cavalcade* in order to become sensitive to the distinctive "ring" to titles from particular periods—the sailor songs of the 1830s, the Italianate opera sentiments of the 1840s, the several characteristic Stephen Foster idioms of the 1850s, the maudlin moth-erishness of the Civil War era, the heavy German parlor spirit of the later decades of the century, the mock-Irish comic and the coon songs of the turn of the century, the engaging intensity of World War I, the clever lyrics that go over one's head but really shouldn't from the 1920s and 1930s, the smoky technicolor titles and phony-Latino moods of the big band era, the airheaded nonsense songs of the 1940s and 1950s, the dull passion of the 1960s. The commonplace notion that a nation's history is written in her songs is nowhere better under-stood than by historians working at the music library inquiry desk.

Bibliographies may be crucial to the search, but often a wide range of other sources is needed as well. Inevitably the present discussion must recite the different kinds—falling short in attempting to describe the most important, varied, and ineffable of all sources, namely, the walking specialized music encyclopedia, whether masquerading as a barroom pianist who needs a good memory to keep the kitty fed, a retired barbershopper with a recall that has outlasted the voice, or an enthusiastic lover of the Broadway or Hollywood musical in pas-sionate search of a kindred spirit. Obviously the diligent reference librarian, out of a strong sense for survival, needs—and out of a sheer joy in a fascinating assignment, wants—to develop sensitivities to the ways in which particular titles will reflect their different musical genres as well as their periods of composition.

Most secular song has appeared—if not at first, at least some time in its history—as "sheet music." Single publications, ephemeral in their profusion, sheet-music editions all demand separate treatment by library cataloguers—they exist at what is known as the "mono-graphic" level. Thus they ought to be in general the most accessible of all forms of song publication. Unfortunately, few libraries have been well enough endowed to afford first-rate cataloguing. If access is measured in terms of our success in locating items actually asked for, then we are perhaps not doing too badly, since to our pleasant surprise we can usually find the popular favorites called for most often. With a bit of further searching, in fact, we can usually find the same information in a goodly number of books. On the other hand, if access is measured in terms of our effective control over the totality of the literature, then our achievement is greatly wanting. Our only salvation is that a high proportion of the repertory is completely forgotten, at least by any kind of an element of recall that might be called for. The most extensive catalogue of sheet music is surely the indexes to the *Catalog of Copyright Entries* (1891– ; see 30 above). When this or other available catalogues fail, American music students typically settle for the less detailed reference sources closer at hand, as described below.

General Directories

The standard strategy is easy to grasp and to adapt to special circumstances. The steps can even be fitted into the following sequence.

1. When the title is definitely or likely American but the century is in doubt, or for titles that sound faintly familiar, start with Mattfeld.

2. When the music is definitely or likely from the twentieth century, use Shapiro or Pollock; consider Lax and Smith as an alternative, then Burton or Spaeth; or if a personal name comes to mind, use vols. 2 and 3 of Kinkle. Thousands of titles are accessible in these books, provided one knows the exact title.

3. However extensive, these indexes unfortunately make little provision for garbled or variant title forms. Unfortunately, the varieties of garbling are infinite, and finding the right statement depends on experience more than on cross-references.

4. Guided by instinct, consider special possible attributes of the title.
   a. If for some reason special musical interest might appear possible, use critical studies like Hamm, Wilder, or Ewen.
   b. On the basis of hunches, try the various show-tune lists (pp. 137–39 below), folksong lists (pp. 120–21 above), topical lists (pp. 139–42 below), personal lists (pp. 86–92 above), or other sources.

5. When in doubt about whether the song is American (rather than British or foreign) in its origins, either look for more information or, failing in this effort, take a chance on the American lists. If British origins seem a strong possibility, consider the BBC *Song Catalogue*.

6. In proceeding through the steps above, keep in mind the importance of the inquiry in general. If the inquiry is extremely important, if no garbling is suspected or if several options are identifiable, and especially if the year is definitely or even approximately known, try the *Catalog of Copyright Entries* (1891–   ; see 30 above). As a last resort short of giving up, try the expensive desperation searches and appeals for help.

7. If the inquiry ends in failure, pay respects to the walking song encyclopedias of yore, and resolve to encourage their cultivation

in the communities of music library users: expertise is never to be sniffed at.

The general reference works—beginning with the most basic of sources from (1) and (2), followed by the critical sources of (4a), and ending with some of the other alternatives—are as follows:

Julius Mattfeld. *Variety Music Cavalcade, 1620–1950: A Chronology of Vocal and Instrumental Music Popular in the United States.* New York: Prentice-Hall, 1952. LC 52-8607. 2d ed., with coverage extending through 1961. Englewood Cliffs, N.J.: Prentice-Hall, 1962. ISBN 0-13-940700-6. 3d ed., with coverage extending through 1969. 1971. ISBN 0-13-940718-9. Brief surveys describing the contexts of concurrent general events are followed by lists of the year's most famous titles, with particulars on the creators and the imprint. The title index reveals about 5,000 entries in the book. [342.

Nat Shapiro. *Popular Music: An Annotated Index of American Popular Songs.* New York: Adrian Press (vols. 1–6); Detroit: Gale (vols. 7–), 1964– . LC 64-23761. Vol. 1 (1964), 1950–59; vol. 2 (1965), 1940–49; vol. 3 (1967), 1960–64; vol. 4 (1968), 1930–39; vol. 5 (1969), 1920–29; vol. 6 (1973), 1965–69; vol. 7 (1984; ISBN 0-8103-0845-2), 1970–74; vol. 8 (1984; ISBN 0-8103-0846-0), 1975–79; vol. 9 (1986; ISBN 0-8103-0848-7), 1980–84; vol. 10 (1986; ISBN 0-8103-0847-5), 1985. Vols. 7–10 by Bruce Pollock. Citations of about 20,000 titles, arranged year by year alphabetically by title, with more particulars on creators and publishers than in Mattfeld. Volumes 1–8 are largely superseded by the new ed. below, except for inquiries involving the context of a single year. [343.

Nat Shapiro and Bruce Pollock. *Popular Music, 1920–1979: A Revised Cumulation.* Detroit: Gale, 1985. ISBN 0-8103-0847-9. A three-vol. reconception of vols. 1–8 above, built around a rearrangement of the citations into one alphabetical sequence. Volume 1 includes the introductory essays to each of the first eight vols. and the song listings for letters A–I; vol. 2 lists the songs J–T; vol. 3 completes the alphabet and features the unified indexes of lyricists and composers and of performers. [344.

Roger D. Kinkle. *The Complete Encyclopedia of Popular Music and Jazz, 1900–1950.* New Rochelle, N.Y.: Arlington House, 1974. ISBN 0-870-00229-5. Volume 1 (pp. 1–476) is a chronicle, listing the Broadway musicals, popular songs, movie musicals (beginning in 1927), and representative recordings (popular and jazz) for each year. Volumes 2 (pp. 477–1266) and 3 (pp. 1277–2000) comprise a biographical dictionary of 2,006 musicians, with added lists of the major songs, appearances, and recordings associated with each. Volume 4 contains the appendixes, including numerical listings for the nine principal record labels (pp. 2043–2282), and indexes, including about 8,000 personal names (pp. 2283–2385), titles of Broadway and movie musicals (pp. 2387–2412), and close to 25,000 song titles (pp. 2413–2638). [345.

Jack Burton. *The Index of American Popular Music*. Watkins Glen, N.Y.: Century House, 1957. LC 57-3788. An alphabetical list of approximately 27,000 titles in *The Blue Book of Tin Pan Alley* (1951 ed.), *The Blue Book of Broadway Musicals* (1952 ed.), and *The Blue Book of Hollywood Musicals* (1953), the first of these cited immediately below, the other two in section 3 below. [346.

Sigmund Spaeth. *A History of Popular Music in America*. New York: Random House, 1948. LC 48-8954. A breezy popularization, still useful for its mention of close to 4,000 titles in the narrative text, accessible through the index on pp. 663–729, as well as for its chronological listings of about 1,400 additional titles on pp. 587–657, the latter unfortunately not indexed. [347.

Jack Burton. *The Blue Book of Tin Pan Alley: A Human Interest Encyclopedia of American Popular Music*. Watkins Glen, N.Y.: Century House, 1951. LC 50-10828. Expanded ed. 2 vols. 1962–65. LC 62-16426. A chronologically organized discussion with listings of about 3,500 songs, 1776–1950, not associated with dramatic productions. [348.

Heaps, *The Singing Sixties* (1960; see 10 above).

David Ewen. *American Popular Songs, from the Revolutionary War to the Present*. New York: Random House, 1966. LC 66-12843. A dictionary with about 5,000 entries under titles and personal names, with facts and anecdotes on each. [349.

Alec Wilder. *American Popular Song: The Great Innovators, 1900–1950*. New York: Oxford University Press, 1972. LC 70-159643. Informal and personal but also respected for its musical insight, with about

131

800 song titles accessible through the index, on pp. 525–36.

[350.

Charles Hamm. *Yesterdays: Popular Song in America.* New York: Norton, 1979. ISBN 0-393-30062-5. Valuable primarily for its trenchant discussion of the contexts of the music, in general and as applicable to the roughly 800 songs that are cited in the index on pp. 507–33.

[351.

British Broadcasting Corporation, Music Library. *Song Catalogue.* London: BBC, 1966. LC 66-5067. Volumes 3 and 4 include a title index of surprising value in locating the Anglo-American repertory that is entered by composer in vols. 1 and 2.

[352.

Warren E. Colbert. *Who Wrote That Song? Or, Who in the Hell Is J. Fred Coots? An Informal Survey of American Popular Songs and Their Composers.* New York: Revisionist Press, 1975. ISBN 0-87700-216-9. The "Alphabetical Listing of Most Popular Songs" (pp. 113–95) assigns composers to about 400 titles, mostly 1920–50.

[353.

David Ewen. *All the Years of American Popular Music.* Englewood Cliffs, N.J.: Prentice-Hall, 1977. ISBN 0-13-022442-1. A narrative history, of no profound distinction but with about 3,000 song titles included in the general index on pp. 779–850.

[354.

Warren Craig. *Sweet and Lowdown: America's Popular Song Writers.* Metuchen, N.J.: Scarecrow, 1978. ISBN 0-8108-1089-1. Brief biographies of 8 composers "before Tin Pan Alley," 30 from during, and about 100 "after Tin Pan Alley," with indexes of about 700 song titles, 2,500 stage productions, and 400 personal names. Among the more significant features of the book is the "Comparative Rankings" of composers (p. 502), in which Duke Ellington is no. 34 while the above-mentioned J. Fred Coots is no. 33.

[355.

Elston Brooks. *I've Heard Those Songs Before: The Weekly Top Ten Tunes from the Past Fifty Years.* New York: Morrow, 1981. ISBN 0-688-00379-6. Citations for titles only, without personal names, with a general index of about 2,500 entries.

[356.

Roger Lax and Frederick Smith. *The Great Song Thesaurus.* New York: Oxford University Press, 1984. ISBN 0-19-503222-5. A vast and generally valuable miscellany of reference features concerning about 10,000 songs, of particular importance here being "The Greatest Songs" (pp. 3–128, a brief chronological list of the songs), "Song Titles" (pp. 159–399, with dates, creators, or other brief particulars), "Lyricists and Composers" (pp. 425–528, with titles after each name), and the "Thesaurus . . . by Subject, Key Word, and Category" (pp. 571–655, a rudimentary subject index).   [357.

Don Tyler. *Hit Parade, 1920–1955: An Encyclopedia of the Top Songs of the Jazz, Depression, Swing, and Sing Eras.* New York: Morrow, 1985. ISBN 0-688-06149-4. General facts on about 1,200 songs; generally unimpressive as a reference source.   [358.

The directories and indexes discussed above are all highly selective in their coverage — necessarily so in keeping with their larger objective, which is to describe the musical panorama itself. Several other directories have the slightly different objective of celebrating the success of the most famous of songs. The reference sources designed to glorify the top-hit tunes range from the expansive and nostalgic, based on sentiment and hearsay, to the dispassionately quantitative, based on the hard facts of broadcast performances and record sales as reflected in the phenomenon today known as the "charts."

John H. Chipman. *Index to Top-Hit Tunes, 1900–1950.* Boston: Bruce Humphries, 1962. LC 61-11711. Details on 3,000 songs that sold at least 100,000 sheet-music copies or recordings, listed alphabetically with an index by year.   [359.

Joel Whitburn. *Top Pop Records, 1940–1955.* Menomonee Falls, Wis.: Record Research, 1973. LC 73-76719.   [360.

ASCAP Hit Songs. New York: ASCAP, [1976?]. A booklet listing about 2,500 titles by year, with a title index.   [361.

80 Years of American Song Hits, 1892–1972: A Comprehensive Yearly Reference Book Listing America's Major Hit Songs and Their Writers. New York: Chappell, 1973. ISBN 0-070789-123. An annalistic listing of about 5,000 titles — a few of them for each of the early years, but approaching 100 for recent years — giving song titles and names of the creators, but with no further particulars and with no indexes.   [362.

Joel Whitburn. *Bubbling under the Hot 100, 1959-1981.* Menomonee Falls, Wis.: Record Research, 1982. ISBN 0-89820-047-4.   [363.

————. *The Billboard Book of Top 40 Hits, 1955 to the Present.* New York: Billboard, 1983. ISBN 0-8230-7511-7.   [364.

Frank Hoffmann. *The "Cash Box" Singles Charts, 1950–1981.* Metuchen, N.J.: Scarecrow, 1983. ISBN 0-8108-1595-8. Rankings of recordings in terms of their popularity as reflected in sales and broadcast frequency, starting not with the earliest charts in 1942 but rather with the system used by the periodical *Cash Box.* The basic "Artist Index" (pp. 1–661) includes the fullest particulars. A "Song-Title Index" (pp. 663–828) covers about 7,400 titles. Several useful appendixes are devoted to chronological listings and special rankings, while the history and rationale of the *Cash Box* system is discussed on pp. ix–xii.   [365.

George Albert and Frank Hoffmann. *The "Cash Box" Country Singles Charts, 1958–1982.* Metuchen, N.J.: Scarecrow, 1984. ISBN 0-8108-1685-7. Similar to the above, with the "Artist Index" on pp. 1–433 and about 5,500 titles in the "Song-Title Index," pp. 435–572.   [366.

————. *The Cash Box Black Contemporary Singles Charts, 1960–1984.* Metuchen, N.J.: Scarecrow, 1986. ISBN 0-8108-1853-1. The main list is arranged alphabetically by the names of about 2,000 performers involved. Under these are the names of about 10,000 best-selling songs, with a "life history" of the popularity of each, i.e., the date when each entered the charts, the artist and song, the label and number, the progress through the charts, and the number of weeks on the charts. The "Song-Title Index" (pp. 559–683) is followed by several summary appendixes.   [367.

From most of the reference sources mentioned above, one might get the notion that the song literature in question is a reasonably homogeneous one. This is certainly not the case. Each of the works cited above will emphasize a particular kind of song, usually to the exclusion of other kinds. There are some song literatures that defy anyone to view them as part of the homogeneous world, which is essentially that of commercial popular sheet music. For this reason users of this book will want to look in chapter 9 for art songs and in chapter 10 for general folksongs (except for regional repertories), in chapter 12 for hymns, in chapter 8 for access through poets and lyricists, and in chapter 16 for the perspectives of the collector.

Analytical Indexes

Valuable as the general directories are, they usually leave us at best with names and dates, not copies of the text: the search for the actual music is ahead of us. As a means of providing immediate access to the words and music itself, analytical indexes of the song anthologies have been developed. The prototype is Sears, developed out of the card file long maintained at the New York Public Library. The value to libraries and their users was as great as the plan was simple: buy all of the books covered, and end up with a completely indexed collection. By the time a successor to Sears was needed, music publishing practices had changed; the song anthology had become, even more than before, a promotional device. The proper successor to Sears is the De Charms and Breed index, although a comparison of its chosen anthologies in 1965 with those in the Leigh index of 1964 (for instance, under Burl Ives) suggests that indexing in the service of library acquisitions programs was now less important. If the two most recent indexes cited below are any indication, the acquisitions program is now quite unfeasible, effectively superseded by library resource-sharing programs. The prospect for computerized updating of the Tennessee index may point to the future, although the advantage of timeliness is certainly not new, having been one of the basic justifications for the loose-leaf *Folio-Dex* notebooks. As its title suggests, this particular service specializes in the popular song folios that are quickly in print and just as quickly out of print. Also to be cited among the indexes to particular literatures are the ancient Cushing and the recent Peterson for children's songs, and the Havlice and the Gargan and Sharma indexes to current popular music.

Minnie Sears. *Song Index.* New York: Wilson, 1926. LC 27-26092. *Supplement.* 1934. Repr. of both vols. Hamden, Conn.: Shoe String, 1966. ISBN 0-209-00548-X. An index to over 12,000 songs in 177 collections, with over 7,000 more songs in 104 collections in the supplement.   [368.

Helen G. Cushing. *Children's Song Index: An Index to More Than 22,000 Songs in 189 Collections Comprising 222 Volumes.* New York: Wilson, 1936. LC 36-27282.   [369.

Finding List of Vocal Music. Rochester, N.Y.: Cook, 1948, 1950–59 annually. LC 49-15085. A title index of the contents of major song folios in print, for the special use of music retailers in filling customer orders for particular songs. Typically about 15,000 titles were listed in each issue, as found in about 500 anthologies. [370.

Robert Leigh. *Index to Song Books: A Title Index to Over 11,000 Copies of Almost 6,800 Songs in 111 Song Books Published between 1933 and 1962.* Stockton, Calif.: Robert Leigh, 1964. LC 64-3837. Repr. New York: Da Capo, 1973. ISBN 0-306-70553-2. Largely eclipsed by De Charms and Breed below. [371.

Desiree De Charms and Paul F. Breed. *Songs in Collections: An Index.* Detroit: Information Service, 1966. LC 65-27601. Covers about 10,000 songs in 411 anthologies, mostly 1940–57, but with a few important earlier ones not previously indexed, the selection based on a survey of librarians. (A counterpart work on piano anthologies, by Rita M. Fuszek in 1982, has a proportionately much smaller amount of American music in it.) [372.

Folio-Dex: Vocal, Piano, and Organ Music Finding List. Loomis, Calif., 1974–   . An updated loose-leaf service indexing the contents of anthologies in print. [373.

Patricia Havlice. *Popular Song Index.* Metuchen, N.J.: Scarecrow, 1975. ISBN 0-8108-0820-X. *First Supplement.* 1978. ISBN 0-8108-1099-9. *Second Supplement.* 1984. ISBN 0-8108-1642-3. Coverage of 529 anthologies issued between 1940 and 1981, with citations of the collections (301, 72, and 156 respectively), an index of somewhat over 50,000 titles and first lines of text and chorus, and a name index of composers and lyricists. [374.

Caralyn Sue Peterson and Ann D. Fenton. *Index to Children's Songs: A Title, First Line, and Subject Index.* New York: Wilson, 1979. ISBN 0-8242-0638-X. Over 5,000 songs are covered, as found in 298 children's books, 1909–77, among them several general folksong anthologies. [375.

Florence E. Brunnings. *Folk Song Index: A Comprehensive Guide to the Florence E. Brunnings Collection.* New York: Garland, 1981. ISBN 0-8240-9462-X. An index of about 50,000 songs in the compiler's collection of books and records. Folk music is a prominent but far from the main feature of the collection, thus making the index at once more widely useful and less intellectually convincing. [376.

UTK Song Index. Knoxville: University of Tennessee Music Library, 1981. The Oct. 1980 COM microfiche indexes cover 13,487 songs in 554 anthologies found in the library, as listed in a supplementary hard copy. The ten indexes cover titles, genres, names, and other features. The anthologies range from operatic collections and song cycles to pedagogical works and sacred selections. [377.

William Gargan and Sue Sharma. *Find That Tune: An Index to Rock, Folk-Rock, Disco, and Soul in Collections.* New York: Neal Shuman, 1984. ISBN 0-918212-70-7. A list of about 4,000 songs as found in 203 anthologies issued 1950–81 (as listed on pp. 3–7), by title (pp. 11–117), first line (pp. 121–90), creator (pp. 193–256), and performer (pp. 259–303). [378.

James Goleeke. *Literature for Voice: An Index of Songs in Collections and Source Book for Teachers of Singing.* Metuchen, N.J.: Scarecrow, 1984. ISBN 0-8108-1782-0. Listing of the contents of about 1,800 titles, as found in thirty-nine collections and class voice anthologies then in print, with particulars on the range of each song, secondary bibliographies following each section, and composer and title indexes to the roughly 1,800 songs involved. [379.

Stage Works

Much as the contents of anthologies are usefully analyzed in the interests of access, the music from operas and musical stage productions is usefully analyzed, thereby identifying the music that was part of the production and the production to which particular musical works belonged. The redundancy on the reference shelf is obviously considerable. Nor is the field quite as neat as the guides may suggest: interpolations, deletions, and alterations have trained the scholar and the experienced reference librarian to look further when scrupulous detail is at stake (as it often is), in biographies, commentaries, even in newspaper sources and programs, or to the accessible aficionados. Among the first sources are the following:

Jack Burton. *The Blue Book of Broadway Musicals.* Watkins Glen, N.Y.: Century House, 1952. LC 52-1432. Rev. ed. 1969. LC 76-76024.

A listing of productions by decade, subdivided by composer, with casts and component music titles, the latter of which can be located through Burton's 1957 *Index* (cited in sec. 1 above). [380.

———. *The Blue Book of Hollywood Musicals.* Watkins Glen, N.Y.: Century House, 1953. LC 53-6568. A chronological list of films, each with its component music titles and singers. Index only of film titles; as with the above, the titles are accessible through the 1957 *Index.* [381.

Richard Lewine and Alfred Simon. *Encyclopedia of Theatre Music: A Comprehensive Listing of More Than 4,000 Songs from Broadway and Hollywood, 1900–1960.* New York: Random House, 1961. LC 61-13837. Useful mostly for more detailed coverage of the period 1900–1924. [382.

———. *Songs of the American Theater: A Comprehensive Listing of More Than 12,000 Songs, Including Selected Titles from Film and Television Productions.* New York: Dodd, Mead, 1973. ISBN 0-396-06657-7. A list of about 12,000 song titles with references to the productions—selective from 1900 to 1925, complete from 1925 to 1971—followed by a list of somewhat under 500 productions (pp. 597–791) with their component musical titles and a chronological list of productions (pp. 795–805). [383.

———. *Songs of the Theater.* New York: Wilson, 1984. ISBN 0-8242-0706-8. A list of over 17,000 songs, ostensibly the successor to the compilers' 1961 and 1973 titles. The more plausible in view of the organization of the present book: theater songs, 1900–1924; theater songs, 1925–60; motion picture songs; and miscellaneous useful features. The earlier books contain much that is not in this volume, which, however, includes a few facts not found in the earlier books. [384.

Ken Bloom. *American Song: The Complete Musical Theater Companion.* New York: Facts on File, 1985. ISBN 0-87196-961-1. Volume 1 lists the titles of 3,283 productions, with particulars on each, while vol. 2 provides an index of about 12,000 personal names and about 17,000 song titles cited in vol. 1, along with a chronological register of the shows. [385.

Allen L. Woll. *Songs from Hollywood Musical Comedies, 1927 to the Present.*

138

New York: Garland, 1976. ISBN 0-8240-9958-3. A list of about 3,500 songs from 1,185 shows, by song (pp. 3–81) and show (pp. 83–213), concluding with a chronological list of shows and a name index.   [386.

Steven N. Suskin. *Show Tunes, 1905–1985: The Songs, Shows and Careers of Broadway's Major Composers.* New York: Dodd, Mead, 1986. ISBN 0-396-08674-8. Different from most of the above reference guides, mainly in its organization in terms of thirty composers, with extensive background details and supplementary information features on Broadway in general.   [387.

The works listed above are complemented by the reference lists devoted to operas, operettas, and musical stage productions themselves (discussed on pp. 102–4 of chapter 9) and occasionally by indexes of films (discussed later in that same chapter on pp. 109–10).

Topical Lists

Inquiries for songs *about* a particular subject are frequent and varied, usually involving casual mention of particular words in the title or text; pervasive portrayal in the content, whether involving a story as narrated in a song or the subject matter of a descriptive piece; or specific intended functions, whether involving original circumstances, modern usages, or both. Easy to answer in a superficial way, questions of content quickly become a matter for logicians, literary critics, linguistic theorists, and social historians to argue over, whether in terms of the theory of reference or the causality of events ("is this song really *about* this topic?"). Bibliographers and library cataloguers argue over them as well, in the interests of providing access ("we have been asked to find music *about* this topic: where can we turn?"). Obviously superficial but still often useful, the following general texts may be worth knowing.

Dichter and Shapiro, *Early American Sheet Music* (1941; see 640 below). Citations for "collectors' items" (pp. 1–163), arranged by topic in a generally chronological sequence.

Dichter, *Handbook of American Sheet Music,* esp. nos. 1–2 (1947–53; see 642 below). Listings of collectors' favorites, by categories that often serve the subject search.

139

Musician's Handbook: Standard Dance Music Guide. [Bayside, N.Y.: Ray de Vita, 1939, 1941, 1944, 1946, 1948, 1951, 1952, 1958, 1962, 1971, 1975, 1980.] A frequently updated list of about 5,000 titles, with keys and composer names, arranged under eighteen categories (including, for instance, "Memory Tunes and Oldies," "Hillbilly Tunes and Cowboy Songs," "Piano Solos"), with "A Handy Fake List and Song Reminder of Top Tunes." [388.

Anthony Stecheson and Anne Stecheson. *Stecheson Classified Song Directory.* Hollywood, Calif.: Music Industry Press, 1961. LC 62-753. *Supplement.* 1978. ISBN 0-910468-08-7. Citations of title, composer, data, and publisher for about 60,000 songs in about 400 categories. The categories, arranged alphabetically and listed on pp. vi–ix, include subjects (e.g., "Acrobat," "Aircraft," "Alimony"), as derived mainly from the titles; genres ("Cha cha cha," "Closing Songs," "War Songs"), keywords ("Beautiful," "Thanks," "Won't," "Tonight"), and other assignments through which flippant inquiries can be served, and in contemplation of which committed devotees of subject access can be reminded of the great difficulties that underlie their cause. Unfortunately the *Supplement* consists solely of a list of about 2,500 titles, arranged alphabetically by year and with no special subject index. [389.

Jeff Green. *The Green Book: Catalog of Songs Categorized by Subject.* Los Angeles: Professional Desk Reference, 1982. LC 82-220575.
[390.

Lax and Smith, *The Great Song Thesaurus* (1984; see 357 above). The subject index (pp. 571–665) covers 10,000 songs. The list is not as large as Stecheson, but perhaps more useful for the standard repertory.

Michael Taft. *Blues Lyric Poetry: An Anthology.* New York: Garland, 1983. ISBN 0-8240-9235-X. *Blues Lyric Poetry: A Concordance.* New York: Garland, 1984. ISBN 0-8240-9236-8. About 2,000 texts, as issued on commercial recordings, 1920–42, are reproduced in the anthology. The set comes to be of particular reference value through the keyword-in-context presentation that makes up the vast and fulsome concordance. [391.

The key to using general topical indexes is to use them quickly —gratefully perhaps, but never to allow time to question the rationale behind the attributions. There are also few topical indexes to specific subjects; but in contrast, these—if one ever has the occasion to use them—are lists one uses with gratitude and respect for their important social perspectives. The first two list titles, while the others cover writings about the music.

Margaret M. Mott. "Transportation in American Popular Songs: A Bibliography of Items in the Grosvenor Library," *Grosvenor Library Bulletin*, vol. 27, no. 3 (1945), pp. 61–106. Also issued separately. Brief citations of topical sheet music, arranged chronologically under the headings "Automobiles" (68 titles), "Aviation" (82 titles), "Bicycles" (33 titles), "Carriages" (26 titles), "Caravans" (2 titles), "Railroads" (94 titles), "Roller Skates" (4 titles), "Ships" (151 titles), "Sleighs" (15 titles), and "Trolley Cars" (22 titles), with illustrations.   [392.

———. "A Bibliography of Song Sheets: Sports and Recreations in American Popular Songs," MLA *Notes*, 2d ser., 6 (1948), 379–418; 7 (1949), 522–61; and 9 (1951), 33–62. Citations, with many illustrations, are classified by topic, e.g., pt. 1 (in vol. 6) covers songs about both drinking—first alcoholic (general; beer, ale, and stout; wine), then nonalcoholic (chocolate, cider, coffee, colas, milk, tea, water)—and not drinking (temperance, prohibition); also songs that mention narcotics (marijuana, opium and derivatives, tobacco). Part 2 (in vol. 7) covers some sports (baseball, football, outdoor swimming—each arranged by date), and pt. 3 (in vol. 9) treats others (archery and target practice, basketball, bicycling, bowling, boxing, crew, fencing, golf, gymnastics, hockey, lacrosse, miscellaneous, mountain climbing, ping-pong, tennis, track, walking, wrestling, yachting).
[Continuation of the above] Gerald D. McDonald, "IV. Songs in the Silent Film," MLA *Notes*, 14 (1957), 325–52, 507–33. Arranged chronologically by film production, 1905–26.   [393.

R. Serge Denisoff. *American Protest Songs of War and Peace: A Selected Bibliography and Discography*. Los Angeles: California State College, Center for the Study of Armament and Disarmament, 1970. LC 73-24735. Rev. ed. as *Songs of Protest, War, and Peace*. Santa Barbara, Calif.: ABC-Clio, 1973. ISBN 0-87436-121-4. The 1st ed. contains a classified, unannotated list of about 250 writings about the topic broadly defined; the rev. ed. has been expanded to include nearly 1,500 titles.   [394.

Foner, *American Labor Songs* (1975; see 11 above).

David King Dunaway. "A Selected Bibliography: Protest Song in the United States," *Folklore Forum*, vol. 10, no. 2 (1977), p. 8. An unannotated listing of about 400 writings about protest song, categorized as general, industrial, Afro-American, and country and western, and including a few titles not in Denisoff.   [395.

In addition several lists devoted to songs about particular regions and areas are cited in chapter 6, while several lists of songs about historic personages are cited in chapter 8. The books by Lester Levy (see 650–62 below passim) help in locating materials about particular subjects, although the absence of detailed subject indexes (which would have been impossible to construct in any event) requires users to read the texts themselves (which is by no means an unrewarding or unpleasant activity). Finally, the informal classification of several personal sheet-music collections — Levy's own at Johns Hopkins, also the Starr at Indiana and the Driscoll at Newberry — includes topical categories, although the assignments are inconsistent and the categories more pragmatic than intellectually convincing.

Patriotic Song

In addition to the works cited above, the literature on the national anthem and other popular patriotic music has its own special bibliographical sources, notably as follows:

Oscar George Theodore Sonneck. *Report on "The Star-Spangled Banner," "Hail Columbia," "America," "Yankee Doodle."* Washington: U.S. Government Printing Office, 1909. LC 9-35010.   [396.

Charles H. Hart. "Hail Columbia and Its First Publication: A Critical Inquiry," *Pennsylvania Magazine of History and Biography*, 34 (1910), 162–65; also "The First Edition of Hail Columbia," ibid., 36 (1912), 126.   [397.

Oscar George Theodore Sonneck. *"The Star Spangled Banner."* Washington: U.S. Government Printing Office, 1914. LC 13-35008. Repr. New York: Da Capo, 1969. ISBN 0-306-71108-7. An expansion of the discussion in the 1909 report of this one text.   [398.

———. "The First Edition of 'Hail Columbia,' " *Pennsylvania Magazine of History and Biography*, 40 (1916), 426–35. Also in his *Miscellaneous Studies in the History of Music* (New York: Macmillan, 1916), pp. 180–89. [399.

Joseph Muller. *The Star Spangled Banner, Words and Music Issued between 1814–1864: An Annotated Bibliographical List with Notices of Different Versions, Texts, Variants, Musical Arrangements, and Notes on Music Publishers in the United States.* New York: G. A. Baker, 1935. LC 35-35354. Repr. New York: Da Capo, 1973. ISBN 0-306-70263-0. The landmark bibliography, with detailed citations and facsimiles. [400.

Richard S. Hill. "The Melody of 'The Star Spangled Banner' in the United States," in *Essays Honoring Lawrence C. Wroth* (Portland, Maine: Anthoensen Press, 1951), pp. 151–93. Particularly valuable for its exploration of the "Anacreon parodies" prior to and about 1814. [401.

The Star-Spangled Banner: Hearings before Subcommittee no. 4 of the Committee on the Judiciary, House of Representatives, Eighty-fifth Congress, Second Session, on H.J. Res. 17, H.J. Res. 517, H.R. 10542, H.J. Res. 558, and H.R. 12231, May 21, 22, and 28, 1958. Washington: U.S. Government Printing Office, 1958. (Printed for the Use of the Committee on the Judiciary, Serial 18.) Interesting evidence on the continuing cultural significance of the national anthem. [402.

[S. Foster Damon.] *Yankee Doodle.* Providence, R.I.: Brown University, John Hay Library, 1968. An exhibition catalogue and keepsake for meetings of the Bibliographical Society of America. [403.

American Patriotic Songs: "Yankee Doodle" to "The Conquered Banner," with Emphasis on "The Star-Spangled Banner." Bloomington: Indiana University, Lilly Library, 1968. LC 73-626178. A well-documented exhibition catalogue. [404.

George J. Svejda. *History of the Star Spangled Banner from 1814 to the Present.* Springfield, Va.: National Technical Information Service, 1969. Report no. FNP-HH-70-5. Compiled for the National Park Service and valuable for its many bibliographical references to developments mostly since the Civil War, especially in the footnotes on pp. 162–414 and in the bibliography on pp. 491–525. Four of the extant holographs are reproduced on pp. 487–90.   [405.

Lester S. Levy and James J. Fuld. "Unrecorded Printings of *The Star-Spangled Banner*," MLA *Notes*, 27 (1970), 245–51. The major updating of the 1935 Muller study.   [406.

P. William Filby and E. G. Howard. *Star-Spangled Books: Books, Sheet Music, Newspapers, Manuscripts, and Persons Associated with "The Star-Spangled Banner."* Baltimore: Maryland Historical Society, 1972. LC 70-187216. An exhibition catalogue describing the major documents illustrating the Fort McHenry context of the national anthem.   [407.

William Lichtenwanger. "Star-Spangled Bibliography," *College Music Symposium*, 12 (1972), 94–102. Useful commentary on major writings about the national anthem.   [408.

Lawrence, *Music for Patriots* (1975; see 659 below).

William Lichtenwanger. "The Music of 'The Star-Spangled Banner': From Ludgate Hill to Capitol Hill," *Quarterly Journal of the Library of Congress*, 34 (1977), 136–70. This will presumably long remain the definitive study of the sources of the tune of the national anthem.   [409.

12

Sacred Music

American printed sacred music falls into two broad categories, not always separable: the hymnals, tunebooks, and related service books that are the subject of this discussion and the concerted sacred art music that is discussed elsewhere in this text (i.e., cantatas, chorale preludes, and other such sacred vocal and instrumental music in chapter 9, folk hymnody in chapter 10, or solo sacred song in chapter 11). Occasional citations of sacred music also will appear in Sonneck-Upton and Wolfe (see chapter 2), their announced emphases on secular music notwithstanding. General writings on hymnology have been collected in several bibliographies:

Ruth Ellis Messenger and Helen E. Pfatteicher. *A Short Bibliography for the Study of Hymns.* New York: Hymn Society of America, 1964. (Papers of the Hymn Society, 25.) LC 66-91961. Includes about 300 titles, a large proportion of them entirely or in part on American topics.   [410.

Hartley, *Theses and Dissertations* (1966; see 507 below).

Samuel J. Rogal. "A Bibliographical Survey of American Hymnody, 1640–1800," *New York Public Library Bulletin,* 78 (1975), 231–52. A short-title list of sources (with one copy located in any of forty-seven libraries) grouped in four categories (psalm, hymn, and anthem collections; psalm and hymn collections for children; single hymns and anthems; and musical collections). The special use of this list will probably be for its frequent citation of those early texts that omitted the musical notation and included words only. [411.

Martha C. Powell. *A Selected Bibliography of Church Music and Music Reference Materials.* Louisville: Southern Baptist Theological Seminary, 1977. (Heintze B16)   [412.

Porter, "Dissertations and Theses" (1979; see 508 below).

Robert de V. Brunkow. *Religion and Society in North America*. Santa
Barbara, Calif.: ABC-Clio, 1983. ISBN 0-87436-042-0. The "Music" section (pp. 146–49) contains fifty-two entries, 1906–57, drawn
from the *America: History and Life* data base. [413.

The bibliographical cornerstone of America's religious music books
is the lineage of ostensibly comprehensive texts detailed in the section
"General Historical Bibliographies," which in its coverage has slowly
moved forward from the beginnings into the nineteenth century. Less
heroic but often of scholarly distinction are the specialized lists cited
under "Denominational and Other Special Lists." Complementing
these are the various special analytical indexes that follow at the end
of the chapter.

General Historical Bibliographies

A classic pattern prevails here: the early work is done by collectors
(as further reflected in the discussion on p. 163 below), the later work
by generalist scholars, who in turn are succeeded by specialized scholars. Warrington's is the first significant list of American titles, appended to a listing of English and Continental titles from earlier
periods, American titles thereafter. Metcalf's 1917 list largely
supersedes Warrington. While Pratt's list gives short titles only for
the period after 1810, it still provides some of the only clues to obscure
titles. Metcalf's second book updates some of the information in his
earlier one, now in a biographical framework.

The modern scholars enter the picture with Britton's ground-break-
ing dissertation of 1949. Here for the first time we have proper
bibliographical citations, along with locations. The subsequent history
of work on the colonial and federal periods, dominated by the efforts
of three persons — Britton, Lowens, and Crawford — is only now coming to completion after nearly four decades. It seems almost churlish
to observe that for the period after 1810 we will still need to use the
ancient Pratt and Metcalf lists, as well as the specialized bibliographies
that are the subject of the next discussion below.

James Warrington. *Short Titles of Books Relating to or Illustrating the
History and Practice of Psalmody in the United States, 1620–1820*. Philadelphia: Author, 1898. LC 5-40490. Repr. New York: Burt Frank-

lin, 1971. ISBN 0-8337-3690-6. A chronological list, 1538–1898, with very brief citations, predominantly of European titles before 1750, mostly American thereafter. [414.

———. "A Bibliography of Church Music Books Issued in Pennsylvania, with Annotations," *Penn Germania*, n.s., 1 [o.s., 13] (1912/13), 170–77, 262–68, 371–74, 460–65, 627–31, 755–58. Essentially a bibliographical essay complementary to the 1898 list, discussing the titles cited there. [415.

Frank J. Metcalf. *American Psalmody; or, Titles of Books Containing Tunes Printed in America from 1721 to 1820*. New York: Charles Heartman, 1917. LC 18-4134. Repr., with a new introduction by Harry Lee Eskew. New York: Da Capo, 1968. ISBN 0-306-71132-X. Citations of somewhat over 200 titles, alphabetically by compiler, extending into the 1830s with references to major bibliographies and holdings in twenty-three libraries. [416.

Waldo Selden Pratt. "Tune Books," in *Grove's Dictionary of Music and Musicians: American Supplement* (New York: Macmillan, 1920), pp. 385–92. Brief citations of about 500 titles, in a broadly chronological arrangement. [417.

Frank J. Metcalf. *American Writers and Compilers of Sacred Music*. New York: Abingdon, 1925. LC 25-18159. Repr. New York: Russell and Russell, 1967. LC 66-24731. A biographical directory, including many titles not cited in the above lists. [418.

Allen P. Britton. "Theoretical Introductions in American Tune-Books to 1800." Ph.D. diss., University of Michigan, 1949. The "Bibliography of Tune Books" (pp. 472–686), with about 200 titles, remains the definitive bibliography as of this writing and is preceded by other useful lists of primary and secondary sources, including a 56-item "Bibliography of Pamphlets and Sermons" that discuss music (pp. 442–71). [419.

Allen P. Britton and Irving Lowens. "Unlocated Titles in Early Sacred American Music," MLA *Notes*, n.s., 11 (1953), 33–48. The first step toward a definitive list (now being completed by Richard Crawford for publication by the American Antiquarian Society). [420.

Denominational and Other Special Lists

Most of the specialized lists are delimited by denomination, published separately or as part of larger denominational bibliographies. Several are devoted to repertories that clearly span sacred art music and service music, while others venture into the vernacular traditions of folk hymnody.

Allen Seipt. *Schwenkfelder Hymnology and the Sources of the First Schwenk-felder Hymn-Book Printed in America.* Philadelphia: Americana Germanica, 1909. LC 9-25119. Repr. New York: AMS Press, 1971. ISBN 0-404-09908-4.   [421.

Ottis J. Knippers. *Who's Who among Southern Singers and Composers.* Hot Springs National Park, Ark.: Knippers Bros., 1937. LC 37-29945. Also issued Lawrenceburg, Tenn.: James D. Vaughan, 1937. Biographical sketches of about 150 early twentieth-century composers, mostly of hymns. Numerous works are listed in the text but without bibliographical particulars, and only a few of these appear in the index (pp. 11–13).   [422.

Nevin Wishard Fisher. *The History of Brethren Hymnals: A Historical, Critical, and Comparative Study.* Bridgewater, Va.: Beacon Publishers, 1950. LC 50-13133. The ten major titles, 1777–1925, are cited in summary on pp. 142–43.   [423.

Sister Mary Camilla Verret. *A Preliminary Survey of Roman Catholic Hymnals Published in the United States of America.* Washington: Catholic University of America Press, 1964. LC 64-18590. A chronological list of 311 titles, 1787–1961, with extensive citations and locations.   [424.

James W. Hall. "The Tune-Book in American Culture, 1800–1820." Ph.D. diss., University of Pennsylvania, 1967. Includes a brief listing of the titles discussed.   [425.

Charles Edward Lindsley. "Early Nineteenth-Century American Collections of Sacred Choral Music, 1800–1810." Ph.D. diss., University of Iowa, 1969. Part 2 consists of "An Annotated Bibliography of Tune-Books, 1800–1810."   [426.

Martin Ressler. *A Bibliography of Mennonite Hymnals and Songbooks,*

1742–1972. [Quarryville, Pa.: Author, 1973.] Citations of eighty-four titles, with extensive and interesting annotations.   [427.

William Burres Garcia. "Church Music by Black Composers: A Bibliography of Choral Music," *Black Perspective in Music,* 2 (1974), 145–57. A list of over 200 available collections and single texts, "selected with the average church choir in mind."   [428.

Kenneth E. Rowe. *Methodist Union Catalog: Pre-1976 Imprints.* Metuchen, N.J.: Scarecrow, 1975– . Projected as a twenty-vol. set plus indexes, of which six vols. (A–I) had appeared to 1985. While the music coverage is difficult to evaluate until the indexes appear, even now many obscure American music titles can be seen. [429.

Showalter, *The Music Books of Ruebush and Kiefer* (1975; see 102 above).

Evelyn Davidson White. *Selected Bibliography of Published Choral Music by Black Composers.* Washington: Howard University, 1975. LC 75-312252. Rev. ed. as *Choral Music by Afro-American Composers: A Selected Annotated Bibliography.* Metuchen, N.J.: Scarecrow, 1981. ISBN 0-8108-1451-X. Whereas the former lists about 600 titles by sixty-three composers, the latter has about 1,000 titles by eighty-five composers. Titles in the earlier edition's "Selected List of Choral Music Permanently Out of Print," now presumably available again, appear in the main list, although other titles from the earlier ed. are omitted from the later. The later ed. also includes selective lists of spiritual collections, source reading, and discography.   [430.

J. Vincent Higginson. *Handbook for American Catholic Hymnals.* N.p.: Hymn Society of America, 1976. LC 76-13307. The "General Bibliography" (pp. 303–9) lists chronologically about 130 hymnals and other writings.   [431.

Cunningham, *The Music Locator* (1976– ; see 54 above).

Nelson P. Springer and A. J. Klassen. *Mennonite Bibliography, 1631–1961.* Scottsdale, Pa.: Herald Press, 1977. ISBN 0-8361-1207-5. Volume 2 lists 365 hymnals, pp. 285–97.   [432.

Edward C. Wolf. "Lutheran Hymnody and Music Published in America, 1700–1850: A Descriptive Bibliography," *Concordia Historical Institute Quarterly,* 50 (1977), 164–85.   [433.

Richard J. Stanislaw. *A Checklist of Four-Shape Shape-Note Tunebooks.* Brooklyn, N.Y.: Institute for Studies in American Music, 1978. (I.S.A.M. Monographs, 10.) ISBN 0-914678-10-8. A list of 305 titles, 1798–1859, with a chronological conspectus, title index, and corrigenda by Paul C. Echols. [434.

Irene V. Jackson. *Afro-American Religious Music: A Bibliography and a Catalogue of Gospel Music.* Westport, Conn.: Greenwood, 1979. ISBN 0-313-20560-4. The bibliography (pp. 3–60) cites 873 writings directly and generally about the topic, arranged in six broad categories without annotations, and with no name index but with a detailed subject index on pp. 187–97. The "Catalogue of the Compositions of Afro-American Gospel Composers (1938–1965)" (pp. 80–184) lists close to 500 composers and about 2,000 titles, with brief information on the sources for each. Unfortunately the "Index to the Catalogue" (pp. 201–10) covers not the titles but rather the composers' names, making it largely redundant. [435.

Samuel J. Rogal. *The Children's Jubilee: A Bibliographical Survey of Hymnals for Infants, Youth, and Sunday Schools Published in Britain and America, 1655–1900.* Westport, Conn.: Greenwood, 1983. ISBN 0-313-23880-4. A short-title list of 301 American titles (pp. 1–26), with biographical annotations on the compilers, indexed by organizational sponsors, personal names, and printers and publishers. [436.

Nicholas Temperley and Charles G. Manns. *Fuging Tunes in the Eighteenth Century.* Detroit: Information Coordinators, 1983. (Detroit Studies in Music Bibliography, 49.) ISBN 0-89990-017-8. A systematic arrangement of 1,239 fuging tunes as located in contemporary sources, 126 of them American (as listed on pp. 68–81), with indexes to the tune names, persons, and modern editions. [437.

Donald R. Hinks. *Brethren Hymn Books and Hymnals, 1720–1884.* Gettysburg, Pa.: Brethren Heritage Press, 1986. The bibliographical appendixes (pp. 119–204) are devoted largely to American editions. [438.

Samuel J. Rogal. *Guide to the Hymns and Tunes of American Methodism.* New York: Greenwood, 1986. ISBN 0-313-25123-1. [439.

In addition twenty-four Confederate hymnals are cited in the Harwell lists (especially those of 1955 and 1957; 100–101 above). Library catalogues with significant sacred music holdings are cited in chapter 13 (notable are those of the American Antiquarian Society, Library of Congress, the Newberry Library, and the New York Public Library — some of whose holdings are cited in the *National Union Catalog: Pre-1956 Imprints;* see 452 below).

Analytical Indexes

Finally, for indexes to the contents of these books, several different lists are available, quite dissimilar in their intention. The strength of the massive *Bibliography of American Hymnals* — a focus on unusual hymnals of limited availability intended for scholarly use — together with the microfiche format, should continue to give the Diehl index a special demand in smaller and more general libraries. Both of these books are general in scope; often, when a denominational context can be understood from the outset, a "companion" volume to the official hymnal will provide the access that is needed. In all of these books the citations must be recognized for what they are and are not. Most of them cite first lines of the text only; a few add first lines of chorus, but very few give the hymn names, if such even exist. All of them cover texts of words, not the music, except implicitly, i.e., unless (as often happens) the same text is invariably associated with the same music. For the variously assigned tune names, the denominational companions provide further access along with background on the circumstances (see Clark, 442 below).

Katherine S. Diehl. *Hymns and Tunes: An Index.* New York: Scarecrow, 1966. LC 66-13743. Included are several indexes (i.e., for titles, tune names, and first lines), as found in seventy-eight major hymnals.   [440.

Hymn Society of America. *Hymnology: North and South America.* Vol. 1, *Bibliography of American Hymnals.* Vol. 2, *Dictionary of American Hymnology: First-Line Index.* Compiled by Leonard Ellinwood and Elizabeth Lockwood. New York: University Music Editions, 1983. The *Bibliography,* on twenty-seven 4" x 6" microfiche, describes 7,500 hymnals published in North and South America between 1640 and 1978, thus reproducing the society's card file. The *Dictionary,* on 179 reels of 16 mm. microfilm, indexes the contents of some 192,000 hymns found in the hymnals described in the *Bib-*

liography. The roughly 1,000,000 entries cover authors, translators, first lines, refrains, titles, and original texts. A printed *Guide* with further explanatory information is also part of the *First-Line Index.* [441.

The song indexes discussed in chapter 11 will often also include hymns and other religious texts.

Invaluable bibliographically, and for reference work in general, are the various "companion" volumes that have been prepared to provide worshipers with background on the texts and contexts of the hymnals. These are often works of painstaking scholarship, typically without heavy sentiment or sectarian bias. The genre has been the subject of a thorough and useful bibliography:

Keith C. Clark. "A Bibliography of Handbooks and Companions to Hymnals: American, Canadian and English," *Hymn,* 30 (1979), 205–9, 269–72, 276; 31 (1980), 41–47, 73–74, 120–26. Citations for thirty current handbooks, 1927– ; seventy-two companions to particular hymnals, 1928– ; thirty-eight early handbooks, 1845–1927; and seventy-three supplementary guides, 1773–1927. Each of the four chronologically arranged lists includes bibliographical particulars on new editions and reissues. [442.

BIBLIOGRAPHICAL FORMS

Sorting out and organizing all the varieties of American music bibliographies may by now have struck the reader as an engaging intellectual game, in which useful results would seem almost a by-product.
By organizing the lists in terms of the major objective of each, however,
an important additional point comes into focus—and by implication
a deserved respect can be paid to the compilers.

Each of the bibliographies described here has a dual role: they
function both as object and as tool. All attempt to define and rationalize—in a sense to canonize—the literature of a particular kind and
also to provide access to that literature. Considering the amount of
labor entailed in preparing each of them, it is obvious that they result
from a mixture of compelling personal intellectual curiosity and hearty
respect for those who need to know more about the subject. In a
sense the compilers of the first group of bibliographies, conceived
chronologically (chapters 2–5), may be seen as motivated by a sense
of the importance of history and historical processes; those conceived
contextually (chapters 6–8) by a sense of the importance of persons,
individually or in groups; those conceived in terms of repertory (chapters 9–12) for the music itself and its users.

Finally, then, we must consider those bibliographies concerned primarily with physical items themselves. The inspiration behind these
lists rarely comes out of any bibliophilic self-indulgence, of course.
Chapters 13, 15, and 16 in particular have probably been inspired
more by affinities, chapters 14 and 17 by responsibilities; in fact, the
two are hardly opposites, as compilers will be quick to insist. Often
the labors behind a bibliography will have been commissioned, for
instance, by a library with an important and well-focused collection
in need of being used. In some cases the compiler seems to have fallen
back on a delimitation in terms of the physical medium almost by
default, all other possible dimensions having failed to provide either

153

the kinds of intellectual coherence that would make for a satisfactory list to read or the kinds of functional rewards that would make for a satisfactory list to consult. It should also be remembered that bibliophiles and discophiles themselves have typically been the most productive, imaginative, and respected scholars of American music.

13

Source Materials

Collections significant for their American music holdings are described in three different kinds of guides. The general guides and the union catalogues are described below. Guides to and catalogues of particular collections are also selectively described below, partly by way of calling special attention to major holdings. The lists and catalogues of particular kinds of materials in libraries are for the most part discussed elsewhere in this book under the material itself.

General Directories and Bibliographies

There is no single guide that briefly summarizes the major repositories of American music—no single essay touching on the high points for the aspiring user of their collections—mostly because the assignment is next to impossible. The holdings are too numerous and diffuse, the needs of readers too varied. Three major sources can be called on, each of considerable length and detail but with limitations of scope that need to be kept in mind. *Resources of American Music History* is the largest of them, covering about 1,500 repositories, sometimes citing specific items but more often describing groups of materials. Its index remains a major source for specialists who ask who has what. At the same time, the word "history" in *RAMH* must be kept clearly in mind: holdings of materials dating past roughly the 1940s could not be described there, although they can often be inferred. Nor does the Lindahl RISM volume pick up all of what *RAMH* omits, for while its coverage includes several repositories not in *RAMH*, its objective is to cover those institutions with holdings to report for an inventory that lists materials before ca. 1800. For general purposes the best survey is probably the one in the Grove set.

Resources of American Music History: A Directory of Source Materials from Colonial Times to World War II [*RAMH*]. Compiled by D. W. Krummel, Jean Geil, Doris J. Dyen, and Deane L. Root. Urbana: University of Illinois Press, 1981. ISBN 0-252-00828-6. A survey of the holdings of 1,689 repositories, with supplemental references to several hundred smaller collections and an extensive index by name and subject.   [443.

Charles Lindahl. *Directory of Music Research Libraries in the United States and Canada.* Kassel: Bärenreiter Verlag, 1983. (Répertoire internationale des sources musicales, C.1) [RISM] ISBN 3-7618-0684-1. A guide to the 457 known repositories with holdings of pre-1800 printed music (superseding Rita Benton's "Preliminary Edition," Iowa City, 1967, with 295 repositories), accessible through a smaller but strategically well-conceived index.   [444.

Mary Wallace Davidson, assisted by D. W. Krummel. "Libraries and Collections," in *The New Grove Dictionary of American Music,* ed. H. Wiley Hitchcock and Stanley Sadie (London: Macmillan; New York: Grove's Dictionaries of Music, 1986), vol. 3, pp. 44–84. More current than either of the above but without the separate indexes.

[445.

It is in deference to the coverage of these lists that the present book has excluded catalogues of particular music collections, except for the several titles noted on pp. 159–60 below.

Other guides (many of them cited on pp. 11–12 of *RAMH,* in the editions cited there or in more current ones) pick up references to unusual materials and further details on important collections. The Downs bibliography cites publications that describe the holdings of particular collections, while the Hamer and NHPRC *Directory* will bring out manuscript and archival material primarily for American historians in general. The *National Union Catalog of Manuscript Collections,* however laudable in its conception, is actually of rather limited usefulness for musical studies because of its restrictive definition of a formal collection. The general subject indexes to collections, of which Ash is the most important, often also turn up interesting materials, although the criterion of inclusion is mostly based on self-selection, and thus many minor collections proud of their limited holdings will be in while major ones that take their vast collections for granted will not. Historical studies on the growth of America's musical collections—of which Bradley is the most important example—are also helpful in suggesting the location of unexpected holdings.

Robert Bingham Downs. *American Library Resources: A Bibliographic Guide.* Urbana, Ill.; Chicago: American Library Association, 1951. LC 51-11156. *First Supplement, 1950–61.* 1961. *Second Supplement, 1961–70.* 1972. ISBN 0-8389-0116-6. *Third Supplement, 1971–80,* with an index to the set by Clara D. Keller. 1982. ISBN 0-8389-0342-8. [446.

Lee Ash. *Subject Collections: A Guide to Special Book Collections and Subject Emphases As Reported by University, College, Public, and Special Libraries in the United States and Canada.* New York: Bowker, 1958. 5th ed., with Dennis J. Lorenz. 1978. ISBN 0-8352-0924-5. 6th ed. 1985. ISBN 0-8352-1917-8. An extensive and useful overview, based, however, on reports of what subjects the collections themselves see as their particular strengths, as listed by subject. The limitations of such an approach were significantly addressed in the 5th ed. (the 6th ed. has not been available for inspection). [447.

Phillip Hamer. *A Guide to Archives and Manuscripts in the United States.* New Haven: Yale University Press, 1961. LC 61-6878. A major source for historians, with music references accessible through the index. [448.

National Union Catalog of Manuscript Collections [NUCMC]. Ann Arbor: J. W. Edwards, 1962; Hamden, Conn.: Shoe String, 1964; Washington: Library of Congress, 1965–   . ISSN 0090-0044. Limited to collections of fifty items or more, as reported by contributing libraries. The indexes bring out relevant holdings through the subject "Music" as well as through more specific headings. The indexes are cumulative within particular spans, however, so that a thorough search must remember the years of cumulation, which to date are 1959–62, 1963–66, 1967–69, 1970–74, and 1975–79. The music holdings in question range from the records of the Juvenile Music Club of Rock Hill, S.C. (MS. 79-1289), to the papers of Waldo Selden Pratt (MS. 77-971), to the papers of the Arizona lawyer Joseph Alexander, whose wife was active in music clubs (MS. 77-59), to papers of William DeVeaux Foulke of Charleston, W.Va., which deal in part with violin making (MS. 78-791). [449.

Directory of Archives and Manuscript Repositories in the United States [NHPRC]. Washington: U.S. National Historic Projects and Records Commission, 1978. LC 78-23870. A supplement to Hamer. [450.

Carol June Bradley. *Music Collections in American Libraries: A Chronology.* Detroit: Information Coordinators, 1981. (Detroit Studies in Music Bibliography, 46.) ISBN 0-89990-002-X. A chronology of institutional activity. The references, in this section and in the "Bibliography" (pp. 213–19), are useful not only for their obscurity but also in their firsthand documentation of the history.   [451.

Due mention should also be made of the monumental and monumentally useful retrospective *National Union Catalog,* cited thus:

National Union Catalog: Pre-1956 Imprints. 685 vols. London: Mansell, 1968–81. *Supplement.* 68 vols. 1980–81.   [452.

This alphabetical main-entry catalogue of books represented in American libraries is based on AACR-1 entry practices. Officially the scope includes musical materials of all kinds. But many of the contributing libraries seem never to have received the message or lacked the resources needed either to copy out the entries in their vast music catalogues or to edit the cataloguing to suit the entry practices for such a reference book — which practices, in fact, were never finally agreed upon. The result is that the holdings of major music repositories are particularly poorly represented, the Library of Congress's being surely most poorly of all. Books about music are fairly well represented, these being the most substantial-looking and least problematic titles for cataloguing. Libretti and treatises are also fairly well represented, along with hymnals, tunebooks, songsters, major anthologies, and historical sets. But the representation of the *NUC*'s quantity of sheet music, and of major musical compositions, is still considerably short of what one should wish for. Below, for instance, are the total entries under several major musicians of the nineteenth century, giving the entries under their names by category: (1) books about music, including tutors; (2) hymnals, tunebooks, and other anthologies, sacred and secular; (3) major works of art music, arbitrarily defined here to consist of single works running to twelve pages or more; (4) sheet music and other short selections in fewer than twelve pages; (5) later (i.e., mostly posthumous) arrangements of favorite popular works by the composer; and (6) libretti, autograph letters, and other miscellaneous works.

	1.	2.	3.	4.	5.	6.	Total
Stephen Collins Foster	—	24	2	265	96	2	388
Lowell Mason	33	252	4	9	1	2	301
George Frederick Root	18	64	36	105	6	8	237
Septimus Winner	83	30	—	51	—	12	176
Henry Russell	—	8	—	139	12	2	161
Charles E. Horn	—	—	17	106	—	28	151
Thomas Hastings	14	105	1	—	—	—	120
Isaac Woodbury	19	39	4	35	1	—	98
John Hill Hewitt	—	2	5	60	—	5	72
Henry Clay Work	—	7	—	49	2	1	59
Charles Zeuner	—	25	4	22	—	3	54

Here one can also find eleven entries for Jesse Aikin's *Christian Minstrel,* six for Francis Allen's *New-York Selection,* and some twenty-odd entries each for the collections of John Cole and Samuel Dyer. Furthermore, the *Pre-1956 NUC* supplement picks up thirty-two more entries for Foster and seventeen more for Mason. These are far from complete holdings, to be sure, but are particularly valuable for what the entries suggest about publishing variants as well as for the convenient prospects for future research that the citations will facilitate.

Particular Collections

Preeminent among the general music libraries of the United States are the Library of Congress and the New York Public Library. While the catalogue cards produced at the former have been widely available since 1900, it should be remembered that only a small portion of the music holdings are included in the printed card program. Most of the music holdings are not catalogued at all, and a large part of that which is catalogued turns up only in the card files of the Music Division itself. Similarly, the immense published catalogue of the New York Public Library, for all its usefulness in work with American music, covers mostly its books, periodicals (titles and many articles), and pamphlets but only a small portion of the vast music collections.

Two other collections that have specialized in early American music in particular are the American Antiquarian Society, devoted to American printed materials before roughly 1880, and the Newberry Library, rich in general holdings up into this century. Both of them have issued printed catalogues, but again covering only parts of the collection, as noted below.

Dictionary Catalog of the Music Division of the New York Public Library. 33 vols. with 10 vols. of supplement. Boston: Hall, 1964. ISBN 0-8161-0709-2. 2d ed. 45 vols. 1982. ISBN 0-8161-0374-1. [453.

A Dictionary Catalog of American Books Pertaining to the 17th through the 19th Centuries in the American Antiquarian Society. 20 vols. Westport, Conn.: Greenwood, 1971. ISBN 0-8371-3265-7. Music materials are most easily accessible through subject headings like "Music" and "Hymns with Music." Complete holdings of later eds. are often cited only under main entries, not under subject headings. [454.

D. W. Krummel. *Bibliographical Inventory to the Early Music in the Newberry Library, Chicago.* Boston: Hall, 1977. ISBN 0-8161-0042-X. American manuscripts before ca. 1860 are listed in class 1.D. (pp. 19–21); American printed materials—all of the books and some sheet music—are in class 9 (pp. 452–525). [455.

Bernard E. Wilson. *The Newberry Library Catalog of Early American Printed Music.* Boston: Hall, 1982. ISBN 0-8161-0389-5. A selection of 3,000 of the more important of the sheet-music editions, mostly from the period before 1850 and of Chicago prefire imprints, by main entry in vol. 1 and by title and imprint in vols. 2–3. [456.

These collections notwithstanding, for the specialized materials of American music, one must look to other libraries as well for any but the most cursory access. All of them have impressive sheet-music collections, for instance; but exceptional holdings are also to be found at U.C.L.A. (the Willson/Ring Collection and the Archive of Popular American Music), Brown University (the Harris Collection in the John Hay Library), Harvard University (the Houghton Library), the Free Library of Philadelphia, the Buffalo and Erie County Public Library (formerly the Grosvenor Library), Indiana University (in the Lilly Library), and the University of Michigan (in the Clements Library). For collections with published catalogues, one must look to smaller institutions, among them Washington University (the Keck dissertation on the Ernst Krohn collection), the University of Virginia (on COM microfiche), or the Houston Public Library.

Among the important collections of hymnals and tunebooks, the four major general repositories share their reputation with such institutions as Yale University (the Lowell Mason collection), the Princeton Theological Seminary (the Louis F. Benson collection), the Pittsburgh Theological Seminary (much of James Warrington's collection), Emory University (other parts of the Warrington collection along with the Paine collection, formerly at the Hartford Theological Seminary in Connecticut), the Clements Library in Ann Arbor, and the Moravian Music Foundation in Winston-Salem (the Irving Lowens collection).

Music Collecting in the United States

It is useful here briefly to trace the history of music collecting in America. The early Boston antiquary Thomas Prince (1687–1758), father of American book collecting, did not collect music as such, although his most notable holdings consisted of no fewer than five (of the eleven extant) copies of the 1640 Bay Psalm Book; and although many of the Bay Psalm Books are today in other libraries, the remainder of his collection forms the nucleus of the rare-book collection at the Boston Public Library. Thomas Jefferson (1743–1826) more plausibly deserves to be honored as the first great music collector in the United States, his material consisting largely of early French chamber music, preserved today at the University of Virginia, separate from the other three major book collections for which he is respected. Several of his noted contemporaries who owned sheet music include Francis Hopkinson (1737–91), now largely at the University of Pennsylvania; Edmond Charles ("Citizen") Genet (1763–1834), whose sheet music is now at the Library of Congress; Caroline Schetky Richardson, niece of the early Philadelphia composer, whose music is now at the Library of Congress and the Newberry Library; and Micah Hawkins (1777–1825), noted in the annals of American opera, whose bound sheet music is now dispersed. Their ownership is attested through their name plates on the covers and their autographs on the front leaves of bound volumes, which between roughly 1790 and 1880 served countless owners as a means for organizing their music. The practice of recent collectors and librarians of disbinding has destroyed much of the evidence of provenance and of tastes in collecting and in music; but the sewing holes and binder's glue on the vast majority of the extant copies of early sheet music remind us of a practice that has assured the survival of copies that otherwise today would likely have been lost.

Several large general music collections date from the mid-nineteenth century, notably those of Lowell Mason (1792–1872), now at Yale University, begun with the en bloc purchase of J. C. H. Rinck's library in Germany in 1852; Boniface Wimmer (1809–87), Archabbot of St. Vincent's in Latrobe, Pennsylvania, where the collection is still extant; Joseph Wilhelm Drexel (1833–88), a Philadelphia banker who had earlier acquired the collection of H. F. Albrecht of the Germania Orchestra, and whose library is now at the New York Public Library; and Allen A. Brown (1835–1916), whose collection was donated to the Boston Public Library in 1894. The presence of earlier music collections of some distinction is attested in several early book auctions, for instance the one in New York on March 17, 1841, at which no fewer than forty-eight lots consist of treatises and instruction books dating from the century before. The last major collection of this character was that of Samuel Prowse Warren (1841–1915), dispersed at auction in 1916 and 1922.

Sheet-music collectors emerged at the turn of the century, most of them enthusiastic amateurs of popular music whose careers were in totally different areas. Their contagious delight led to the informal confraternity that gathered around Joseph Muller (1877–1939), who served both as cook on the personal yacht of J. P. Morgan and as bibliographical consultant to the New York Public Library, where the collection largely resides today. No less important in the group was the Philadelphia antiquarian dealer Harry Dichter (1900–1976), whose final stock largely went to the Free Library of Philadelphia.

Other prominent early sheet-music aficionados included J. Francis Driscoll (1875–1959), a civil engineer from Brookline, Massachusetts, whose collection is now at the Newberry Library; Carl H. Tollefson (1882–1963), a Brooklyn chamber-music enthusiast whose collection is now at Southern Illinois University in Edwardsville; Walter N. H. Harding (1883–1973), a Chicago free-lance pianist and organist whose collection is now in the Bodleian Library, Oxford; W. Lloyd Keepers (1886?–1978) of New York, whose collection now seems to be mostly at the University of California, Los Angeles; Ernst C. Krohn (1888–1975), a St. Louis music teacher whose collection is now at Washington University; Arthur Billings Hunt (1890–1967), a New York musician whose collection is now at Columbia University; Edward Raymond Sanger Wilkins (1891–1971), a Boston judge whose collection is now at Harvard University; Abbé Niles (1894–1963), a Hartford journalist whose collection is now at Trinity College; Elliott Shapiro (1896–1956), a New York music publisher whose collection is now at the New York Public Library; S. Foster Damon (1893–1971), a Providence English professor active in developing the collection at Brown University; Lester S. Levy, a Baltimore textile executive whose collection is now at Johns Hopkins University; Harry F. Bruning of San Francisco, whose collection is now at Brigham Young University;

Saul Starr, an Eastchester, New York, doctor whose collection is now at Indiana University; and Richard E. Townsend of Buffalo, New York, and Malcolm Stone of Englewood, New Jersey, both of whose collections are now largely dispersed.

Women who collected sheet music included Clara de Windt of Boston, whose library is now at Harvard University; Mrs. R. Kay Spencer of San Antonio, whose library is now at Baylor University; Bella C. Landauer, whose library is now dispersed but with much of it at the New-York Historical Society; and Josephine McDevitt and Edith A. Wright, whose collection is now at the Free Library of Philadelphia. Later important collections were assembled by George Goodwin (now at the New York Public Library), Carl Haverlin (now with the BMI Archives in New York), and Sam Di Vincent (in Fort Wayne, Ind.) or were acquired circumstantially by Bly Corning (part of it now at the Clements Library in Ann Arbor).

Other collectors specialized in hymnals, beginning with the music publisher Hubert P. Main (1839–1925), whose tunebooks are now at the Newberry Library; James Warrington (1841–1915), Silas K. Paine, and Waldo Selden Pratt, whose collections were partly merged at the Hartford Theological Seminary but are now largely divided between the Western Theological Seminary in Pittsburgh and Emory University; the hymnologist Louis F. Benson (1855–1930), whose books are now at the Princeton Theological Seminary; Canon Charles Winfred Douglas (1867–1944), who built the collection now at the National Cathedral in Washington; George Pullen Jackson (1874–1953), whose southern shape-note materials are now at the University of California, Los Angeles; Robert G. McCutchan (1877–1958), whose books are now at the Claremont Colleges in California; and Irving Lowens (1916–83), whose tunebooks are now at the Moravian Music Foundation in Winston-Salem. Among the major active collectors today is Martin Ressler in Pennsylvania.

While the traditions of musical bibliophily are not as deep in North America as in Europe, many precious treasures have come to the United States through private collectors. A number of major composers' autographs were assembled by the Boston pianist Johann Ernst Perabo (1845–1920), whose collection is today dispersed mostly through European libraries. The popular composer Jerome Kern (1885–1945) is prominently known as a bibliophile, although he deliberately avoided collecting in the field of music and is famous for the prices fetched at his auction, which took place just before the 1929 stock market crash. The Italian music library of Frank V. de Bellis (d. 1968), now at San Francisco State University, deserves special

163

praise, as does the collection of first editions assembled by James J. Fuld. Manuscripts of rarity and importance have been collected by Danny Heineman (1872–1962), now at the Morgan Library in New York; Mary Louise Curtis Bok (1876–1970), until recently at the Curtis Institute in Philadelphia; George T. Keating (1892–196?), now at Stanford University; Mary Flagler Cary (1901–67), now at the Morgan Library; James M. Osborn (1906–76), now at Yale University; and the music publisher Walter Hinrichsen (1907–69). Prominent materials are today owned by Reginald Allen, Rudolf Kallir, Louis Krasner, Jacob Lateiner, Robert O. Lehman, Hans Moldenhauer, and William H. Scheide.

General collections of distinction were also assembled by critics and scholars, among those of the former, Philip Hale (1854–1934) and Richard Aldrich (1863–1937), the latter now at Harvard University. The superb library of books on the flute, assembled by the physicist Dayton C. Miller (1866–1941), is now at the Library of Congress along with his flutes, while the opera scores assembled by Harry Schumer (d. 1971), longtime librarian for the Metropolitan Opera, are now at the New York Public Library. Major collections are continuing to be assembled by musicologists today, usually reflecting their special scholarly interests. Among the notable musicians who took special efforts to document their own careers were the conductor Theodore Thomas (1835–1905) and the composer Frederick Grant Gleason (1849–1903), both of whose memorabilia are at the Newberry; the Damrosch family and the soprano Geraldine Farrar (1882–1967), both now at the Library of Congress; and the composer Arnold Schoenberg, whose papers now form the nucleus of the institute in Los Angeles that bears his name.

Finally, special honor should be given to the collectors of musical ephemera and miscellanea, of programs, posters, tickets, catalogues, and other documents intended to be discarded, but which for that reason alone provide an immediacy to our understanding of the American musical experience not typically found in more official documents. Their activities rank alongside those of the unsung volunteers, working independently in libraries, historical societies, or privately, in compiling the miscellaneous indexes, registers, calendars, and checklists that will be a continuing bridge between surviving historical evidence and the processes of historical scholarship.

This survey of American music collecting, however interesting in its own right, further bears a lesson for music bibliographers to remember. The lesson is perhaps suggested by the entries that follow, citing virtually the only general source for and about American book collectors that contains some identifiable mention of music. (There are others, numerous and venerable, like Wright Howes's *US-iana*, in which the mention is either missing entirely or at least unidentifiable.) The slim pickings for the field of music are scarcely evidence of inactivity: the previous discussion tells us that. Rather they suggest that the character of the major community of American collecting came to be oriented toward printed books from the outset, leaving music as something to be, if not scorned, at least ignored. The bound sheet-music volumes belonged on the piano bench, not in the library. Meanwhile, the rise of the special music collectors — concomitant with the emergence of our nation's social historians, but I suspect largely separate from it — has erected a small side-chapel in the cathedral of American civilization: its relics, consisting mostly of phonograph records (along with its peripheries) and sheet music, have been venerated mainly in the sources cited in chapters 15 and the first part of 16. The next direction for music collectors is widely thought to involve musical graphics and ephemera; indeed a few music collectors are said to be already active in the field. In the meantime the following texts are relevant to the above discussion:

Joseph Sabin. *Dictionary of Books Relating to America, from Its Discovery to the Present Time.* [Commonly known as the "Bibliotheca Americana."] New York: Sabin, 1868–92; completed by the Bibliographical Society of America, 1928–36. LC 1-26958. Repr. Metuchen, N.J.: Scarecrow, 1966. ISBN 0-8108-0033-0. A monumental list of somewhat over 100,000 books relating to or published in the Americas (North and South). Appropriate to its intended audience of the antiquarian book world, the set is particularly useful for its descriptive annotations, insofar as the basis for special interest of collectors is a likely indication of the importance of the book to general historians. The arrangement tends to limit the value of the set to subject specialists of all kinds, although the title that follows is often helpful. [457.

John Edgar Molnar. *Author-Title Index to Joseph Sabin's Dictionary of Books Relating to America.* Metuchen, N.J.: Scarecrow, 1974. ISBN 0-8108-0652-5. Over 270,000 author and title references to Sabin numbers, including extensive identifications of anonymous and pseudonymous writings, as well as titles beginning with "Music" and other appropriate words. [458.

Special Materials

It is perhaps debatable whether the source materials for the study of music extend further afield than for other domains. The fact remains that little effort has been given over to the rich domain of musical ephemera. Once the object of rich sentimental affection, the autographed program book, the gaudy concert poster, the well-cherished torn ticket stub, the glossy portrait of a forgotten artiste, the manuscript commonplace book of an aspiring contributor to the Sunday hymn singing or of a serenading swain, the inventory of the long-lost sheet-music or 78-RPM record collection, the street-corner missive attacking the latest political injustice, and the newspaper clipping yellowed on high-acid paper and protective scotch tape all come to be preserved by the world's musical community, even if they are generally held in ruthless contempt by our space-sensitive, cataloguing-conscious, and preservation-minded library community. The result is that we know precious little about the history and importance of this material. Sheet music and sound recordings, as discussed mostly in chapters 16 and 15, respectively, are generally the fortunate exceptions. Under the circumstances blessings are to be counted for the few titles listed below, Fuld-Davidson and Keller for their coverage of manuscripts, Anderson for calling attention to newspaper materials, Wolf and Rudolph for descriptions of broadsides, McNeil and Olson for suggesting the relevance of forgotten materials in general.

Earle Leighton Rudolph. *Confederate Broadside Verse: A Bibliography and Finding List.* New Braunfels, Tex.: Book Farm, 1950. LC 50-4085. A list of 318 titles held in twenty-four libraries, with an index to 67 of the tunes specified. [459.

Edwin Wolf II. *American Song Sheets, Slip Ballads, and Poetical Broadsides, 1850–1870.* Philadelphia: Library Company of Philadelphia, 1963. LC 63-23661. Repr. New York: Kraus, 1970. ISBN 0-527-70950-6. Cites nearly 4,000 sheets as found in the library's collection, arranged by title with name indexes with a "photo-bibliography" of selected items. [460.

W. K. McNeil. "Popular Songs from New York Autograph Albums, 1820–1900," *Journal of Popular Culture,* 3 (Summer 1969), 46–56. A discussion of several collections and a defense of their significance: while printed materials represent physical possession and perhaps nothing more, a manuscript copy reflects the conscious desire to preserve and the activity of saving particular texts.   [461.

Gillian Anderson. *Freedom's Voice in Poetry and Song.* Wilmington, Del.: Scholarly Resources, 1977. ISBN 0-8420-2124-8. Part 1 is "An Inventory of Political and Patriotic Lyrics in Colonial American Newspapers, 1773–1783," citing 1,455 titles, with indexes to first lines, titles, authors, composition places and dates, and tunes.   [462.

Irving Lowens. *A Bibliography of Songsters Printed in America before 1821.* Worcester, Mass.: American Antiquarian Society, 1976. ISBN 0-912296-05-4. Meticulously compiled list of 649 books, typically devoted to secular texts and with words only. Facsimiles of the title pages of thirty-seven of the Massachusetts songsters are reproduced in the author's "Eighteenth-Century Massachusetts Songsters," in *Music in Colonial Massachusetts, 1630–1820, II: Music in Homes and Churches,* ed. Barbara Lambert (Boston: Colonial Society of Massachusetts, 1985), pp. 547–81.   [463.

James J. Fuld and Mary Wallace Davidson. *18th-Century Secular Music Manuscripts: An Inventory.* Philadelphia: Music Library Association, 1980. (MLA Index and Bibliography Series, 20.) ISBN 0-914954-16-4. Ample citations of eighty-five manuscripts, with detailed lists of contents and an index of the roughly 5,000 names, titles, and genres contained in them.   [464.

Kate Van Winkle Keller. *Popular Secular Music in America through 1800: A Checklist of Manuscripts in North American Collections.* Philadelphia: Music Library Association, 1981. (MLA Index and Bibliography Series, 21.) ISBN 0-914954-22-9. A location list for almost 400 manuscripts, arranged by repository.   [465.

Kenneth E. Olson. *Music and Musket: Bands and Bandsmen of the American Civil War.* Westport, Conn.: Greenwood, 1981. ISBN 0-313-22112-X. The bibliography (pp. 267–86) calls particular attention to some of the unusual forms of materials important for historians, among them memoirs, journals, government documents, newspapers, archives, and other sources.   [466.

Keith David Eiten. "The American Musical Amateur, 1860–1920: A Photographic Iconography." M.A. thesis, University of Iowa, 1986.

A study of the photographic evidence preserved in one private and four public collections.   [467.

The bibliographical control of manuscript materials is in a particularly unhappy state, again in large part because the genre itself is so diverse—from massive opera full scores to commonplace books, from autograph letters (often from and to persons outside the field of music but with interesting things to say about music) to account books of musical organizations, from performance parts to literary sketches. Under the circumstances, for music manuscripts the general bibliographical record (see 448–50 above) is shamefully unaccommodating: *NUCMC* is limited to collections with fifty items or more, Hamer and *NHPRC* essentially serve American historians, RISM for musicologists mainly concerned with European topics. In time union catalogues may come to supersede the valuable catalogues prepared for the rich Moravian manuscript holdings at Bethlehem and at Winston-Salem, as well as the surviving documents of the nineteenth century in general. The music manuscript holdings of several major libraries are described mostly, if at all, in their own catalogues; choice items from the Library of Congress are also listed in early volumes of the *National Union Catalog* (see 33 above). European music manuscripts in American libraries, finally, were the subject of the interesting work cited below, the second edition of which deserves to be completed:

Otto E. Albrecht. *A Census of Autograph Music Manuscripts of European Composers in American Libraries.* Philadelphia: University of Pennsylvania Press, 1953. LC 53-1163. A composer catalogue of 2,017 items, with indexes for present and former owners.   [468.

14

Writings about Music

The bibliographical record of writings about American music often seems thin on the top and thick on the bottom. We have too few works of substance, of scholarship and sympathetic critical insight— so our premonitions suggest—although happily the quality is improving. Instead of quality we have much sheer bulk, consisting mostly of factual statements for the mass audience, their content typically contaminated by vacuity, puffery, and absence of authority—although the picture seems also to be improving. Few students and scholars today would dare to question these sentiments. What is particularly important, then, is the recognition that similar statements are so often, thoughtlessly, and painfully made about America's music itself. American music's cultural inferiority complex is true no less of its written record than of its sounds; it is about as deserved as we may wish to make it. Although there are few imposing arguments and rich perspectives, more useful background work has been done than one at first might suspect—or such, it is hoped, may be the conclusion to be drawn from a better use of the writings in the bibliographies cited below.

In surveying the record in terms of the different kinds of documents, one should begin with the periodical literature, in which the quantity promises to be greatest and the cumulative quality the lowest. From here we will proceed to those forms generally thought to be characterized by scholarship—namely, the dissertations—and critical insight—namely, essays, analyses, histories, and biographies. Readers should not need to be reminded that the distinctions apply in the broadest and most general terms. They may wish to recall that writings about music are also cited in other sources discussed elsewhere in this handbook.

Music Periodical Titles

Continuations need to be considered first, as broadly defined here to include not only quarterlies, monthlies, and weeklies but ideally also annuals, occasionals, and even daily newspapers, whether concerned with music mainly, partly, or even infrequently. They may be surveyed in two ways: as titles (one entry for each work, preferably with locations of holdings) and as contents (analytically, according to the articles and contributions, ideally with subject coverage). The major general lists— the *Union List of Serials* and its updatings in *New Serial Titles*—by policy generally exclude annuals and newspapers but still manage to pick up a respectable proportion of the rest.

The difference between the respectable proportion and the totality becomes very clear when one compares the holdings in the *Union List of Serials* with the two main nineteenth-century music lists, by Wunderlich for the period up to 1850 and by his mentor Weichlein for the rest of the century. The same point can be made, however less disturbingly, as one compares the coverage in *New Serial Titles* with the occasional essays and lists that have appeared over the past several decades in MLA *Notes.* The proliferation has been awesome. Like most other subject fields, music has witnessed the rise of its own specialty organizations: fan clubs, professional associations, lobbying alliances, and groups of performers on a particular instrument or of a particular repertory or in a certain style, many of these at the local, regional, national, and international levels, often with special joint committees negotiating with each other. Each of them typically needs not only a journal for prestige but also a newsletter for membership communication and a monographic series for major studies that respected scholarly publishers would hesitate to consider in view of the small audience involved. A cursory glance at the titles of Wunderlich and Weichlein will suggest that this situation is nothing new.

Joan Meggett. *Music Periodical Literature: An Annotated Bibliography of Indexes and Bibliographies.* Metuchen, N.J.: Scarecrow, 1978. ISBN 0-8108-1109-X. A guide to the major directories, article indexes, and reviewing media, complementing this present discussion.

[469.

Vera S. Flandorf. "Music Periodicals in the United States: A Survey of Their History and Content." M.A. thesis, University of Chicago, 1952. (Heintze 2013) [470.

Wunderlich, "Early American Music Periodicals" (1962; see 20 above).

Weichlein, *American Music Periodicals, 1850–1900* (1970; see 21 above).

Union List of Serials in American Libraries. 3d ed. Washington: Library of Congress, 1967. LC 65-10150. Alphabetical listing of journals held in American libraries. There is no special access to the music titles, and the holdings reported are often abbreviated in their particulars. The set remains nevertheless the indispensable first place to start with most inquiries.   [471.

New Serial Titles in American Libraries. 3d ed. Washington: Library of Congress, 1953– . ISSN 0028-6680. Issued quarterly, with cumulations for 1950–70, 1971–75, and 1976–80, and annually so as to pick up all entries since the previous major cumulation. Entries are by title, so there is no way to survey the American music holdings other than through title or through the subject headings at the foot of each entry, as facilitated by on-line access, or in the title below.   [472.

New Serial Titles, 1950–1970: Subject Guide. New York: Bowker, 1975. ISBN 0-8352-0820-6. An arrangement of the entries in the above by Dewey decimal number, in which about 2,800 music entries appear under the 780s. Additional peripheral materials may be located through the subject heading index.   [473.

Musician's Guide (1954– ; see 48 above for its directories of current music periodicals).

Music Library Association. *Notes* (2d ser., 1943–). The special concerns of music libraries have led to an array of listings, beginning with Jessica M. Fredricks, "Music Magazines of Britain and the U.S.," vol. 6 (1949), pp. 329–63 and 457–79, and vol. 7 (1950), pp. 372–76, which cites, describes, and indexes about 200 titles. Articles on new music periodicals before 1976 are mentioned in vol. 21 (1963–64), pp. 58–60, and vol. 41 (1984), p. 14. The extensive coverage between 1976 and 1982, prepared under the supervision of Charles Lindahl, has been cited and indexed by Linda Solow in vol. 39 (1983), pp. 585–90. Since 1982 the annotated lists have been assembled by Stephen M. Fry and published in the June and Dec. issues.   [474.

Joseph V. Marconi. *Indexed Periodicals: A Guide to 170 Years of Coverage in 33 Indexing Services.* Ann Arbor: Pierian Press, 1976. ISBN 0-87650-005-X. An alphabetical record of the periodicals covered in the best-known general indexes, 1802–1973. [475.

Imogen Fellinger and John Shepard. "Periodicals," in *The New Grove Dictionary of American Music,* ed. H. Wiley Hitchcock and Stanley Sadie (London: Macmillan; New York: Grove's Dictionaries of Music, 1986), vol. 3, pp. 505–35. A brief historical introduction, followed by a list of 1,113 titles arranged chronologically by first publication, followed by an alphabetical index of titles and related particulars. [476.

Analytical Access to Writings about Music

Music periodical articles are covered in the music indexing programs discussed in chapter 5 and in several general indexing programs, as noted below. Historically the general coverage involves the following three titles:

Early American Periodicals Index to 1850 (1964; see 27 above).

Poole's Index to Periodical Literature (1852, 1891–1908; see 23 above).

Nineteenth-Century Readers' Guide to Periodical Literature, 1890–1899 (1944; see 26 above).

Current coverage of the general literature involves the following:

Readers' Guide to Periodical Literature. New York: Wilson, 1905– . ISSN 0034-0464. Standard guide for general articles appropriate to small public library collections. The music content is accessible through the general heading "Music," as well as through specific subjects and occasionally author. [477.

Annual Magazine Subject Index, 1907– : A Subject Index to a Selected List of American and English Periodicals and Society Publications. Boston: Faxon, 1908– . ISBN 0-8161-0401-8. Now collected into the *Cumulated Magazine Subject Index, 1907–1949.* Boston: Hall, 1964. A few music articles appear under such headings as "Music," "Bands," "Choirs," "Hymns," and the like. [478.

172

Humanities Index [as *Readers' Guide to Periodical Literature: Supplement,*
1907–19; *International Index,* variously, 1920–65; *Social Sciences and
Humanities Index,* 1965–74]. New York: Wilson, 1975– . ISSN
0095-5981. An extension of coverage of the *Reader's Guide* to more
specialized journals, with occasional entries under music headings.   [479.

As for the coverage devoted particularly to music, mention should
be made of the vast card index prepared under WPA auspices about
1940, formerly in the Newberry Library and at DePaul University
in Chicago and now at Northwestern University in Evanston, and to
the following less expansive lists:

D. H. Daugherty. *A Bibliography of Periodical Literature in Musicology
and Allied Fields and a Record of Graduate Theses Accepted.* Washington:
American Council of Learned Societies, 1940–43. Repr. New York:
Da Capo, 1971. ISBN 0-306-70413-7. Volume 1 covers about 700
articles and just over 100 theses, 1938–39, while vol. 2 covers 930
articles, 1939–40, with detailed author and subject indexes but
without the dissertation list.   [480.

Lowens, "Writings about Music in the Periodicals of American Transcendentalism" (1957; see 28 above).

Mussulman, *Music in the Cultured Generation* (1971; see 29 above).

The following indexes to particular journals are also notable:

John Louis Sievert. "A Classified Annotated Bibliography of Materials
Contained in Issues of *The Diapason* from 1934 to 1954." M.M.
paper, Northwestern University, 1955. (Heintze 33)   [481.

Hazel G. Kinscella. "Americana Index to *The Musical Quarterly,*
1915–1957," *Journal of Research in Music Education,* vol. 6, no. 2
(Fall 1958), pp. 3–144. Essentially the entire issue is devoted to the
detailed subject index.   [482.

Wayne D. Shirley. *Modern Music, Published by the League of Composers,
1926–1946: An Analytic Index.* Edited by William Lichtenwanger
and Carolyn Lichtenwanger. New York: AMS Press, 1976. ISBN
0-404-13217-0. An exemplary name and subject index, in awesome

and gratifyingly thorough detail, covering a particularly important recent music journal. [483.

Michael Yaffe. *Annotated Bibliography of Publications, 1943–1976.* Reston, Va.: National Association of Schools of Music, 1976. LC 76-53707. An annotated author list, with subject index, covering about 400 articles in the association's sixty-four *Bulletins* and *Proceedings,* mostly devoted to the programs for accreditation of institutions of higher education. [484.

Ann P. Basart. *Perspectives of New Music: An Index, 1962–1982.* Berkeley, Calif.: Fallen Leaf Press, 1984. ISBN 0-914913-00-X. Includes separate author, work, and subject indexes. [485.

James Farrington and Jon L. Piersol. "Index," *Journal of Band Research,* vol. 20, no. 1 (Fall 1984), pp. 41–78. Includes fifteen bibliographies, as cited on pp. 70–71, and numerous references to writings on American band music accessible through the title, keyword, and subject indexes. [486.

The bibliographical control of reviews of new scores and books on music is discussed on pp. 35–40 above, that of sound recordings on pp. 196–99 below. Two other sources are appropriately mentioned here, the first of them strictly not a bibliography at all but rather a useful model that one hopes may be revived, either in connection with on-line newspaper data bases or even better in a journal devoted to publicizing the varied musical activities throughout the country.

Music Reporter. New York: City Center of Music and Drama, 1948–49. LC 49-3613. A montage of New York reviews (excluding articles and news notices) in the *Times, Herald-Tribune, Sun,* and *World-Telegram* between Sept. 1947 and Aug. 1949, with indexes of major performers and of works first performed. [487.

American Musical Digest. New York: Music Critics Association, 1969–70. Not strictly speaking bibliographical but rather an anthology of selected reviews from across the country. Through such laudable efforts the dispersal of American musical activity comes to be suggested. [488.

James M. Salem. *A Guide to Critical Reviews.* Pt. 2, *The Musical from Rodgers-and-Hart to Lerner-and-Loewe.* Metuchen, N.J.: Scarecrow,

1967. LC 70-41109. 2d ed. as pt. 2, *The Musical, 1909–1974*. 1976. ISBN 0-8108-0959-1. 3d ed. 1984– . Part 1 covers American drama, while pts. 3 and 4 cover British and Continental drama and screenplays, respectively. Part 2 of the 3d ed. has not appeared as of this writing. The 1976 ed. of pt. 2 provides an alphabetical title listing of about 1,800 stage works, with particulars on the text and production and references to over 10,000 reviews.   [489.

Combined Retrospective Index to Book Reviews in Scholarly Journals, 1886–[1974]. Arlington, Va.: Carrollton; Woodbridge, Conn.: Research Publications, 1979– .
Combined Retrospective Index to Book Reviews in Humanities Journals, 1802–1974. Arlington, Va.: Carrollton; Woodbridge, Conn.: Research Publications, 1979– . Two complementary lists, the second somewhat more extensive for music than the first, covering reviews of the major American books on music.   [490.

Avery T. Sharp. *Choral Music Review Index, 1983–1985*. New York: Garland, 1986. ISBN 0-8240-8553-1. A listing of the reviews of some 2,038 choral octavos, 212 extended works, and 175 anthologies, citing the coverage in fifteen English-language journals.
                [491.

Dissertations

Theses and dissertations are often cited along with books and articles, but not always. Thus the assembly of special bibliographies will provide access to a good many studies that explore unusual and obscure topics. These lists may address the auspices of music departments as such, musical subject matter regardless of the department, or a mixture of the two. The musicology compilations are central to the genre, although important works in peripheral subject areas are excluded from their purview (music education perhaps most notably), with the result that many important music works need to be located through other specialized subject lists. Furthermore, while the Ph.D. dissertation continues as the primary exposition of serious musical scholarship, important texts occasionally come from other doctoral dissertations (Ed.D., D.M.A., D.A.) and from theses or papers for master's degree work. The comprehensive guides are cited below first, followed by specialized subject lists and regional enumerations:

175

Michael M. Reynolds. *Guide to Theses and Dissertations: An International Bibliography of Bibliographies.* Detroit: Gale, 1975. ISBN 0-8103-0976-9; 2d ed. Phoenix, Ariz.: Oryx, 1986. ISBN 0-89774-149-8. A classified overview, with general guides cited on pp. 1–4 of the 2d ed.; fourteen American music education lists on pp. 109–10; about thirty general music lists on pp. 119–23; regional studies on pp. 28–33; and several others most conveniently accessible through the index.   [492.

Dissertation Abstracts International [*Microfilm Abstracts*, 1938–51; *Dissertation Abstracts*, 1952–66]. Ann Arbor: University Microfilms, 1938– . The vast set has since 1966 included most of its music abstracts in ser. A. Access is usually most convenient through the following:

Comprehensive Dissertation Index, 1861–1972. 37 vols. Ann Arbor: University Microfilms, 1973. ISBN 0-8357-0080-1/-0116-6. Musicology titles are listed by subject in vol. 31 (pp. 269–599), on the psychology of music in vols. 20–24, on music education in vols. 25–26, and elsewhere as accessible through the author indexes in vols. 33–37. Supersedes the publisher's 1970 *Dissertation Abstracts International Retrospective Index.*

Comprehensive Dissertation Index: Ten-Year Cumulation, 1973–82. ISBN 0-8357-0639-7/-0676-1. Largely supersedes the annual supplements, in which music is again assigned to vol. 31; *1983 Cumulation,* in which music appears in vol. 3, pp. 471–95; *1984 Cumulation,* in which music appears in vol. 3, pp. 493–520.   [493.

Musicology

Oliver Strunk. *State and Resources of Musicology in the United States.* Washington: American Council of Learned Societies, 1932. (Bulletin, 19.) LC A33-1170. About 175 music theses and dissertations (1919–32) on history, psychology, and education topics are cited on pp. 43–51.   [494.

A Report on Publication and Research in Musicology and Allied Fields in the United States, 1932–1938. Washington: American Council of Learned Societies, 1938. LC 39-32447. A report by the Committee on Musicology, which cites additional "Graduate Theses Related Directly or Indirectly to Musicology. . ." (pp. 57–74).   [495.

Daugherty, *Bibliography of Periodical Literature* (1940; see 480 above), continues the coverage with about 100 titles, 1938–39.

Doctoral Dissertations in Musicology. Preliminary ed., comp. Hans T. David. N.p.: Music Teachers National Association, American Musicological Society, 1951. 1st ed. Philadelphia: American Musicological Society, Music Teachers National Association, 1952. LC A54-5165. 2d ed., comp. Helen Hewitt. Baldwin, N.Y.: Music Teachers National Association, 1957. LC 58-13151. 3d ed., comp. Helen Hewitt. Philadelphia: American Musicological Society, 1961. LC 61-65077. 4th ed., comp. Helen Hewitt. Philadelphia: American Musicological Society, 1965. LC 66-1684. 5th ed., comp. Cecil Adkins. Philadelphia: American Musicological Society, 1971. Listings of dissertations both completed and in progress, the 2d through 4th eds. cumulating the interim supplements appearing in the *American Music Teacher* (1953–59) and in the *Journal of the American Musicological Society* (1954–69). [496.

Cecil Adkins. *International Index of Dissertations and Musicological Works in Progress.* Philadelphia: American Musicological Society, 1977. LC 78-109440. In effect the 6th ed., cumulating the lists of "American Doctoral Dissertations in Musicology," *Journal of the American Musicological Society* (1969–74), as well as those from abroad in the issues of *Acta Musicologica* and the 5th ed. above. A classified list mostly by period, with author and subject indexes.
———. *International Index of Dissertations and Musicological Works in Progress: American-Canadian Supplement.* Philadelphia: American Musicological Society, 1979. A list of about 600 titles, jointly edited by Alis Dickinson. LC 79-120603. [497.

———. *Doctoral Dissertations in Musicology.* 7th North American ed., 2d International ed. Philadelphia: American Musicological Society; Basel: International Musicological Society, 1984. LC 84-229167. Further annual supplements are now issued by the American Musicological Society, 1984– . [498.

Dominique-René de Lerma. *A Selective List of Master's Theses in Musicology.* Bloomington, Ind.: Denia Press, 1970. LC 77-130048. A list of 257 titles, with author, subject, and institutional indexes. [499.

D. Jay Rahn. "Master's Theses in Musicology: First Installment," *Current Musicology,* 12 (1971), 7–37; Douglass Seaton, "Master's Theses in Musicology: Second Installment," 17 (1974), 69–76. Between the two, records of more than 600 titles, 1965–72. [500.

American Music

Rita H. Mead. *Doctoral Dissertations in American Music: A Classified Bibliography.* Brooklyn, N.Y.: Institute for Studies in American Music, 1974. (I.S.A.M. Monographs, 3.) ISBN 0-914678-02-7. A classified list of 1,226 titles, drawn from all disciplines, with author and subject indexes. [501.

James R. Heintze. *American Music Studies: A Classified Bibliography of Master's Theses.* Detroit: Information Coordinators, 1984. (Bibliographies in American Music, 8.) ISBN 0-89990-021-6. A list of 2,370 titles, arranged by subject, with author and subject indexes. [502.

Band Music

Frank J. Cipolla. "A Bibliography of Dissertations Relative to the Study of Bands and Band Music," *Journal of Band Research,* 15 (1979), 1–31; addenda, 16 (1980), 29–36. [503.

Black Music

West, *Bibliography of Doctoral Research on the Negro* (1969; see 142 above).

Eddie S. Meadows. *Theses and Dissertations on Black American Music.* Beverly Hills, Calif.: Front, 1980. ISBN 0-934082-01-4. Brief citations of about 300 master's and doctoral projects, listed by author under fourteen broad subject headings. [504.

Ethnomusicology

Frank Gillis and Alan P. Merriam. *Ethnomusicology and Folk Music: An International Bibliography of Dissertations and Theses.* Middletown, Conn.: Wesleyan University Press, for the Society for Ethnomusicology, 1966. LC 66-23459. An alphabetical author list of 873 titles, of which over 500 are concerned with U.S. topics, as accessible through the subject index (pp. 123–48). Continued by Gillis, Joseph C. Hickerson, Don L. Roberts, and Neil Rosenberg, as "Current Bibliography and Discography: Dissertations and Theses" [title varies], *Ethnomusicology,* 11 (1967), 121, 255–56; 12 (1968), 138–39, 276, 440; 13 (1969), 348; 14 (1970), 350–51, 496–97; 19 (1975), 134–36; 20 (1976), 588–89; 21 (1977), 495–96; 22 (1978), 512–13; 23 (1979), 324–25, 457; and 24 (1980), 103–4, 284–85. [505.

Alan Dundes. *Folklore Theses and Dissertations in the United States.* Austin:
University of Texas Press, 1976. ISBN 0-292-72413-6. An annalistic
list, 1860–1967, of about 3,500 master's and doctoral studies in all
areas, with subject, name, and institutional indexes. The subject
index includes numerous general references (folk music, folksong,
ballad), a few under specific genres (chantey, hymns), personal names,
and geographical headings. [506.

Hymnology and Sacred Music

Kenneth R. Hartley. *Bibliography of Theses and Dissertations in Sacred
Music.* Detroit: Information Coordinators, 1966. (Detroit Studies
in Music Bibliography, 9.) LC 64-20649. A list of 1,525 master's
and doctoral projects, arranged by institution, with author and
subject indexes. [507.

Thomas H. Porter. "Dissertations and Theses Related to American
Hymnody, 1964–1978," *Hymn,* 30 (1979), 199–204, 221. A list of
85 titles, supplemented in vol. 31 (1980), pp. 48–53 (91 titles); vol.
32 (1981), pp. 35–36 (26 titles); vol. 33 (1982), pp. 41–43 (28
titles); vol. 34 (1983), pp. 40–41 (22 titles); and vol. 35 (1984), pp.
102–4 (31 titles). [508.

Jewish Music

Albert Weisser. "Theses and Dissertations of Jewish Music Accepted
at American Universities," in his *Bibliography of Publications and Other
Resources on Jewish Music* (New York: National Jewish Welfare Board,
1969), pp. 75–80. A list of fifty-eight titles. [509.

Music Education

[Clara Kjerstad.] [*Bibliography of Music Researches.*] Evanston: Northwestern University, School of Education, 1932. Fifty entries for
"Music Researches in Educational Publications" are followed by
"Master's and Doctor's Theses," 150 in music education and 112
in music theory, as reported by thirty-five universities. [510.

Arnold M. Small. *Bibliography of Research Studies in Music Education,
1932–1944.* Iowa City: State University of Iowa Press, [1944]. LC
45-7497. Prepared for the Music Educators National Conference,

179

listing about 1,200 theses and dissertations, arranged by institution. [511.

William S. Larson. *Bibliography of Research Studies in Music Education, 1932–1948.* Chicago: MENC, 1949. LC 49-6749. Small's successor cites about 1,600 theses and dissertations, arranged geographically, with a subject index. Larson also prepared a supplement for 1949–56 in the *Journal of Research in Music Education,* 5 (1957), 63–225, similarly laid out and with about 1,700 entries. Roderick D. Gordon published the supplements for 1957–63, now entitled "Doctoral Dissertations in Music and Music Education," in vol. 12 (1964), pp. 2–122, with about 1,000 entries; for 1963–67 in vol. 16 (1968), pp. 87–216, with about 1,100 entries; for 1968–71 in vol. 20 (1972), pp. 2–185, with about 1,300 entries; and for 1972–77, in vol. 26 (1978), pp. 135–415, with about 2,000 entries — each of these constituting the cumulations, with topical indexes, of the journal's annual author listings, 1964– . [512.

Earl Ronald Borg. "A Codified Bibliography of Music Education Research at the Master's Level in Selected Institutions of the North Central Association." Ph.D. diss., Northwestern University, 1964. Volume 2, bibliography and appendixes with supplement. (Heintze B2) [513.

Council for Research in Music Education. *Directory of International Music Education Dissertations in Progress, 1969/1971– .* Urbana: University of Illinois, School of Music, 1971– . Annual listings, in which about 700 works are cited for 1986, arranged by subject category with author and institutional indexes at the front. [514.

———. *Comprehensive Listing of Dissertations Available for Review.* Urbana: University of Illinois, School of Music, 1971– . Occasional listings by way of updating the above. [515.

Music Educators National Conference. [Special Research Interest Groups, *Newsletters.*] The Historical Research in Music Education *Newsletter* maintained "A Bibliography of Doctoral Dissertations in the History of Music Education and Related Topics" beginning with vol. 2, no. 2 (July 1979). These are continued in the *Bulletin of Historical Research in Music Education* (University of Kansas, Department of Music Education and Music Therapy, 1980–). [516.

————. [Special Research Interest Groups, *Newsletters.*] The Social Sciences Special Research Interest Group *Newsletter* includes "A Bibliography of Doctoral Dissertations in Music Education Relating to Sociology, Social Psychology, and Anthropology, 1948–1969," in vol. 3, nos. 1–4 (Sept.-Dec. 1982 and Mar.-June 1983); also "A Bibliography . . . in Anthropology, 1972–1977," and ". . . , 1968–71," in vol. 1, nos. 1–4 (Sept. 1980–June 1981) and vol. 2, nos. 1–4 (Sept. 1981–June 1982).   [517.

A Bibliography of Music Research Done in the Southern Division. [N.p.:] MENC, Southern Division, Research Committee, 1961. 2d ed. 1963. 3d ed. 1968. The 1968 list includes 1,221 items of all kinds, arranged by state and institution, with indexes of authors (pp. 124–49) and keywords (pp. 150–282).   [518.

A Bibliography of Master's Theses and Doctoral Dissertations in Music Completed at Texas Colleges and Universities, 1919–62. Houston: Texas Music Educators Association, Research in Music Education Committee, 1964. LC 64-56610. About 1,000 titles are listed chronologically by institution with subject and name indexes.   [519.

Suzanne Snyder. *University of Iowa Theses in American Music.* Iowa City: University of Iowa, 1985. A list of 162 master's and doctoral projects.   [520.

Music Education, Pedagogy, and Testing

A good deal of pedagogical material, particularly for performance, is accessible by period in this book in chapters 2–5 (in chapter 5 particularly), by source in chapters 6–8, and by genre in chapters 9–12. Such materials are often covered from the special vantage of the educator in the titles listed below, along with other writings and teaching materials:

Hazel N. Morgan. *Music Education Source Book [no. 1].* Chicago: MENC, 1947. LC 48-202. Reissued with appendix revisions, 1951. LC 52-2150. Assembled by the organization's Curriculum Committee, with short lists at the ends of many chapters along with "Library Book Lists" for collections designed for particular age levels.   [521.

Selected Bibliography: Music Education Materials. Chicago: MENC, 1952. Prepared "as a guide in the selection of materials which are distributed . . . by the Department of State to cultural institutes of the U.S. in other countries," containing about 1,200 entries arranged by five school levels. [522.

Katherine C. Modisett. "Bibliography of Sources, 1930–1952, Relating to the Teaching of Choral Music in the Secondary Schools," *Journal of Research in Music Education,* 3 (1955), 51–60. Includes 236 items, not annotated, organized around broad topics. [523.

Music in American Education: Music Education Source Book [no. 2]. Chicago: MENC, 1955. LC 56-399. Essentially a new ed. of the 1951 Morgan committee book, now assembled by the Music in American Education Committee, and containing seventeen lists at the ends of chapters, unannotated but highly respected if by no means exhaustive. [524.

Albert W. Wassell and Walter L. Haderer. *Bibliography for String Teachers.* Washington: MENC, 1957. Rev. ed., by Wassell and Charles H. Wertman. 1964. LC 67-49283. A classified list, with about 250 titles in the 1964 ed. [525.

"Music Education Materials: A Selected Bibliography," *Journal of Research in Music Education,* vol. 7, no. 1 (Spring 1959). A useful annotated list of about 1,000 titles, grouped around broad topics, with a supplementary list of "State Music Educators Association Official Publications." [526.

Harold W. Arberg and Sarah P. Wood. *Music Curriculum Guides.* Washington: Government Printing Office, 1964. (U.S. Office of Education, Bulletin 1964, no. 14; Superintendent of Documents Catalog No. FS 5:233:33032.) An annotated list of 491 guides, mostly prepared 1950–63 by school systems for classroom use. Classified by level and purpose, with an added subject index. [527.

T. C. Collins. *Music Education Materials: A Selected Annotated Bibliography.* Washington: MENC, 1968. LC 68-2190. A classified and annotated list, in three parts. Part 1 cites about 800 works for teacher use, i.e., the major titles of interest to music educators. Part 2 cites about 600 works for the student, i.e., "basic series," method books, miscellaneous other class songbooks and the like. Part 3 covers "Instructional Resources," mostly on access to audiovisual material. [528.

Educational Resources Information Clearinghouse [ERIC]. *Educational Document Index, 1966/69– *. New York: CCM Information [later Macmillan], 1970– . LC 71-130348. Monthly issues, cumulated annually, covering the documents entered into the ERIC data base and available on demand. Three alphabets at first — "Major Descriptors," "Minor Descriptors," and "Author Index" — are later supplemented by an "Institutional Index." Typically over 100 documents, mostly but not entirely on music education topics, are covered each year. [529.

Peggy Flanagan Baird. *Music Books for the Elementary School Library.* Washington: MENC, 1972. LC 72-77124. An annotated list of about 250 titles. [530.

Charles Sollinger. *String Class Publications in the United States, 1851–1951.* Detroit: Information Coordinators, 1974. (Detroit Studies in Music Bibliography, 30.) ISBN 0-911772-61-8. Several hundred titles are listed on pp. 23–71, often with valuable bibliographical and critical annotations, but in a classified arrangement that makes the titles difficult to locate in the absence of any indexes. [531.

National Endowment for the Arts, Research Division, *List of Publications* (1976; see 554 below).

Gene M. Simons. *Early Childhood Musical Development: A Bibliography of Research Abstracts, 1960–1973.* [Athens: University of Georgia, 1976.] *Supplement, 1960–75.* (Mathemagenic Activities Program — Follow Through, Research Report 23.) Detailed abstracts, with extensive methodological particulars, of sixty-three studies in the main set and thirteen more in the *Supplement.* Also issued Reston, Va.: MENC, 1975. (*RILM* 1978:4587) [532.

Arts and Aesthetics: An Agenda for the Future. Edited by Stanley S. Madeja. St. Louis: CEMREL, 1977. LC 77-75363. Based on a conference held at Aspen, Colo., June 22–25, 1976, cosponsored by CEMREL, Inc. (the Central Mid-Western Regional Educational Laboratory), and the Education Program of the Aspen Institute for Humanistic Studies. The literature of music in the area of aesthetic education is presented in the list of 143 references (pp. 101–8) in

Charles Leonhard's and Richard J. Colwell's survey of "Research in Music Education," by way of complementing the art list on pp. 119–47 and the general list on p. 80.   [533.

James C. Carlsen. *A Computer Annotated Bibliography: Music Research in Programmed Instruction, 1952–1972.* Reston, Va.: MENC, 1978. A chronological list of fifty-one titles annotated with extensive keyword lists, supplemented by twenty-five titles not available for review. The keywords become the basis for an extensive index; the computerization is nevertheless at so perfunctory a level (even by mid-1970s standards) as to leave the reader to ask of the title, "Who's kidding who?"   [534.

Ernest Harris. *Music Education: A Guide to Information Sources.* Detroit: Gale, 1978. ISBN 0-8103-1309-X. A classified list of about 2,000 entries, thoughtfully annotated. The scope is broadly defined, making for a reference source of general usefulness, specifically for its coverage of music education materials.   [535.

Margaret Chase Diaz. "An Analysis of Elementary School Music Series Published in the United States from 1926 to 1976." Ed.D. thesis, University of Illinois, 1980. The books under discussion are listed alphabetically by editor, with particulars on the various editions, on pp. 515–34—this being probably the best bibliographical survey of the "basic series" books.   [536.

The literature of testing is much like music itself in that it is twofold, involving the tests themselves and also the literature about tests and testing. Insofar as the tests involve privileged information, however (whether the answers, the questions, or the format), the field is unlike that of musical editions—except to the extent that some music is published on paper but capable of effective realization only in the hands of a recognized virtuoso or apostle. Music tests are rarely listed in any of the titles cited elsewhere in this book, except for a few of the music education sources immediately above; writings on music testing appear only slightly more often. For these materials one starts and ends with bibliographies like the following:

Cecile Woodard Flemming and Marion Flagg. *A Descriptive Bibliography of Prognostic and Achievement Tests in Music.* New York: Columbia University, Teachers College, 1936. Lists fifty-seven tests on pp. 1–20.   [537.

Oscar Krisen Buros. "Music Tests," in *Mental Measurements Yearbook*, 1938–78.   [538.

Tests in Print: A Comprehensive Bibliography. Highland Park, N.J.: Gryphon, 1961. LC 61-16302. Compiled by Oscar Krisen Buros, with nineteen music tests listed on pp. 83–85.
Tests in Print II. Highland Park, N.J.: Gryphon, 1974. ISBN 0-910674-14-0. Twenty-four music tests on pp. 43–49.
Tests in Print III: An Index to Tests, Test Reviews, and the Literature on Specific Tests. Lincoln: University of Nebraska Press, 1983. ISBN 0-910674-52-3. Compiled by James V. Mitchell, Jr., with twenty-four music tests listed on p. 527.   [539.

Paul R. Lehman. *Tests and Measurements in Music.* Englewood Cliffs, N.J.: Prentice-Hall, 1968. LC 68-10416. Chapters 6–8 (pp. 37–62) consist largely of annotated bibliographies of thirty tests, while the app. (pp. 89–90) lists twenty out-of-print music tests. The list is complemented by Lehman's "A Selected Bibliography of Works on Music Testing," *Journal of Research in Music Education,* 17 (1969), 427–42.   [540.

William J. Bullock. "A Review of Measures of Musico-Aesthetic Attitude," *Journal of Research in Music Education,* 21 (1973), 331–44.   [541.

Rosamund Shuter-Dyson. *The Psychology of Musical Ability.* London, New York: Methuen, 1968. LC 68-122648. 2d ed., with Clive Gabriel. 1981. ISBN 0-416-71300-9. Appendix 1 ("Description of Tests"; pp. 272–301 in the 2d ed.) evaluates the major available tests in print, while the "Bibliography of References Cited" (pp. 302–37) lists about 500 titles relevant to the topic of music testing.   [542.

Essential to the world of the music educator, meanwhile, are the audiovisual materials described in bibliographical sources such as the following:

Music Educators National Conference, Committee on Audio-Visual Aids. *Handbook of 16mm. Films for Music Education.* Prepared by Lilla Belle Pitts. Chicago: MENC, 1952.   [543.

National Information Center for Educational Media. *NICEM Media*

Indexes. Los Angeles: University of Southern California, 1967– .
Miscellaneous guides to filmstrips, videotapes, audiotapes, and slides,
usually arranged by subject with title indexes. [544.

Media Review Digest. Ann Arbor: Pierian Press, 1970– . ISBN 0-
87650-198-6. Annual coverage of reviews, containing entries arranged by medium (film and video, filmstrips, and so on) and often
annotated, with alphabetical subject indexes that include numerous
entries beginning "Music." [545.

Mary Robinson Sive. *Educators' Guide to Media Lists.* Littleton, Colo.:
Libraries Unlimited, 1975. ISBN 0-87287-181-9. 2d ed. as *Selecting
Instructional Media: A Guide to Audiovisual and Other Instructional
Media Lists.* 1978. ISBN 0-87287-122-3. 3d ed. 1983. ISBN 0-
87287-342-0. Arranged by subject, with twenty-six, fourteen, and
twenty-eight music entries, respectively. [546.

Margaret I. Rufsvold. *Guides to Newer Educational Media.* Chicago:
American Library Association, 1961. 2d ed. 1967. 3d ed. as *Guides
to Educational Media.* Compiled by Carolyn Guss. 1971. 4th ed.
[covering 1972–76]. 1977. ISBN 0-8389-0232-4. An index of catalogues, indexes, and reviewing services, with title, address, scope,
and arrangement under each entry. The subject indexes to each
vol. cite upwards of a dozen music entries. [547.

Music from the Perspective of Other Disciplines

Writings about music are often buried in the bibliographies of other
disciplines. By way of complementing *Music Index* and *RILM Abstracts,*
such tools as the Beers bibliographies, *America: History and Life, Resources in Education,* and *Popular Culture Abstracts* are often worth
checking.

Writings on American History. Washington: American Historical Association, 1906– . ISBN 0-527-00373-5. Annual bibliography of
writings, 1902–76 (with cumulation for 1962–73), of likely interest
to American historians. Since 1961 coverage has been limited to
the U.S. sections of *Recently Published Articles,* in which 4,000 journals are covered, many of them obscure, regional, or institutional
publications with occasional music entries. The "Music" heading
in the subject index, along with other headings, calls attention to

a vast number of writings on American music not easily accessible
elsewhere.   [548.

Appleton Prentiss Clark Griffin. *Bibliography of American Historical Societies.* Washington: Government Printing Office, 1907. (American
Historical Association, Annual Report, 1905, vol. 2.) "2d ed." LC
8-7356. Vast and inadequately indexed, but with occasional early
curiosities of musical scholarship.   [549.

Henry Putney Beers. *Bibliographies in American History: Guide to Materials for Research.* New York: Wilson, 1938. LC 38-27119. Rev. ed.
1942. LC 42-23899. Repr. Paterson, N.J.: Pageant Books, 1959.
LC 59-14179. Repr. New York: Octagon Books, 1973. ISBN 0-274-
90515-0. The 1942 ed.—expanded by roughly a third over the
1938 ed. and with much improved indexes—includes sixty-six bibliographical items relating to music on pp. 253–55 and a few others
accessible through the index. The scope of the bibliographical items
in question is rather unsettled: several of the works seem to have
been included because they were bibliographies compiled by Americans, without any special concern for American topics.
———. *Bibliographies in American History, 1942–1978.* Woodbridge,
Conn.: Research Publications, 1982. ISBN 0-89235-038-5. Includes
121 additional items on pp. 397–406. (The headings "Printing"
on p. 400 and "Lists" on p. 406 would seem to have been switched
by mistake.)   [550.

David R. Weimer. *Bibliography of American Culture, 1493–1875.* Ann
Arbor: University Microfilms, 1957. LC 57-4827. A list of titles
prepared by the American Studies Association of works made available on film, including sixty-one unusual music titles on pp.
105–7.   [551.

America: History and Life. Santa Barbara, Calif.: ABC-Clio Press,
1964– . ISSN 0002-7065. The set has grown from a modest
monthly list to a massive on-line service today. Before 1974 music
subjects were collected in the indexes at the end of each number
under the heading "Music," with further titles often buried under
the names of states and territories but with no further guidance on
matters of precise subject coverage. The two five-year cumulative
indexes use "—Music" as a subdivision under the general heading
"United States" and for specific state and territory headings. Beginning in 1974, pt. D of the annual index includes entries under

"Music," as well as guidance to more specific entries like "Composers," "Folk Songs," "Musicians," "Opera," and "Radio." A selected sampling turned up several music articles not covered in *Music Index* or *RILM Abstracts,* in such journals as *Labor History, Palimpsest* (State Historical Society of Iowa), and *Mississippi Quarterly.* Several bibliographies with music entries have been compiled from the data base, among them Brye on urban ethnicity (1983; see 177 above), Shumsky and Crimmins on urban studies in general (1983; see 178 above), Wertheim on popular culture (1984; see 303 above), and Harrison on women's studies (1979; see 184 above).   [552.

Charlotte Georgi. *The Arts and the World of Business: A Selected Bibliography.* Metuchen, N.J.: Scarecrow, 1973. ISBN 0-8108-0611-8. A classified list of about 500 titles.   [553.

National Endowment for the Arts, Research Division. [*List of Publications.*] Washington, 1976–   . The program has issued four series: (1) *Research Reports* (1976–   ; eighteen titles to date), occasional summaries distributed by the Publishing Center for Cultural Resources, New York (and cited in *PTLA,* 49 above) as well as the American Council for the Arts; (2) *Notes* (1982–   ; eighteen titles to date), brief occasional pamphlets on current topics, and available through the Washington office; (3) full texts, distributed through ERIC (and hence cited in 529 above); and (4) computer tapes of research data, also available through the Washington office. Annotated listings have also been prepared, with particulars on availability, of the various studies on "American arts, artists, and audiences—who they are; how they relate to the total economy; and what their prospects are for growth and development."   [554.

Marion K. Whalen. *Performing Arts Research: A Guide to Information Sources.* Detroit: Gale, 1976. ISBN 0-8103-1364-2. A classified list that includes several dozen basic or popularized music sources, accessible through the table of contents or the index.   [555.

Jeannette L. Cook. "Documents on Music Issued by the United States Government: An Annotated Bibliography." Master's thesis, University of Nebraska, 1978. (Heintze 5)   [556.

Gail Fleming Winson, "Music and the Law: A Comprehensive Bibliography of Law-Related Materials," *COMM/ENT: A Journal of Communications and Entertainment Law,* 4 (1982), 489–551. A list of about 700 titles, a few of them annotated, classified by form and topic, without indexes. [557.

Of more modest and questionable value are a number of other guides that profess to cover all aspects of American culture. The Ireland indexes can serve as cases in point. Their objective is entirely laudable: to give general readers a detailed index to the subject coverage provided in comprehensive popularizations—just over 100 of these books for each century. But the inclusion of several specifically musical titles—in the first volumes John Tasker Howard, in the last volume Chase (but in a superseded edition), and a few other titles both respected and dubious—suggests an amateurishness that scarcely endorses the volumes. But as one examines the popularizations themselves—scanning their indexes by genre or personal name—one comes to realize how little there is in any of the sources other than these few music books. The general reader indeed deserves better than this, beginning with better popularizations that do take music seriously.

Norma Olin Ireland. *Index to America: Life and Customs, 17th Century.* Westwood, Mass.: Faxon, 1978. ISBN 0-87305-107-6.
———. *Index to America: Life and Customs, 18th Century.* Westwood, Mass.: Faxon, 1976. ISBN 0-87305-108-4.
———. *Index to America: Life and Customs, 19th Century.* Metuchen, N.J.: Scarecrow, 1984. ISBN 0-8108-1661-X. [558.

On-Line Data Bases

The conception, reconception, and conversion of major continuing services has proceeded apace over the past decade and can be expected to continue. Although the present discussion will no doubt be out of date when it appears in print, for now it is possible to distinguish several kinds of sources. First are the directories that cover data bases in general, each containing some entries not found in the others. (The citations and annotations below, unlike most others in this book, are constructed from the perspective of the latest edition in its own right and wherever possible as relevant to likely future editions; a survey of the coverage in previous editions would be useful mostly as a reflection of the history of the directories themselves rather than of the emergence and evolution of the data bases.)

Encyclopedia of Information Systems and Services. 6th ed. Detroit: Gale,

1985–86. ISSN 0734-9068. (1st ed. 1971.) An alphabetical listing of files accessible both commercially and locally only, with nine music-specific projects indexed on p. 1208.   [559.

Martha E. Williams [earlier eds. by Carolyn G. Robbins]. *Computer-Readable Databases*. Chicago: American Library Association, 1985. ISBN 0-444-87615-4. Volume 2, devoted to business, law, the humanities, and the social sciences, includes eight music-specific data bases, of which only two are also listed in the above.   [560.

Directory of Online Databases. Santa Monica, Calif.: Cuadra Associates, 1979– . ISSN 0193-6840. Issued quarterly, with each issue superseding all previous numbers, but limited in its coverage to those data bases available "for interactive access by users from remote computer terminals and microcomputers." An alphabetical listing, with its specific music data bases accessible through subject entries such as "Music and Music Industry," "Entertainment Industry," "Performing Arts," and "Library Holdings—Catalogs."
                    [561.

Data Base Directory, 1984. [2d ed.] White Plains, N.Y.: Knowledge Industry Publications, 1984. ISSN 0749-6680. Generated from the Data Base User Service on-line files, to which subscribers have access, and updated through a monthly *Data Base Alert*. The several entries specific to music, such as *RILM*, *Hollywood Hotline*, and *Billboard Information Network*, are all included in the lists above. [562.

The following texts summarize the recent state of the art, as they analyze the ways in which the major music data bases now serve their users and might in the future better serve those users:

David Brian Williams and I. Sue Beasley. "Computer Information Search and Retrieval: A Guide for the Music Educator," Council for Research in Music Education, *Bulletin no. 51* (1977).   [563.

Michael Keller and Carol A. Lawrence. "Music Literature Indexes in Review," MLA *Notes*, 36 (1980), 575–600.   [564.

Allie Wise Goudy. "Music Coverage in Online Databases," *Database*, vol. 5, no. 4 (Dec. 1982), pp. 39–57.   [565.

Thomas F. Heck. "Computerized Bibliographic Retrieval of Music," in Sarah K. Burton and Douglas D. Short, *Sixth International Conference of Computers and the Humanities* (Rockville, Md.: Computer Science Press, 1983), pp. 249–52.   [566.

David Ossenkop. "Computerized Bibliographic Retrieval of Music Literature: An Annotated Bibliography," *Cum Notis Variorum* (University of California Music Library, Berkeley), 96 (Oct. 1985), 11–17. A discussion of the state of the art, reflecting the texts of nearly fifty writings in music and related fields.   [567.

Of the major continuing bibliographical series, the most important ones now on-line are, through the DIALOG system, *RILM Abstracts* (see 45 above), *America: History and Life* (see 552 above), and ERIC (see 529 above); through the WILSONLINE system, the various Wilson indexes, notably the *Book Review Digest* (73 above), the *Readers' Guide to Periodical Literature* (477 above), and the *Humanities Index* (479 above); the *Arts and Humanities Citation Index* (below); in various ways the *National Union Catalog* (see 33 above) and *Union List of Serials / New Serial Titles* (see 471–72); also the *Catalog of Copyright Entries* (see 30 above). Of special interest in its own right, and nowhere else in this book as appropriately accommodated as here, is the following:

Arts and Humanities Citation Index. Philadelphia: Institute for Scientific Information, 1977– . A vast index to works cited in other writings, perhaps best defended in Thomas G. Heck, "The Relevance of the 'Arts and Humanities' Data Base to Musicological Research," *Fontes Artis Musicae*, 28 (1981), 81–87.   [568.

How well is American music represented in other data bases? A search of the BRS CROS data base, performed in spring 1986 and based on the strategy of using "America$ AND Music$," turns up the following total numbers of entries:

MAGS (*Magazine Index:* General interest magazines)	2,931
AHCI (*Arts and Humanities Citation Index*) [568 above]	2,225
PETE (*National College Databank*)	1,367
DISS (*Dissertation Abstracts*) [493 above]	1,208
ERIC (*Educational Research Information Clearinghouse*)	1,159
BOOK (*Booksinfo:* Brodart list of U.S. books in print)	854
BBIP (*Books in Print:* Bowker list) [49 above]	774
A400 (*Abstrax 400:* Popular periodical literature)	665
NOOZ (*National Newspaper Index:* 5 major U.S. papers)	584
BIZZ (*Trade and Industry Directory*)	536
AAED (*Academic American Encyclopedia Database*)	522
OCLC (*Online Computer Library Center, Inc.*)	475

191

The figures are obviously too raw to be meaningful—except for purposes of suggesting that American music is, in various ways, finding its way into the files. Perhaps strategically even more promising are the prospects for wider coverage of American newspapers (for instance, by way of reviving the *Music Reporter;* see 487 above), of popular music (for instance, through the *Billboard Information Network, Hollywood Hotline,* and the like), or of biographical information on musicians through general biographical sources. At some point the data bases cease to become essentially bibliographical, while at some point they may cease to be essentially either musical or American—although perhaps not to the detriment of use by the American music community, except insofar as they may require the mediation of librarians able to access and interpret them and sources of funds to pay for them.

Music bibliographies in print or on-line, meanwhile, benefit from a broad strategy of subject searching that readers may wish to adapt for their own special needs. The formulation of headings is difficult for the compiler of bibliographies, partly because of the ambiguity created by an overabundance of terms, partly because one never knows whether to settle for headings that are either too broad or too particular to be of much help. At the most general level, readers will automatically think to look up "Music" in Americana sources and either "U.S." or "America" in music sources. As refinements are appropriate, a list of useful subdivisions is worth having in reserve, for instance the names of plausible cities, states, or regions (New England, Appalachia, Pacific Northwest); of musical mediums, genres, and forms (band, church, chor—, folk—, hymn, jazz, opera, rock, sing—, song, violin); of particular composers or performers, appropriately popular or obscure or intermixed; or even of particular musical titles. Lists of subject headings, thesauri, and musical dictionaries can be helpful, but usually more for compilers than for users. As systematic hierarchies might appear enlightening (perhaps in the manner one uses Roget's *Thesaurus*), the classification of members' interests used in the Sonneck Society membership lists (since 1986) offers the first model comprehensive to the field of American music. Others, no doubt equally valid to particular perspectives, will presumably continue to be developed—one hopes with a view to bringing out the character of the material being described, as reflected in the attitudes and presentations of respected scholars.

15

Discography

Sound recordings are a particularly awkward world for music bibliography, thanks in some part to the historic concern of bibliographers with printed materials. No less troublesome is a fundamental bibliographical awkwardness of the material itself—it simply does not "cite" well—partly, perhaps, because of its historic patterns of commercial distribution—involving objects that, for reasons that are obscure but probably significant, are not "published" but instead are "released." Furthermore the medium is continually changing in its forms—from cylinder to 78 disc to LP to stereo to cassette to compact disc—transformations the likes of which, it is reasonable to expect, will most certainly continue. Obviously recordings are here to stay, and to be used in whatever form, although their relegation en bloc to a separate chapter of this book is evidence of the continuing awkwardness in dealing with them.

In what sense may a discography be said to be concerned with American music? It is convenient here to separate three kinds of national identity: producer, performer, and repertory. The distinction of discographical genres proposed in 1975 by J. F. Weber (*Recorded Sound*, nos. 57–58, pp. 380–82) is appropriate to adapt here: discographies may emphasize the producer, in this discussion the output of American record companies; they may emphasize the performers, however Americans are to be identified; or they may emphasize the works performed, in this instance repertories or composers indigenous to or associated with the United States. Fitting the literature of American music discography under these three rubrics admittedly results in inevitable overlaps—the instances, particularly in recent pop music, of performers who compose their own music and own their own record companies, for example—but in the classification scheme of this book, overlaps by now are neither new nor unexpected.

The abundance of lists necessitates a discussion mostly of types, leaving particular representative or laudable titles to passing mention only. It is useful to begin by citing the several major bibliographies devoted to discographies.

Lewis Foreman. *Discographies: A Bibliography of Catalogues of Recordings, Mainly Relating to Specific Musical Subjects, Composers and Performers.* London: Triad Press, 1974. LC 74-174493. A list of 388 titles, with several American music entries accessible either through the systematic arrangement or the index. [569.

David Edwin Cooper. *International Bibliography of Discographies.* Littleton, Colo.: Libraries Unlimited, 1975. ISBN 0-87287-108-8. A list of about 2,000 citations, arranged topically under broad categories, with detailed subject and compiler indexes. Of particular value to the American music in the "Classical" section are the "Subjects and Genres" section (pp. 31–52, including eight "American music entries," and others under "Band Music" and "Musical Comedy"), historical recordings (pp. 53–62), and a list of composers and performers (pp. 63–142). The "Jazz and Blues" section includes 62 blues (pp. 145–52) and 204 general jazz sources (pp. 153–74), as well as a composer and performer section (pp. 175–220). A brief concluding summary of national discographic sources includes thirteen U.S. titles (pp. 233–34). Generally superseded by the title below, this text continues to be valuable for its conciseness and for its variant subject arrangements. [570.

Bibliography of Discographies. New York: Bowker, 1977–   . Vol. 1, *Classical Music, 1925–1975.* Edited by Gerald D. Gibson and Michael H. Gray. 1977. ISBN 0-8352-1023-5. Vol. 2, *Jazz.* Edited by Daniel Allen. 1981. ISBN 0-8352-1342-0. Vol. 3, *Popular Music.* Edited by Michael H. Gray. 1983. ISBN 0-8352-1683-7. Volume 1 covers 3,307 lists, vol. 2 cites 3,842 from the period 1935–80, and vol. 3 includes 3,831 from the period up to 1982. Volume 4 is projected to cover ethnic and folk music, while vol. 5 is to cover general sources, label lists, and nonmusic recordings. Each vol. is arranged alphabetically by topic (i.e., composer, performer, repertory, label), with detailed indexes by subject and compiler. [571.

David Hall, Gary-Gabriel Gisondi, and Edward Berger, "Discographies," in *The New Grove Dictionary of American Music,* ed. H. Wiley Hitchcock and Stanley Sadie (London: Macmillan; New York: Grove's Dictionaries of Music, 1986), vol. 1, pp. 627–32. A list of about 200 titles, preceded by a brief but authoritative survey. [572.

Association for Recorded Sound Collections [ARSC]. *Journal.* 1967– .
These listings of recent discographies serve to extend the coverage
of the Bowker *Bibliography of Discographies.* The cumulations to date
(in the second number of the vols. in question) are in vol. 10 (1979),
pp. 128–62 (1976 cumulation, with 429 entries, also 37 additional
titles for 1975); vol. 11 (1979), pp. 152–90 (1977 cumulation, with
638 entries); and vol. 13 (1981), pp. 29–75 (1978–79 cumulation,
with 809 entries). Complemented at first, and now largely superseded
by the Brooks lists that follow.
Tim Brooks. "Current Bibliography," ARSC *Journal,* vol. 10, nos. 2/
3 (1979), pp. 123–27; 11 (1979), 144–51; 12 (1980), 174–83; 13
(1981), 19–28, 80–89; vol. 14 (1982), no. 1, pp. 47–56, no. 2, pp.
43–50, no. 3, pp. 62–67; 15 (1983), 15–24, 66–80; and 16 (1984),
33–45, 79–98. Devoted to "recent English-language articles dealing
with recording history," with added listings of "labels" (i.e., in effect,
new catalogues of record companies), also new books, discographies,
and miscellaneous timely announcements.   [573.

B. Lee Cooper. "Discographies of Contemporary Music, 1965–1980:
A Selected Bibliography," *Popular Music and Society,* 7 (1980), 253–69.
A list of nearly 300 discographies of current popular music, arranged under broad topics (general, topical, by style, composer,
performer, and record company), to facilitate general subject
access.   [574.

Pete Moon. *A Bibliography of Jazz Discographies Published since 1960.*
Edited by Barry Witherden. 2d ed. South Harrow [Middlesex, En-
gland]: British Institute of Jazz Studies, 1969, 1972 (with supplements announced). LC 75-301663. Presumably largely superseded
by the titles above, although of possible continuing use for references to European work.   [575.

Source Discographies

At the outset the totality of American sound recording activity needs
to be viewed in brief perspective. Parallel in a sense to the distinction
between printed and manuscript music, for instance, is that between
so-called commercial recordings and the other kind, variously designated as noncommercial, unissued, archival, or instantaneous recordings. The former are offered for sale to the general public or
otherwise issued in multiple copies. The auspices range in size and

objectives from the major mass-audience record companies (of which there are at any time in history between half a dozen and two dozen that dominate the market), to the smaller specialty companies that aspire to major success but usually by emphasizing particular performers or repertories, or to those persons or institutions that issue occasional recordings as part of their mandate in serving particular musical repertories. The "unissued" recordings, in contrast, are those in archival collections, piracies, studio versions, and aspiring releases not yet accepted or rejected by commercial firms. A particular discography may exclude or exclusively describe any of these. Pervading the field, meanwhile, is the basic distinction between classical and popular music, the latter of which subsumes a wide range of repertories from jazz to ethnic to current rock, with the repertories of salon music and its derivatives, background music, and "old favorites" falling in the midst of everything.

As with bibliographies of printed music and books, discographies may be devoted either to current or retrospective listings. The current listings, again, address questions of what may be new, available, or good. The best general listing of new releases is still the starred items in the monthly Schwann catalogues, notwithstanding their primary purpose of listing the recordings that are available (and for this function it has no peers). The Library of Congress cataloguing provides more access points and reflects better authority work, appropriate to the needs of libraries in cataloguing their collections; but only the small proportion of the recordings likely to end up in major collections is given the fairly high level of description. Furthermore, even library cataloguing necessarily involves many compromises of the discographer's ideal and often provides inadequate contents listings as well.

Library of Congress. *Printed Music, Books on Music, and Sound Recordings* (1953–   ; formerly *Music and Phonorecords;* see 33 above).

Schwann Long Playing Record Catalog. Boston: W. Schwann [ABC Schwann since 1977], 1949–   . The invaluable monthly listing of what is currently available for sale in American record shops. Arranged by genre, e.g., classical (by composer), electronic, collections, musicals, popular (including band music), pop collections, jazz, jazz anthologies, spoken and miscellaneous, and international pop and folk. Between 1968 and 1985 the current and older listings were further separated. A summary history of the set appears in vol. 36, no. 12 (Dec. 1984), pp. 6–7; a detailed history would be extremely desirable.   [576.

Phonolog: The All in One Record Reporter. Los Angeles: Trade Service Publications, 1948– . A loose-leaf service with weekly updatings of selected pages, as explained in the introductory material. These are followed by a list of labels, with current names and addresses. The entries themselves are cited under the following categories: pop titles, pop artists, pop albums, band, Christmas albums and singles, children's, Hawaiian, Latin American, motion pictures, sacred, show tunes, specialties and miscellaneous, theme songs, classical titles, classical composers, and classical artists.   [577.

Catalog of Copyright Entries, 3d ser., pt. 4 [since 1978, 4th ser., pt. 7]: *Sound Recordings, 1973–* . Washington: Library of Congress, Copyright Office, 1975– . The first vol. includes about 8,400 titles, arranged by registration number, with indexes by name, title, and record label and number. The 4th ser., beginning with 53,000 entries in 1978, is arranged alphabetically by title, with a claimant index. The most recent vol. in this ser., covering the first half of 1979, already has reached 100,000 entries, with no index. [578.

List-o-Tapes "All in One" Tape Catalog. San Diego, Calif.: Trade Service Publications, 1964– . A counterpart to *Phonolog,* updated weekly, attempting to cover the output of all manufacturers of prerecorded tapes, arranged in sections devoted mostly to broad types of material, with a classified genre index.   [579.

Equally important and also valuable as historical summaries are two older sets designed in their day as guides to the purchaser and aspiring to international coverage:

The Gramophone Shop Encyclopedia of Recorded Music. Edited by R. D. Darrell. New York: Gramophone Shop, 1936. LC 36-27336. 2d ed., by George C. Leslie. New York: Simon and Schuster, 1942. LC 42-24376; 3d ed., by Robert H. Reid. New York: Crown, 1948; LC 48-7633. Repr. of 3d ed. Westport, Conn.: Greenwood, 1970. LC 70-95122. Composer listings, with a performer index in the 3d ed. The three sets, each of which includes some information not in the other two, often provide the sole citations of classical music recordings of the day.   [580.

David Hall. *The Record Book: A Music Lover's Guide to the World of the Phonograph.* New York: Smith and Durrell, 1940. LC 41-1274. Supplements (1941, 1943) merged in the "Complete Edition." New

York: Citadel Press, 1946. LC 46-11855. All effectively superseded by the "International Edition." New York: Oliver Durrell, 1948. LC 48-5666. While many of the citations also appear in the *Gramophone Shop Encyclopedia*, the authoritative annotations in this set are of continuing usefulness. [581.

Qualitative considerations are addressed in reviewing journals, for which special indexes have proven particularly useful. Those assembled by Kurtz Myers are the models, both in priority and quality. The information cited in his entries often exceeds that provided by current library cataloguing standards in authority and detail and thus makes for an especially respected reference guide.

Kurtz Myers. "Index to Record Reviews," MLA *Notes* (1948–). Quarterly lists, with annual indexes to composite listings. Since June 1981 (vol. 37), every fourth quarterly issue has also included William C. Rorick's "Manufacturer's Numerical Index." The indexes themselves have been cumulated into the three titles below.
Kurtz Myers and Richard S. Hill. *Record Ratings*. Boston: Hall, 1956. LC 54-12064. A cumulation of the above, through June 1955.
———. *Index to Record Reviews*. Boston: Hall, 1978. ISBN 0-8161-0087-X. An extension of the above to include all LP recordings reviews between 1949 and 1977.
———. *Index to Record Reviews, 1978–83*. Boston: Hall, 1985. ISBN 0-8161-0435-2. A further supplement, covering the reviews cited 1978–83. [582.

Antoinette O. Maleady. *Record and Tape Reviews Index, 1971–74*. Metuchen, N.J.: Scarecrow, 1972–75. LC 72-3355.
———. *Index to Record and Tape Reviews, 1975–82*(?). San Anselmo, Calif.: Chulainn Press, 1976–83(?). ISSN 0097-8256, 0147-5983 (after 1974). An annual index to reviews of particular recordings, largely duplicating Myers's indexes, somewhat more convenient than Myers for being in one annual list rather than several, with more accessible coverage of collections and anonyma and with a useful performer index. It remains questionable whether the enhancements are sufficient to justify two indexes that duplicate each other almost completely. [583.

Annual Index to Popular Music Record Reviews, 1972–77. Variously edited by Andrew D. Armitage, Dean Tudor, Linda Biesenthal, and Nancy Tudor. Metuchen, N.J.: Scarecrow, 1973–78. ISSN 0092-

3486. Beginning in 1972 with 7,307 reviews in thirty-five journals, and reaching a high of seventy-one journals in 1977, and 14,214 reviews in 1974. Arranged by genre, with various useful indexes.

[584.

Cooper, *International Bibliography of Discographies* (1975; 570 above). The section of U.S. national discographies (pp. 233–34) cites five catalogues and eight reviewing sources.

The best-known general retrospective discographies—at least the ones that leap to mind to most users and reference librarians—are the works above. The retrospective discographies most respected by discographic scholars, on the other hand, are the catalogues and promotional literature of the record companies themselves. Working from these and other sources, discographers have slowly begun to assemble secondary, and often definitive, historical listings, typically arranged in the chronological numerical sequences of the firms in question. Some of these are cited in the several standard bibliographies noted first below.

Cooper, *International Bibliography of Discographies* (1975; see 570 above). Sections on "Historical Recordings and Label Discography" are for classical music (pp. 53–62), blues (pp. 149–52), and jazz (pp. 166–74).

Bibliography of Discographies (1975; see 571 above). The relevant lists are to appear in vol. 5. Until this appears Cooper remains the major source, supplemented by other continuing lists such as the ARSC *Journal* (see 573 above).

Other particularly important works that follow deserve to be cited, either for their general acclaimed excellence or for the significance of their subject or their conception. Discography, like American music bibliography in general, finds its best efforts concentrated largely on the earliest periods. The landmark studies of this era are those of Deakins, now extended and largely superseded by the work of Annand, Koenigsberg, Wile, and Dethlefson. Recently several of the peripheries distinctive to the medium of sound recordings—for instance, special issues (such as Sears on V-discs) and piracies (such as Reinhart on Beatles pressings)—have also begun to be addressed. The titles cited here reflect mostly the main history, as suggested in their titles.

199

Julian Morton Moses. *The Record Collector's Guide.* New York: College of the City of New York, Concert Bureau, 1936. LC 36-35208. Rev. ed. as *Collector's Guide to American Recordings, 1895–1925.* New York: American Record Collector's Exchange, 1949. LC 50-5022. Repr. New York: Dover, 1977. ISBN 0-486-23448-7. A first attempt "to piece together a complete account of all American recordings of celebrated singers." [585.

Duane D. Deakins. *Cylinder Records: A Description of the Numbering Systems, Physical Appearance, and Other Aspects of Cylinder Records Made by the Major American Companies, with Brief Remarks about the Earliest American Companies and the Foreign Record Manufacturers.* Stockton, Calif.: Author, 1956. LC 57-26790. 2d ed. 1958. LC 58-22781. The basic text, supplemented by the title that follows below.
Thomas Grattelo and Duane D. Deakins. *Comprehensive Cylinder Record Index.* Stockton, Calif.: Author [i.e., Deakins], 1956. LC 61-33158. In five parts: (1) "Edison Amberol Records," (2) "Edison Standard Records," (3) "Edison Blue Amberol Records," (4) "Indestructible Cylinder Records," and (5) "U.S. Everlasting Cylinder Records." Complementary numerical listings, with dating chart and indexes by author and title for each company/record series. [586.

Victor Girard and Harold M. Barnes. *Vertical-Cut Cylinders and Discs, a Catalogue of All "Hill & Dale" Recordings of Serious Worth Made and Issued between 1897–1932 circa.* London: British Institute of Recorded Sound, 1964. LC 66-13807. 2d ed. 1971. LC 72-187040. [587.

Major H. H. Annand. *The Complete Catalogue of the United States Everlasting Indestructible Cylinders, 1908–1913: [A Numerical List].* London: City of London Phonograph and Gramophone Society, 1966. LC 66-67437. [588.

Allen Koenigsberg. *Edison Cylinder Records, 1889–1912: With an Illustrated History of the Phonograph.* New York: Stellar Productions, 1969. LC 70-8824. Includes a numerical index, with a dating chart similar to Deakins's. [589.

Brian Rust. *The American Record Label Book.* New Rochelle, N.Y.: Arlington House, 1978. ISBN 0-87000-414-X. For all its problems, this book remains the best source for identifying labels, ca.

1896–1942, against the photographic copies reproduced here.

[590.

Ronald Dethlefson. *Edison Blue Amberol Recordings.* Brooklyn, N.Y.: APM Press, 1980. ISBN 0-937612-00-6. Volume 1 is devoted to Edison Blue Amberol recordings, 1912–1914, "live" recordings, and selected recordings, 1915–28, while vol. 2 (ISBN 0-937612-01-4) covers the Blue Amberol recordings, 1915–29. Profusely illustrated, with a history of Edison's cylinder works, numerical dating charts, chronologies, miscellaneous charts, and indexes for artists and titles. [591.

Kenneth M. Lorenz. *Two-Minute Brown Wax and XP Cylinder Records of the Columbia Phonograph Company: Numerical Catalogue, August, 1908–ca. March, 1909.* Wilmington, Del.: Kastlemusick, 1981. Numerical listings, with a "Special List of 1908 Presidential Election Campaign Cylinders" added, along with dating charts and an introductory chart in the company's "Cylinder Block System Distribution." Highly respected despite the absence of a performer index, known take numbers, and a correlation of contemporaneous disc issues. [592.

Paul C. Mawhinney. *MusicMaster: The 45 RPM Record Directory, 1947–1982.* Alison Park, Pa.: Record-Rama, 1983. ISBN 0-910925-00-3. Also issued, New York: Facts on File, 1983. ISBN 0-87196-939-4. A listing of about 100,000 recordings, by performer in vol. 1 and by title in vol. 2, of special value for particulars of interest to collectors. [593.

Ted Fagan and William R. Moran. *The Encyclopedic Discography of Victor Recordings: Pre-Matrix Series.* Westport, Conn.: Greenwood, 1983. ISBN 0-313-23003-X. Includes a reprint of Benjamin L. Aldridge's book *The Victor Talking Machine Company* (1964), with a serial-number listing for over 3,000 recordings and with artist and title indexes, largely 1900–1903. [594.

Ronald Dethlefson and Ray Wile. *Edison Disc Artists and Records, 1910–1929.* Brooklyn, N.Y.: APM Press, 1986. This recently announced work promises to supplement Wile's *Edison Disc Recordings* with additional technical and discographic data. [595.

Finally, due mention should be made of the great catalogues, in-

201

valuable as a record of library holdings and as a source of discographic information:

Sibley Music Library. *Catalog of Sound Recordings, the University of Rochester, Eastman School of Music, Rochester, N.Y.* Boston: Hall, 1977. ISBN 0-8161-0063-2. A massive reproduction of the cards that cover the vast dictionary catalogue of the collection.   [596.

New York Public Library, Library and Museum of the Performing Arts. *Dictionary Catalogue of the Rodgers and Hammerstein Archives of Recorded Sound.* Boston: Hall, 1981. ISBN 0-8161-0359-3. An equally important reference source. The Rochester cataloguing is more orthodox in its conformity to AACR practices and more useful through its more numerous access points, whereas the New York collection is considerably larger and stronger in rarities.   [597.

Lloyd E. Rigler and Lawrence E. Deutsch. *Rigler and Deutsch Record Index.* Syracuse, N.Y.: Mi-kal County-Matic, 1983. A preliminary ed., on thirty reels of 16-mm microfilm, is now available on about 1,350 microfiche. A vast catalogue of about 275,000 78-RPM titles, ca. 1895–mid-1950s (representing 615,000 discs, of which some 345,000 are estimated to be duplicate holdings) at the five major repositories that make up the Associated Audio Archives — Yale University, New York Public Library, Syracuse University, the Library of Congress, and Stanford University. The six indexes cover label/issue, label/matrix, composer/author, title/composer, performer/composer, and repository. Its numerous errors and omissions notwithstanding, the set is invaluable if mostly for minimal information such as can lead to fuller investigation as the inquiry may demand. The best brief evaluation of the set is probably Richard Koprowski's, in MLA *Notes,* 42 (1986), 535–37.   [598.

In addition to these are numerous other scholarly discographies — whether for companies and labels (the difference may be important) or performers or repertory as discussed below — and in this burgeoning field the scholar learns to keep up with current announcements of publications from Greenwood (Discography series, ISSN 0192-334X), Arlington House, Kastlemusick (Pioneer Discography Series), Scarecrow (Studies in Jazz, from the Institute of Jazz Studies at Rutgers University, Newark campus), and Babylon (Hot Wacks books), which are the successors to the Oakwood Press's *Voices of the Past* series (see 601 below). Here as elsewhere, the endorsement of publication in a series being no stronger than the weakest work in the series, it is useful to know about the retrospective series listings, for which the best source at present (and in an otherwise rather disappointing book) is the incomplete list in chapter 7 ("A Bibliography of Booklength Discographies," pp. 89–106) of *Brian Rust's Guide to Discography* (1980).

Performer Discographies

American performers and performances are described in a wide range of specialized lists. For the strictly defined purposes of this present text, an awkward question has to be asked: When should a performer or performance be seen as truly American? Some musicians are born and perform mostly in America; but a few Americans have worked mainly in Europe, while numerous foreigners have done their best work—and most of their recordings—in the United States. Many have worked back and forth, usually, of course, in performance of European repertories. Classical music performers generally pose more problems than popular music performers, although there can still be awkward moments in accommodating Latin American dance music of the 1940s, West Indian calypso during the 1950s, or almost every kind of transplanted ethnic folk music during any period. Happiest perhaps are the discographers who can ignore the question entirely, in the likely assumption that most users really do not care.

The Cooper bibliography, for instance, includes many discographies of American performers, their names cited in the index. Gray and Gibson mention even more in the course of their topical alphabet in the Bowker classical volume, while Allen and Gray include still more in the jazz and popular volumes. These lists are clearly the place to start. It would be wrong, however, to leave the topic without a special word of respect for the following particular discographies:

Roberto Bauer. *Historical Records.* Milan: Martucci, 1937. LC 39-870. Repr. as *The New Catalogue of Historical Records, 1898–1908/9.* London: Sidgwick and Jackson, 1947. LC 48-1665. Repr. 1970, 1972. ISBN 283-48420-9. Repr. Westport, Conn.: Greenwood, 1970. ISBN 0-8371-9104-1. International in scope and still not superseded for its American coverage.   [599.

Frederick P. Fellers. *The Metropolitan Opera on Record: A Discography of the Commercial Recordings.* Westport, Conn.: Greenwood, 1984.

ISBN 0-313-23952-5. A scrupulously assembled chronological list of the 477 authorized recordings, 1906–72, with indexes. Excluded are pressings taken from radio broadcasts now being issued, as well as the important early materials described in David Hall's "Mapleson Cylinder Project (Repertoire, Performers and Recording Dates)," *Recorded Sound*, 83 (Jan. 1983), 21–55. [600.

J. R. Bennett. *Voices of the Past*. 11 vols. to date. Lingfield (Surrey): Oakwood, 1956– . LC 58-21632. An extensive project organized around the catalogues of major European firms (notably the Gramophone Company of various countries, English Columbia, and Societa Italiana di Fonotipia), with indexes to performers, many of them Americans who recorded in Europe. Also included are European releases of many American recordings. [601.

Repertory Discographies

Among the lists devoted to the music of American composers or particular American genres are the following:

Brian Rust. *Jazz Records: A–Z, 1897–1931*. Hatch End, Middlesex [England]: Author, 1961. LC 61-45695. 2d ed. 1962. LC 65-53104.
———. *Jazz Records: A–Z, 1897–1931. Index*, comp. Richard Grandarge. Hatch End, Middlesex: Author, 1963.
———. *Jazz Records, 1932–1942*. Hatch End, Middlesex: Author, 1965. LC 66-49990.
———. *Jazz Records, 1897–1942*. New rev. [3d] ed. London: Storyville, 1969. LC 72-7388. 4th rev. and expanded ed. New Rochelle, N.Y.: Arlington House, 1978. ISBN 0-87000-404-2. A venerable master jazz discography, running in its latest form to 1,996 pages with over 200 pages of indexes. [602.

Richard Spottswood. "A Catalog of American Folk Music on Commercial Recordings at the Library of Congress, 1923–40." Master's thesis, Dept. of Library Science, Catholic University of America, 1962. [603.

John Godrich and Robert M. W. Dixon. *Blues and Gospel Records, 1902–1943*. N.p.: Privately printed, 1963. LC 64-6615. 2d ed. Chigwell, Essex: Storyville, 1969. LC 68-58241. 3d rev. ed., with the authorship now listed as Robert M. W. Dixon and John Godrich.

1982. ISBN 0-902391-03-8. A comprehensive and scrupulously authoritative listing of recordings by black performers, ca. 1902–42.   [604.

Archie Green. *Only a Miner: Studies in Recorded Coal-Mining Songs.* Urbana: University of Illinois Press, 1972. ISBN 0-252-00181-8. A study of how the recordings, as issued between 1925 and 1970, complement the written documentation, as assembled most notably by George Korson among other scholars—thereby complementing the author's earlier "A Discography of American Coal Miners' Songs," *Labor History,* 2 (1961), 101–15.   [605.

Frederick P. Williams. "The Times As Reflected in the Victor Black Label Military Band Recordings from 1900 to 1927," ARSC *Journal,* 4 (1972), 33–46; vol. 8, no. 1 (1976), pp. 4–14; and vol. 13, no. 3 (1981), pp. 21–59. A narrative tour through the author's private collection. The valuable incidental facts include bibliographical and discographic particulars, also details of and perspectives on the repertory itself.   [606.

Dominique-René de Lerma. "The Teacher's Guide to Recent Recordings of Music by Black Composers," *College Music Symposium,* 13 (1973), 114–19. Seventy-five titles, supplemented by the list of fifty-three titles in "Recent Recordings," *Black Perspective in Music,* 5 (Fall 1977), 225–27, and eventually by *Concert Music and Spirituals: A Selective Discography* (Nashville: Institute for Research in Black American Music, Fisk University, 1981), a list of about 500 works by nearly 100 composers.   [607.

Brian Rust and Allen G. Debus. *The Complete Entertainment Discography, from the Mid-1890s to 1942.* New Rochelle, N.Y.: Arlington House, 1973. ISBN 0-87000-150-7. A collection of performer discographies, concentrating on the range of "minstrel pioneers, the vaudevillians, the film stars and radio personalities, and the straight actors and actresses" (p. 7), mostly American. Excluded are jazz and blues musicians, some entertainers already covered by discographies, and, more ambiguously, "artists whose fame spread through their records."   [608.

Kinkle, *The Complete Encyclopedia of Popular Music and Jazz* (1974; see 345 above). The indexes to recordings are particularly useful.

Brian Rust. *The American Dance Band Discography, 1917–1942.* New Rochelle, N.Y.: Arlington House, 1975. ISBN 0-87000-248-1. Citations are arranged under the names of particular bands, with a performer index on pp. 2006–66. [609.

David Hummel. *The Collector's Guide to the American Musical Theatre.* Grown, Mich.: D. H. Enterprises, 1977. 2d ed. 1978. LC 79-100313. *Supplement.* 1979. ISBN 0-934628-02-5. New ed. (referred to on p. x of the author's introduction as the "current expanded edition"). Metuchen, N.J.: Scarecrow, 1984. ISBN 0-8108-1637-7. A listing of several thousand recordings, arranged by show and including British, Canadian, and Australian theater as well. Strong in its coverage of LPs, both commercial and noncommercial, weaker for 78s. The name index, which comprises vol. 2 of the 1984 ed., is particularly impressive in its detail. [610.

B. Lee Cooper. "Rock Discographies: Exploring the Iceberg's Tip," *JEMF Quarterly,* 15 (1979), 115–20; and "Rock Discographies Revisited," 16 (1980), 89–94. Annotations for the most important of the 130 titles cited here, brief entries for others. Largely subsumed in the author's 1984 *Popular Music Handbook* (see 302 above). [611.

Dean Tudor and Nancy Tudor. [Popular music series; 4 vols.] Littleton, Colo.: Libraries Unlimited, 1979. *Jazz* (ISBN 0-87287-148-7), *Black Music* (ISBN 0-87287-147-9), *Grass Roots* (ISBN 0-87287-133-5), and *Contemporary Popular Music* (ISBN 0-87287-191-6). "Buying guides," covering in all about 5,000 recordings selected on grounds of significance, justified through descriptive and critical annotations, arranged by broad genres. The "series" is not identified as a unity except through its uniformity of design and auspices, and through the set below:
———. *Popular Music: An Annotated Guide to Recordings.* 1983. ISBN 0-87287-395-1. A one-vol., rev. ed. of the above, from which about 1,000 entries were deleted and replaced by about 2,000 new ones, with new annotations for many of the remaining titles. The prose texts and annotations for continuing entries are generally about the same, however. [612.

American Music before 1865 in Print and on Records: A Biblio-Discography. Brooklyn, N.Y.: Institute for Studies in American Music, 1976. (I.S.A.M. Monographs, 6.) ISBN 0-914678-05-1. Section 4 ("Music on Records," pp. 67–92) is a composer list of 543 titles, followed by the record label and number. [613.

Norm Cohen. *Long Steel Rail: The Railroad in American Folksong.* Urbana: University of Illinois Press, 1981. ISBN 0-252-00343-8. Following the model of Green (1972; see 605 above), a study of a folk genre through its recorded materials. [614.

Elizabeth A. Davis. *Index to the New World Recorded Anthology of American Music: A User's Guide to the Initial One Hundred Records.* New York: Norton, 1981. ISBN 0-393-95172-3. A praiseworthy program, its achievements set forth in this collection of five indexes: a "Master" numerical list to the contents; an "Index to Recorded Materials" with access to works and performers; an "Index to Printed Materials" covering liner notes and related subjects; an "Index to Genres and Performing Media," i.e., the repertories covered; and a "Chronological Index" by date of composition or, for works in the "oral tradition," by dates of recording. [615.

Terry Hounsome and Tim Chambre. *Rock Record.* New York: Facts on File, 1981. ISBN 0-87196-547-X and -548-8. 2d ed. as *New Rock Record.* Poole, Dorset [England]: Blandford, 1983. ISBN 0-7137-1305-4. Based on the compilers' 1978 *Rockmaster,* the set now includes 6,000 entries, for 40,000 recordings of 35,000 musicians, with an index of the musicians (pp. 624–719). Rock is defined broadly, and reissues are included, bootlegs not. A hastily edited computer-generated production, somewhat confusing in its layout, with numerous typos and omissions, on poor paper, but still an essential text in its area. [616.

Ethnic Recordings in America: A Neglected Heritage. Washington: Library of Congress, American Folklife Center, 1982. ISBN 0-8444-0339-9. Not a discography but rather the proceedings of a conference, at which the speakers provided valuable discographic facts and perspectives. Of special interest is "Recorded Ethnic Music: A Guide to Resources" by Norm Cohen and Paul Wells (pp. 175–250). [617.

Carol J. Oja. *American Music Recordings: A Discography of 20th-Century U.S. Composers.* Brooklyn, N.Y.: Institute for Studies in American Music, 1982. ISBN 0-914678-19-1. An extensive list of importance for providing access to the music, discographically drawn mostly from the *Gramophone Shop Encyclopedia, Schwann,* and other secondary sources, with datings accordingly. Included are about 13,000 recordings of 8,000 works by about 1,300 composers, with performer indexes. [618.

Beverly B. Boggs and Daniel W. Patterson. *An Index of Selected Folk Recordings.* Chapel Hill: University of North Carolina, Curriculum in Folklore, 1984. A microfiche index to the titles and key lines, performers' names, geographic sources, and subjects of 8,350 performances in 500 published recordings, accompanied by a seventy-five-page printed manual that spells out the indexing procedures and lists the terms used in the subject index. [619.

Jack Raymond. *Show Music on Record from the 1890s to the 1980s.* New York: Ungar, 1982. ISBN 0-8044-5734-3. A chronological listing by show (making the index of "key" numbers on pp. 11–25 indispensable), covering recorded selections only, but particularly strong for the early 78s. Discographic information is minimal, and there are omissions. [620.

Catalog of the William Ransom Hogan Jazz Archive: The Collection of Seventy-Eight RPM Phonograph Recordings. Boston: Hall, 1984. ISBN 0-8161-0434-4. Catalogue of the impressive collection of about 27,000 records and 1,500 "live interview" tapes at the Howard-Tilton Library of Tulane University, poorly reproduced and difficult to read, but with useful dating and other discographic detail. [621.

IJS Jazz Register and Indexes. Newark, N.J.: Rutgers University, Institute of Jazz Studies, 1982– . A COM microfiche, describing the Rutgers collection through scrupulously detailed cataloguing, updated quarterly and (as of Feb. 5, 1987) running to sixteen cards. The shelf list ("Jazz Register") is indexed by (1) performer/performer group, (2) performer/title, (3) performing group, (4) title, (5) label name and issue number, and (6) composer. [622.

Many of the bibliographies cited elsewhere in this book will include discographies as well. Limbacher's *Keeping Score* (1981; see 287 above), for instance, includes a 177-page list of recordings of film music, while a good many of the composer bibliographies mentioned in passing in chapter 8 include discographies. The indexes of folksongs discussed in chapter 10 (pp. 120–21) are often based on sound recordings archives, it should be remembered, while the charts of popular songs discussed in chapter 11 (pp. 133–35) are today based on sales and performances of sound recordings.

Other Discographical Materials

The present survey would not be complete without mention of the following miscellaneous titles:

Oliver Read and Walter L. Welch. *From Tin-Foil to Stereo: Evolution of the Phonograph.* Indianapolis: Sams, Bobbs-Merrill, 1959. LC 59-15832. 2d ed., with an added chap. on recent technological developments. 1976. ISBN 0-672-21206-4. The bibliography (pp. 495–502 and 521–28 in the two eds.) provides the best source of writings relating to the early history of sound recording. [623.

Steven Smolian. *A Handbook of Film, Theater, and Television Music on Record, 1948–1969.* New York: Record Undertaker, 1970. LC 76-20001. Volume 1 cites about 2,000 recordings, listed alphabetically by show title, with a vast range of information condensed into single-line entries. Volume 2 consists of a manufacturer and composer index. Complemented by the compiler's *Show and Soundtrack List,* nos. 1–2. [624.

Carol Mekkawi. "Music Periodicals: Popular and Classical Record Reviews," MLA *Notes,* 34 (1977), 92–107. A survey describing twelve general indexes and twenty-seven major periodicals with new record reviews and lists, followed by an extended essay that, in effect, annotates the works cited. An invaluable source, still useful but in need of updating. [625.

Gary-Gabriel Gisondi. "Sound Recording Periodicals: A Preliminary Union Catalog of Pre-LP-Related Holdings in Member Libraries of the Associated Audio Archives," ARSC *Journal,* 10 (1978), 37–65. Citations and locations of 126 journals, many of them early, specialized, and obscure. [626.

Tim Brooks. "The Artifacts of Recording History: Creators, Users, Losers, Keepers," ARSC *Journal,* 11 (1979), 18–29. A brief essay on the sources and their need for preservation. [627.

L. R. Docks. *American Premium Record Guide: Identification and Values,*

78's, 45's and LP's, 1915–1965. Florence, Ala.: Books Americana, 1980. ISBN 0-89689-012-0. 2d ed. 1982 (distributed New York: Crown). ISBN 0-89689-023-6. 3d ed. 1986. ISBN 0-89689-054-6. Perhaps the best of the "price guides," classified by genres, with discographic features, such as the forty-five-page section on label illustrations and the eight-page introduction, that are useful although not always definitive. [628.

Sheldon L. Tarakan. *Directory of Recorded Specialties.* Port Washington, N.Y.: Sound Advice Enterprises, 1982. ISBN 0-943668-00-X. A listing of some of the less well known labels. [629.

William R. Daniels. *The American 45 and 78 RPM Record Dating Guide, 1940–1959.* Westport, Conn.: Greenwood, 1985. ISBN 0-313-24232-1. A handy text for library cataloguers in particular, as they need to assign dates on the basis of label numbers. [630.

Among the less common genres of physical documents in special need of bibliographical coverage, meanwhile, the "liner notes" for record jackets clearly rank near the top of the list. Their importance for both scholarly and general informational purposes, while considerable, is yet to be defended; furthermore, the very model for a useful survey can be cited in a counterpart article by G. Thomas Tanselle on book jackets (*Library*, 5th ser., 26 [1971], 91–134). The problems with the genre, to be sure, are daunting indeed. The content varies from major scholarly or otherwise critically perceptive essays to sloppy hackwork. Library cataloguing has been concentrated on the disc, typically at the expense of any concern for the names of major contributors of the liner texts, while no models in bibliographical citation practice have ever been devised. The record companies themselves have been indifferent, often using variant (successive or even simultaneous) jackets for the very same recording issue. At the same time it should be remembered that liner notes are often a source of perceptive statements about the music and sometimes the only place to find particulars about a composer or arranger, lists of contents, timings, biographical information on performers, and the specifics of the recording circumstances.

16

The Literature for Music Bibliophiles and Bibliographers

Three kinds of music collectors have arisen in the United States (as suggested in chapter 13 above), specializing in hymnals, sheet music, and records. The first of these has enjoyed a quiet history, involving mostly the literature discussed in chapter 12, while the third has involved the diffuse specialties discussed in the preceding chapter. Sheet-music collectors have been largely distinctive to the United States (English interest in nineteenth-century illustrated covers notwithstanding). Their collections, numbered in the tens of thousands of items and even more, are today mostly the cornerstones of the great musical Americana research collections. Their successors, amateur hobbyists or research scholars or librarians with special institutional interests to serve, still find valuable and enticing materials in odd places; the search merely becomes the more romantic as the looking gets harder. Thanks to the illustrious forebears, the search is also more learned, with the establishment of "points" that separate the breathtakingly exciting (and valuable) variants from the common copies. The specialized literature—and, by extension, the literature on American music publishing itself—is the topic of this chapter.

The Sheet Music Collector's Literature

Typical of collectors' literatures in general, the material is often as elusive as the music itself—and often clearly as learned as the literature for the scholars. The 1941 Dichter and Shapiro *Early American Sheet Music* is difficult to locate now, as are the major dealers' catalogues, including Dichter's three rather ambiguously titled *Handbooks*. Fortunately the 1941 book has now been reprinted. Other books variously reflect the enthusiasm and the search for context that mark our most respected collectors, those of Bella Landauer's being among the first of these, those by Lester S. Levy clearly the most engagingly presented. Recent books include the Westin guide and the Klamkin anthology, both sadly oblivious to their lack of context; and the superb Lawrence volume, rich in graphic and historical context. Among the books on music illustration as such, Harry Peters's is a treasure, Tatham's a delight to own. It may be tempting to pass off the whole lot of these as "coffee-table books"; they still bring out a characteristic of our country's musical heritage that is easily forgotten. Even in its day sheet music was acquired and cherished not only for performance but also for a vague but real "cultural delight." It is easy to disparage a preoccupation with personal property; but it is important, too, to understand that the possession of items of beauty should be seen as serving to elevate the owner, the listener, or the beholder. Historical collections reflect and foster owners who are thereby the more humane, more filled with delight, good taste, and understanding of human history, and thus more responsive to one's fellow citizenry and the democratic society that was part of the collective national vision.

Elizabeth Lounsbery. "Early Illustrated Music Titles," *American Homes and Gardens,* Jan. 1914, pp. 22–25.   [631.

Aaron Davis. "Music Covers," *Antiques,* 12 (1927), 394–96.   [632.

Harry T. Peters. *America on Stone.* New York: Doubleday, Doran, 1931. LC 31-33726. In this venerated study of early American lithography in general, "Music Sheets" are discussed briefly on p. 48. The author's *California on Stone* (New York: Doubleday, Doran, 1935; LC 35-37866) also discusses sheet music, with twenty-two illustrations accessible through the index on p. 216. The same is also true of his *Currier and Ives: Printmakers to the American People* (Garden City, N.Y.: Doubleday, 1929; also New York: Doubleday, Doran, 1942; LC 42-24944), in which sheet music is very briefly discussed on pp. 37–38 and illustrated on plates 91–94.   [633.

Bella C. Landauer. *Some Aeronautical Music.* Paris: Privately printed, 1933.   [634.

Edith A. Wright and Josephine McDevitt. "Early American Sheet-Music Lithographs," *Antiques,* 23 (1933), 50–53, 99–102.   [635.

S. Foster Damon. *Series of Old American Songs, Reproduced in Facsimile from Original or Early Editions in the Harris Collection of American Poetry and Plays.* Providence, R.I.: Brown University Library, 1936. Reproductions of fifty items, five from the colonial period, seven from the early nineteenth century, thirty-eight from pre–Civil War minstrelsy, with Damon's annotations.   [636.

Edith A. Wright and Josephine McDevitt. "Collecting Early American Sheet Music," *Antiques,* 29 (1936), 202–5.   [637.

———. "What's in a Name Plate," *Antiques,* 36 (1939), 182–83.
                                                              [638.

Marian Hannah Winter. *Art Scores for Music.* Brooklyn, N.Y.: Brooklyn Museum, 1939. LC 40-10130. Catalogue of an exhibition, in which American titles are discussed on pp. 41–47.   [639.

Harry Dichter and Elliot Shapiro. *Early American Sheet Music: Its Lure and Its Lore, 1768–1889.* New York: Bowker, 1941. LC 41-7397. Repr. as *Handbook of Early American Sheet Music.* New York: Dover, 1977. ISBN 0-486-23364-2. The 1941 ed. includes lists of the famous "collectors' items" arranged by period, a directory of music publishers' addresses, a list of illustrators, and thirty-two illustrations of famous American music covers. The reprint has some corrections by Dichter, and the illustrations have been rearranged and extended.   [640.

Edith A. Wright and Josephine McDevitt. "Music Sheets for Stamp Collectors," *Antiques,* 41 (1942), 183–85.   [641.

Harry Dichter. *Handbook of American Sheet Music,* nos. 1–3. Philadelphia: Harry Dichter, 1947, 1953, 1966. The title notwithstanding, the "First Annual Issue" is, in fact, a list of somewhat over 2,000 items offered for sale, the second a list of 1,451 titles, the third a desiderata list of titles being sought for Dichter's customers. The classification by categories along with Dichter's blurbs make the first two of these particularly useful for the bibliographer, collector, and historian. Several volumes and numbers of the *Musical Americana Newsletter* also appeared over this same period.   [642.

Bella C. Landauer. *My City 'Tis of Thee.* New York: Privately printed, 1951. LC 52-2489. Songs relating to New York City, from a collection now in the New-York Historical Society.   [643.

————. *Striking the Right Note in Advertising.* New York: Privately printed, 1951. LC 51-4216. Music covers illustrating the history of advertising. [644.

————. *Some Terpsichorean Ephemera.* New York: Privately printed, 1953. LC 53-3182. Illustrations of the dance, mostly reproduced from sheet music. [645.

[*Baseball in Music and Song.*] Philadelphia: Musical Americana (Harry Dichter), ca. 1954. Reproductions, in color but reduced in size, of nine "collector's items," 1860–94. [646.

[*Musical Americana's One Hundred Great American Songs.*] Philadelphia: Musical Americana (Harry Dichter), 1956–57. Reproductions, in black and white and at or close to full size, of the sheet-music collector's major "high spots." [647.

Lester S. Levy. "Music Had Charms," *American Heritage,* Apr. 1958, pp. 53–61. [648.

Edward P. Soule. "Tutte le forze imaginevole," *Call Number* (University of Oregon Library), 28 (1967), 5–20. [649.

Lester S. Levy. *Grace Notes in American History: Popular Sheet Music from 1820 to 1900.* Norman: University of Oklahoma Press, 1967. LC 67-24623. Stories behind historically important or interesting works, with many illustrations. [650.

Oral S. Coad. "Songs America Used to Sing," *Rutgers University Library Journal,* 31 (1968), 33–45. [651.

"Chicago: A Musical Accompaniment" (1969; see 115 above).

David Tatham. "Some Apprentice Lithographs of Winslow Homer: Ten Pictorial Title Pages for Sheet Music," *Old-Time New England,* 59 (1969), 87–104. The pictures date from the mid-1850s. [652.

Nancy R. Davison. "The Grand Triumphal Quick-Step; or, Sheet Music Covers in America," in John D. Morse, *Prints in and of America to 1850* (Charlottesville: University Press of Virginia, 1970), pp. 257–89. A lecture held at a Winterthur Conference on early American prints. [653.

214

Lester S. Levy. *Flashes of Merriment: A Century of Humorous Song in America, 1805–1905.* Norman: University of Oklahoma Press, 1971. ISBN 0-8061-0714-9. Comic songs discussed, quoted, and illustrated, often in color. [654.

Nancy R. Davison. *American Sheet Music Illustration: Reflections of the Nineteenth Century.* Ann Arbor: William L. Clements Library, 1973. LC 74-620850. Text of a lecture to accompany an exhibition. [655.

David Tatham. *The Lure of the Striped Pig: The Illustration of Popular Music in America, 1820–1870.* Barre, Mass.: Imprint Society, 1973. ISBN 0-87636-051-7. The golden age of early and color lithography, as evidenced particularly in the output of the major Boston shops. [656.

Dunn, "A Century of Song . . . in Minnesota" (1974; see 109 above).

Collectors Guide to Sheet Music. Gas City, Ind.: L-W Publications, 1975. LC 80-260326. A price guide to about 1,500 song sheets, arranged alphabetically under broad topical subject headings. The authority of the pricing is not attested, nor is the authenticity of the 350 sheets that are illustrated. [657.

Marian Klamkin. *Old Sheet Music: A Pictorial History.* New York: Hawthorn, 1975. ISBN 0-8015-5500-0. Mostly on twentieth-century pictorial covers, with little text and, in fact, little emphasis on the history. [658.

Vera B. Lawrence. *Music for Patriots, Politicians, and Presidents: Harmonies and Discords of the First Hundred Years.* New York: Macmillan, 1975. ISBN 0-02-569390-5. A superb pictorial treasury of historically important musical documents of all kinds. [659.

Lester S. Levy. *Give Me Yesterday: American History in Song, 1890–1920.* Norman: University of Oklahoma Press, 1975. ISBN 0-8061-1241-7. Stories of songs of the recent past. [660.

L. Edward Purcell. "Songs for the Parlor," *Palimpsest* (State Historical Society of Iowa), 56 (1975), 46–55. [661.

Lester S. Levy. *Picture the Songs: Lithographs from the Sheet Music of*

Nineteenth-Century America. Baltimore: Johns Hopkins University Press, 1976. ISBN 0-8018-1814-1. Interesting stories behind selected sheet-music illustrations.   [662.

David Tatham. "John Henry Bufford, American Lithographer," *Proceedings of the American Antiquarian Society,* 86 (1976), 47–73. Summary of the career of one of the leading sheet-music illustrators of mid-nineteenth-century America.   [663.

Helen Westin. *Introducing the Song Sheet: A Collector's Guide, with Current Price List.* Nashville, New York: Thomas Nelson, 1976. ISBN 0-8407-4325-4. Generally weak in musical and historical matters, but valuable for the insights of collectors, e.g., in chaps. 2 ("Do, Re, Mi's of Song Sheet Collecting," pp. 15–25), 5 ("Miscellaneous Categories," pp. 59–99, for lists of titles on particular subjects), and 6–7 ("The Cover Artists" and "Special Covers," pp. 101–18, on illustration and its collecting, with facsimiles of artists' signatures), as well as in the supplementary suggestions of "Current Values by Category" (pp. 143–51).   [664.

Daniel B. Priest. *American Sheet Music: A Guide to Collecting Sheet Music from 1775 to 1975, with Prices.* Des Moines, Iowa: Wallace-Holmstead, 1978. ISBN 0-87069-205-4. Breezy and superficial in style, but with many useful illustrations.   [665.

Caroline Moseley. "Music in a Nineteenth-Century Parlor," *Princeton University Library Chronicle,* 41 (1980), 231–42.   [666.

Sheet Music Exchange. Winchester, Va., 1982– . ISSN 0741-7780. Issued bimonthly, consisting of brief illustrated notices and short essays, along with notices from and for dealers and collectors.

[667.

Lester S. Levy, "Sheet Music Buffs and Their Collections" (1983; see 744 below).

Currier and Ives: A Catalogue Raisonné. With an introduction by Bernard E. Reilly, Jr. Detroit: Gale, 1984. ISBN 0-8103-1638-2. A bibliography of 7,450 prints, of which about 1,000 are illustrated, greatly reduced and in black and white but generally serviceable. While the arrangement is by the title, close to 100 sheet-music covers are accessible through the subject index, most of them under "Music

Sheets." A valuable concordance correlates the entries in this book with those in the 1929–31 Harry Peters checklist (see 633 above) and with Frederic A. Conningham's *Currier and Ives Prints: An Illustrated Checklist* (in the 1930 and 1970 rather than the 1983 ed.).   [668.

Paul O. Pryor, "Collecting American Sheet Music," *AB Bookman's Weekly*, vol. 74, no. 24 (Dec. 10, 1984), pp. 4163–86. Featured in the second of the journal's annual music issues, which are of interest to music collectors and dealers most specifically but also to the American music community at large.   [669.

The dividing line is obviously tenuous between titles appropriate to the list above, concerned with visual materials or otherwise addressed to collectors, and those appropriate to the ones that follow, concerned with printing and publishing history or otherwise addressed to scholars. Many of the titles listed above are more scrupulously documented and useful for scholars than those below, while many of those below are more engaging and enticing than those cited above. The point is important to concede, both because the authors of works like those above may be unnecessarily proud of their thin skins and because the authors of works like those below may be unnecessarily proud of their thick skins.

The Scholar's Literature

Music bibliographers — whether analytical bibliographers studying the production of particular printed documents; historical bibliographers probing the relationships between society and its printed documents; descriptive bibliographers defining the appropriate statements that establish the identity of particular copies; or textual bibliographers looking for the authentic statement of musical texts — also have their own literatures (or at least the beginnings of their own literatures) that document the slowly expanding record of musical scholarship. Among the most important writings, and in addition to works cited elsewhere in this book but particularly in chapters 6 and 13, are the following:

Oscar G. Sonneck. "The Bibliography of American Music," *Papers of the Bibliographical Society of America*, 1 (1904–6), 50–64.   [670.

William Arms Fisher. "The American Music Publisher and His Relationship to the Music Teacher and the Composers," *Music Teachers National Association Proceedings*, 13 (1918), 96–105.   [671.

————. *One Hundred and Fifty Years of Music Publishing in the United States*. Boston: Ditson, 1933. LC 33-12389. Ostensibly a survey of the whole history but, in fact, a rather superficial overview from the perspective of the Ditson firm, soon to disappear from the scene.   [672.

Oliver Strunk. "Early Music Publishing in the United States," *Papers of the Bibliographical Society of America*, 31 (1937), 176–79.   [673.

American Society of Composers, Authors, and Publishers. *Copyright Law Symposium*. New York: Columbia University Press, 1939–   . LC 40-8341. ISSN 0069-9950. An irregular series (usually annual, with thirty-one vols. through 1984), devoted to the award-winning essays submitted for the Nathan Burkan Memorial Competition. A survey of the published papers (typically listed as an appendix to each vol.) suggests that close to half are devoted to matters specifically involving the legal protection of published music.   [674.

Dichter and Shapiro, *Early American Sheet Music* (1941; see 640 above).

William Treat Upton. "Secular Music in the United States 150 Years Ago," *Papers of the American Musicological Society*, 1941, pp. 105–11.   [675.

————. "Early American Publications in the Field of Music," in *Music and Libraries*, ed. Richard S. Hill (Washington: Music Library Association, 1943), pp. 60–69.   [676.

Musician's Guide (1954–   ; see 40 above for its directories of current music publishers).

James J. Fuld. *American Popular Music (Reference Book), 1875–1950*. Philadelphia: Musical Americana, 1955. *Supplement*. 1956. LC 55-5415. Perhaps the closest thing the field has seen to a proper descriptive bibliography, with citations for the earliest published sources of 252 of our country's most popular songs, most of them originally issued as sheet music.   [677.

James H. Stone. "The Merchant and the Muse: Commercial Influences on American Popular Music before the Civil War," *Business History Review*, 30 (1956), 1–17.   [678.

D. W. Krummel. "Graphic Analysis: Its Application to Early American Sheet Music," MLA *Notes*, 2d ser., 16 (1959), 213–33.   [679.

Dena J. Epstein. "Introduction" to the reprint of the U.S. Board of Music Trade, *Complete Catalogue* (New York: Da Capo, 1973), pp. v–xxvi. See also her revised text, "Music Publishing in the Age of Piracy," MLA *Notes*, 31 (1974), 7–29.   [680.

D. W. Krummel. "Quantitative Evaluation of a Sheet-Music Collection (American Music Bibliography, III.)," *Yearbook for Inter-American Musical Research*, 9 (1973), 177–81.   [681.

Guide for Dating Early Published Music: A Manual of Bibliographical Practices. Compiled by D. W. Krummel. Hackensack, N.J.: Joseph Boonin, 1974. (International Association of Music Libraries, Commission for Bibliographical Research.) ISBN 0-913574-25-2. American music is discussed and illustrated on pp. 229–42. See also the "Supplement," *Fontes Artis Musicae*, 24 (1977), 175–84, in which the updated list of plate numbers of American music publishers (pp. 180–81) is useful in dating imprints.   [682.

D. W. Krummel. "Counting Every Star; or, Historical Statistics on Music Publishing in the United States (American Music Bibliography, IV.)," *Yearbook for Inter-American Musical Research*, 10 (1974), 175–93.   [683.

Christopher Pavlakis. *The American Music Handbook*. New York: Free Press, 1974. LC 73-2127. An invaluable reference book, in which the section on "Music Publishers" (pp. 624–46) includes useful details on about 150 major firms of the day.   [684.

Paula Dranov. *Inside the Music Publishing Industry*. White Plains, N.Y.: Knowledge Industry Publications, 1980. ISBN 0-914236-40-7. An analysis of the business side.   [685.

Leonard Feist. *An Introduction to Popular Music Publishing in America*. New York: National Music Publishers Association, 1980. LC 80-

116943. A brief history of popular music publishing, put together by one of its eminent leaders.   [686.

Richard J. Wolfe. *Early American Music Engraving and Printing.* Urbana: University of Illinois Press, 1980. ISBN 0-252-80726-3. A detailed technical account of the early processes from a historical perspective.   [687.

An Introduction to Music Publishing. Edited by Carolyn Sachs. New York: C. F. Peters, 1981. ISBN 0-938856-00-6. Brief perspectives by eminent figures honoring the firm's anniversary.   [688.

Richard Crawford and D. W. Krummel. "Early American Music Printing and the Founding of Its Two Practices," in *Printing and Society in Early America,* ed. William L. Joyce et al. (Worcester, Mass.: American Antiquarian Society, 1983), pp. 186–207.   [689.

Russell Sanjek. *From Print to Plastic: Publishing and Promoting America's Popular Music (1900–1980).* Brooklyn, N.Y.: Institute for Studies in American Music, 1983. (I.S.A.M. Monographs, 20.) ISBN 0-914678-22-1. Experienced observations on how things today came to be the way they are.   [690.

Sarah J. Shaw and Lauralee Shiere. *Sheet Music Cataloging and Processing: A Manual.* Canton, Mass.: Music Library Association, 1984. (MLA Technical Report, 15.) ISBN 0-914954-34-2.   [691.

[Reports on American sheet-music bibliography, prepared 1983–86 under the auspices of the Music Library Association for the National Endowment for the Humanities:] D. W. Krummel, *Early American Sheet Music: Serving Its Scholars through a Bibliographical Program;* Jean Geil, *Major Repositories of Early American Sheet Music;* and Mary Kay Duggan, *Levels of Bibliographic Control of Early American Sheet Music.*   [692.

In addition to the writings on music publishing in general are the various studies of particular firms and groups of firms, along with the writings by music printers and publishers themselves describing their work. The list below updates Tanselle's (*Guide to the Study of United States Imprints,* sec. G., vol. 2, pp. 405–762) and complements the imprint lists cited in chapter 6. In overview, the literature may be seen to be of several kinds. The giants among music publishers, like most of their European counterparts, have enjoyed celebrating their anniversaries without divulging any of their processes or problems. The 1957 Schirmer festschrift (its scholarly essays on other topics notwithstanding), the Peters *Introduction,* and the Rorick essay on Presser are essentially of this kind. In contrast, Ernst Krohn's study of early midwestern publishing is among the books that mention many titles and provide invaluable background information but include no lists; the several directories, by Howe and Redway for New York and Duggan for San Francisco, are useful sources for which future scholars will be much indebted. Having established here a dichotomy between the laudatory and the descriptive, it is necessary to point out that the Heinsheimer volumes properly fit both and neither of these categories, being instead the personal recollections of a respected music publisher, primary source material of the most delightful kind (Max Winkler's protestations perhaps notwithstanding).

"Music Engraving and Printing," *New-York Mirror: A Weekly Gazette of Literature and the Fine Arts,* 19 (Aug. 28, 1841), 279. Perhaps the first American text devoted to the topic. [693.

"W. W." [brief note on the first music books printed in America], *Notes and Queries,* 16 (1857), 105, 126. [694.

Ammon Stapleton. "Early German Musical Publications in Pennsylvania," *Pennsylvania German,* 7 (1906), 174–76. [695.

Mabel Almy Howe. *Music Publishers in New York City before 1850.* New York: New York Public Library, 1917. LC 18-4333. Also issued in the *Bulletin of the New York Public Library,* 21 (1917), 589–604. [696.

Frank J. Metcalf. "Cut Hymn Books," *American Collector,* 3 (1926–27), 159–61. Discussion of an 1818 "Dutch-door hymnal," with pages slit across the middle to allow the words above to be matched with different music below. [697.

———. "Early Hymn Books Printed in Washington, D.C.," *American Collector,* 5 (1927–28), 144–50. [698.

Isaac Goldberg. *Tin Pan Alley: A Chronicle of the American Popular Music Racket.* New York: John Day, 1930. LC 30-31878. Repr., with a supplement, "From Sweet and Swing to Rock 'n' Roll," by Edward Jablonski. New York: Ungar, 1961. LC 60-53364. While the role of the music publisher pervades the event described in this book, chap. 5 ("The Rise of Tin Pan Alley," pp. 84–138) discusses publishing specifically.   [699.

Matt B. Jones. "Bibliographical Notes on Thomas Walter's Grounds and Rules of Musick Explained," *Proceedings of the American Antiquarian Society*, 41 (1932), 235–46.   [700.

Virginia Larkin Redway. "The Carrs, American Music Publishers," *Musical Quarterly*, 18 (1932), 150–77.   [701.

———. "James Parker and the 'Dutch Church,' " *Musical Quarterly*, 24 (1938), 481–500.   [702.

Edith A. Wright and Josephine McDevitt. "Henry Stone, Lithographer," *Antiques*, 34 (1938), 16–19.   [703.

Isadore Witmark and Isaac Goldberg. *From Ragtime to Swingtime: The Story of the House of Witmark*. New York: Lee Furman, 1939. LC 39-15198. Repr. New York: Da Capo, 1976. ISBN 0-306-70686-5.
[704.

Margaret E. Lippencott. "Dearborn's Musical *Scheme*," *New-York State Historical Society Bulletin*, 25 (1941), 134–42.   [705.

Virginia Larkin Redway. *Music Directory of Early New York City: A File of Musicians, Music Publishers and Music Instrument-Makers Listed in New York Directories from 1786 to 1835, Together with the Most Important Music Publishers from 1836 through 1875*. New York: New York Public Library, 1941. LC A41-674.   [706.

Dena J. Epstein. "Music Publishing in Chicago prior to 1871: The Firm of Root & Cady, 1858–1871." Master's thesis, University of Illinois, 1943. Also published in MLA *Notes*, n.s., 1 (1943), 3–11, 43–59; 2 (1944–45), 16–26, 124–48, 201–26, 310–24; and 3 (1945–46), 80–98, 101–9, 193–215, 299–308. (See also the revised study of 1969; 104 above.)   [707.

Evan Klock. "Music Merchandising Moves into a House of Many

Mansions," MLA *Notes*, n.s., 1 (1943), 16–23. On the Chicago firm of Lyon and Healy. [708.

Edward N. Waters. "The Wa-Wan Press: An Adventure in Musical Idealism," in *A Birthday Offering for Carl Engel* (New York: Schirmer, 1943), pp. 9–21. [709.

H. W. Heinsheimer. *Menagerie in F Sharp.* Garden City, N.Y.: Doubleday, 1947. LC 47-4000. [710.

R. B. Brown and Frank X. Braun. "The Tunebook of Conrad Doll," *Papers of the Bibliographical Society of America*, 42 (1948), 229–38. [711.

Thelma Lynn. "History of William A. Pond and Company: Publishers of the Music of Stephen Foster." Master's thesis, Columbia University, 1948. [712.

Carleton Sprague Smith. "The 1774 Psalm Book of the Reformed Protestant Dutch Church in New York City," *Musical Quarterly*, 34 (1948), 84–96. [713.

Josephene C. White. "Music Printing and Publishing in Philadelphia: A Technical and Sociological Study." Master's thesis, Columbia University, 1949. [714.

Max Winkler. *A Penny from Heaven.* New York: Appleton-Century-Crofts, 1951. LC 51-10743. Recollections of a music publisher, active in the United States at first with Carl Fischer, later on his own. [715.

Irving Lowens. "John Wyeth's *Repository of Sacred Music, Part Second* (1813): A Northern Precursor of Southern Folk-Hymnody," *Journal of the American Musicological Society*, 5 (1952), 114–31. Also in his *Music and Musicians in Early America* (New York: Norton, 1964), pp. 138–54. [716.

H. W. Heinsheimer. *Fanfare for Two Pigeons.* Garden City, N.Y.: Doubleday, 1952. LC 52-5750. [717.

Allen P. Britton and Irving Lowens. "*The Easy Instructor* (1798–1831): A History and Bibliography of the First Shape-Note Tune-Book,"

Journal of Research in Music Education, 1 (1953), 30–55. Updated by Lowens in his *Music and Musicians in Early America* (New York: Norton, 1964), pp. 115–37, 292–310.   [718.

Kenneth C. Hanson. "Finis: A Century of Gospel Music Publishing," *Harbinger and Discipliana,* 13 (1953), 44. A short account of the career of the Cincinnati firm of Fillmore Brothers.   [719.

Irving Lowens. "John Tufts's Introduction to the Singing of Psalm Tunes," *Journal of Research in Music Education,* 2 (1954), 89–102. Also in his *Music and Musicians in Early America* (New York: Norton, 1964), pp. 39–57, 289–91.   [720.

———. "The Bay Psalm Book in 17th Century New England," *Journal of the American Musicological Society,* 8 (1955), 22–29. Also in his *Music and Musicians in Early America* (New York: Norton, 1964), pp. 25–38.   [721.

B. M. Woodward. "Theodore Presser: Master of American Music Publishing." Master's thesis, Drexel Institute of Technology, 1955.   [722.

Madeleine B. Stern. *Imprints on History.* Bloomington: Indiana University Press, 1956. LC 56-11995. Includes brief sketches of thirteen music publishers (Boston Music Co., Carl Fischer, J. Fischer, H. W. Gray, E. B. Marks, Theodore Presser, G. Ricordi, G. Schirmer, Arthur P. Schmidt, Silver Burdett, Clayton F. Summy, M. Witmark, and B. F. Wood).   [723.

Max Winkler. *From A to X: Reminiscences.* New York: Crown, 1957. LC 57-8701.   [724.

One Hundred Years of Music in America. Edited by Paul Henry Lang. New York: G. Schirmer, Grosset and Dunlap, 1961. LC 61-65802. Repr. New York: Da Capo, 1984. ISBN 0-306-76242-0. A festschrift for the Schirmer firm, including the editor's "Portrait of a Publishing House" (pp. 9–21) and Richard F. French, "The Dilemma of the Music Publishing Industry" (pp. 171–85), Roland Gelatt, "Music on Records—1877–1961" (pp. 186–93), R. D. Darrell, "Neither Quick nor Dead: The Music Book Paradox" (pp. 194–208), Richard Gilmore Appel, "The American Music Library, Past, Present, and Future" (pp. 245–56), and Hans W. Heinsheimer, "Epilogue" (pp. 305–22), as well as eleven other articles.   [725.

Theodore W. Thorson. "A History of Music Publishing in Chicago, 1850–1960." Ph.D. diss., Northwestern University, 1961.   [726.

Harry Eskew. "Joseph Funk's *Allgemein nützliche Choral-Music* (1816)," *Report of the Society for the History of the Germans in Maryland,* 32 (1966), 38–46. On the work of Laurentz Wartmann and other early German music printers in the Shenandoah valley of Virginia.   [727.

Mary Teal. "Couse's Bazaar: Detroit's First Successful Music Store," *Among Friends* (Detroit Public Library), 44 (1966), 2–5.   [728.

J. Murray Barbour. "The Unpartheyisches Gesangbuch," in *Cantors at the Crossroads: Festschrift for Walter E. Buszin* (St. Louis: Concordia, 1967), pp. 87–93.   [729.

H. W. Heinsheimer. *Best Regards to Aida: The Defeats and Victories of a Music Man on Two Continents.* New York: Alfred A. Knopf, 1968. LC 68-23964.   [730.

Ernst C. Krohn. *Music Publishing in the Middle Western States before the Civil War.* Detroit: Information Coordinators, 1972. (Detroit Studies in Music Bibliography, 23.) ISBN 9-11772-47-2.   [731.

Karl Kroeger. "Isaiah Thomas as a Music Publisher," *Proceedings of the American Antiquarian Society,* 86 (1976), 321–41.   [732.

Peggy Cecile Boudreaux. "Music Publishing in New Orleans in the Nineteenth Century." M.A. thesis, Louisiana State University, 1977. (Heintze 2007)   [733.

Joann Taricani. "Music in Colonial Philadelphia and Michael Hillegas." M.A. thesis, University of Pennsylvania, 1977. Covers the story of one of America's first music shops. (Heintze 195)   [734.

Patricia Gray Tipton. "The Contributions of Charles Kunkel to Musical Life in St. Louis." Ph.D. diss., Washington University, 1977. (*RILM* 1978:5207)   [735.

Vivian Perlis. *Two Men for Modern Music: E. Robert Schmitz and Herman Langinger.* Brooklyn, N.Y.: Institute for Studies in American Music, 1978. (I.S.A.M. Monographs, 9.) ISBN 0-914678-09-4. A summary of Langinger's activities in support of Henry Cowell's *New Music.*
[736.

Chris Yoder. "Theodore Presser, Educator, Publisher, Philanthropist: Selected Contributions to the Music Teaching Profession in America." Ed.D. diss., University of Illinois, 1978. (*RILM* 1978:6209)
[737.

Charles R. Bauerlein. "Origins of the Popular Music Press in America." Master's thesis, University of Pennsylvania, 1979. (Heintze 2005)
[738.

Mary Kay Duggan. "Music Publishing and Printing in San Francisco before the Earthquake and Fire of 1906," *Kemble Occasional,* no. 24 (Autumn 1980). [739.

Jean W. Thomas. "A Pittsburgh Collection of Nineteenth Century Household Music." M.A. thesis, University of Pittsburgh, 1981. (Heintze 2080) [740.

William C. Rorick. "Galaxy Music Corporation: The First Fifty Years," *Fontes Artis Musicae,* 29 (1982), 125–28. [741.

Sylvia Craft. "The Music Publishing Experience," *AB Bookman's Weekly,* 72 (Dec. 12, 1983), 4155–61. On the firm of G. Schirmer. [742.

Mary Kay Duggan. "A Provisional Directory of Music Publishers, Music Printers, and Sheet-Music Cover Artists in San Francisco, 1850–1906," *Kemble Occasional,* no. 30 (Summer 1983), 1–8.
[743.

"Music Printing and Publishing" issue of *American Music* (vol. 1, no. 4, for Winter 1983), ed. D. W. Krummel. Includes Paul R. Osterhout, "Andrew Wright: Northampton Music Printer" (pp. 5–26); Richard D. Wetzel, "The Search for William Cumming Peters" (pp. 27–41); Diane Parr Walker, "From 'Hawk-Eye March and Quick Step' to 'Caprice Hongrois': Music Publishing in Iowa" (pp. 42–62); Rita H. Mead, "The Amazing Mr. Cowell" (pp. 63–89); and others. [744.

William C. Rorick. "Theodore Presser Company: A Bicentennial Retrospect," *Fontes Artis Musicae,* 31 (1984), 118–25.   [745.

Excluded from this list are a number of studies concerned primarily with music copyright, with the economics of music publishing, and with matters of politics, censorship, and dialectics. The first of these is usually best surveyed through specialized legal bibliography, the second through business sources, the third extensively through writings on popular music cited in chapter 10.

17

Bibliographical Guides

In summary it is useful and proper to mention the predecessors to the present text, those major bibliographical lists that cover the whole of American music in general terms. Their differing plans of organization will inevitably reflect their somewhat different intended readerships, as well as their compilers' contrasting conceptions of the totality of the field. For a convenient selective guide for the general reader, involving a broad overview of the whole, the Kroeger guide can still be recommended despite its date. Among a number of other selective guides that include American music sections, the Library of Congress *Guide* enjoys high respect, although it, too, now stands in need of an updating. Horn's special focus on popular music is at once both its weakness and its strength: for while the list should hardly purport to address the whole, its many references to popular musical articles in the general press are a special virtue. Tanselle's concern for imprints makes for a work of special importance to the historical bibliographer in general, whether in search of printing and publishing history or of evidence of the broader impact of documents on our country's musical life. Gleason's course syllabus is of special value not only for its panoramic display but also for the convenience with which the reader can move from the general to the specific level of primary source materials.

Passing mention should also be made of Richard Jackson's "The Bibliography That Might Have Been" (MLA *Notes*, 27 [1971], 453–60), in which the strange, fond dreams of the music bibliographer are set forth — the strange dreams in perhaps an unorthodox way, the fond dreams in a distinctively catholic way.

Closer in objectives to the present list are those by Jackson and Marco, the first with a special concern for biography, the second as part of a Pan-American perspective. In both cases the scope includes reference sources in general, e.g., directories, dictionaries, and even a few essays as well as bibliographies. Marco's classified arrangement is laid out below to suggest an alternative to the one devised for this handbook. The present author's essay in the 1986 Grove set mirrors the present list in many particulars, although it is delimited along somewhat different lines, reflecting the overall plan of the dictionary as a whole. While the 1947 Hitchcock bibliography is an intellectual progenitor of the present book, equal respect must be paid to John Davies's *Musicalia* (Oxford: Pergamon, 1966, 1969), which conceptually addresses the specialized needs of different communities as its basis for organizing the bibliographical record.

Bio-Bibliographical Index of Musicians (1940; see 188 above). The "Bibliography" (pp. xvii–xxiii) lists the sixty-six titles indexed along with twelve supplementary titles, these constituting the generally recognized corpus of American musical scholarship at the time.

Bibliographic Index: A Cumulative Bibliography of Bibliographies, 1937– .
New York: Wilson, 1938– . LC 46-41034. ISSN 0006-1255. A miscellany of lists can be found under "Music" and related subject headings, mostly of interest to general readers, a few of the lists not accessible elsewhere.   [746.

H. Wiley Hitchcock. "A Bibliography of American Music." Unpublished syllabus for the course Music Literature 125 at the University of Michigan, dated Dec. 1, 1947, and covering about 1,200 books, articles, and recordings.   [747.

Harold Gleason. *Music Literature Outlines [Series III]: Early American Music.* Rochester, N.Y.: Levis Music Stores, 1955. LC 71-209504. 2d ed., with C. Warren Becker. Bloomington, Ind.: Frangipani Press, 1981. ISBN 0-89917-265-2. Numerous bibliographical references are cited in context in the text and in separate lists.   [748.

Julius R. Chitwood. "The Development of Music Bibliography in the United States." M.A. thesis, University of Chicago, 1954. Includes a "Bibliography of Bibliographies of Music Literature Separately Published in the United States before 1955" (pp. 57–63), listing seventy-six titles.   [749.

Library of Congress, General Reference and Bibliography Division. *A Guide to the Study of the United States of America: Representative Books Reflecting the Development of American Life and Thought.* Washington: Government Printing Office, 1960. LC 60-60009. *Supplement.* 1976.

The music section in the original set includes eighty-two well-selected titles with careful annotations, the *Supplement* thirty-five more. [750.

Karl Kroeger. "Bibliography," in John Tasker Howard, *Our American Music*, 4th ed. (New York: Thomas Y. Crowell, 1965), pp. 769–845. Although now somewhat out-of-date, the list of about 1,000 titles in this particular ed. can still serve as a model for a general selective bibliography of the field. [751.

Edward N. Waters. "Problems of Music Bibliography in the United States," in *Papers of the Yugoslav-American Seminar on Music*, ed. Malcolm H. Brown (Bloomington: Indiana University, School of Music and Russian and East European Institute, 1970), pp. 95–112. Observations on recent scholarly studies, some of them only indirectly bibliographical or otherwise related mostly to European music. [752.

G. Thomas Tanselle. *Guide to the Study of United States Imprints.* Cambridge: Harvard University Press, 1971. ISBN 0-674-36761-8. Organized by A: "Regional Lists" (pp. 1–67); B: "Genre Lists" (pp. 68–161); C: "Author Lists" (pp. 162–302); D: "Copyright Records" (pp. 303–6); E: "Catalogues" (pp. 307–97); F: "Book-Trade Directories" (pp. 398–403); G: "Studies of Individual Printers and Publishers" (beginning vol. 2; pp. 405–762); H: "General Studies" (pp. 763–887); and I: "Checklists of Secondary Material" (pp. 888–94). Music entries are cited mostly under the region, genre, and publisher, accessible through the index. See the present author's analysis of the music coverage, with addenda, *Yearbook for Inter-American Music Research*, 8 (1972), 140–46. [753.

David Horn. *The Literature of American Music* (1972, 1977; see 296 above).

Richard Jackson. *United States Music: Sources of Bibliography and Collective Biography.* Brooklyn, N.Y.: Institute for Studies in American Music, 1973. LC 73-80637. Covers ninety major reference sources, with annotations at once both delightfully opinionated and highly authoritative. [754.

Frederick Freedman. "Some Publishers of Books (and Anthologies) in American Music." Handout for a meeting of the Music Library

Association, Urbana, Ill., Feb. 2, 1974, with brief citations of about 500 titles, arranged by publisher and useful as a record of the intentions of publishers during the heyday of reprinting. The reprint business of the "post-Sputnik era" and its impact on American music studies are also discussed in the present author's "The Facsimiliad," *Yearbook for Inter-American Musical Research,* 7 (1971), 135–60.   [755.

H. Wiley Hitchcock. "Sources for the Study of American Music," *American Studies International,* vol. 14, no. 2 (Winter 1975), pp. 3–9. Commentary on the state of scholarship as reflected in major studies.   [756.

Guy A. Marco, Ann M. Garfield, and Sharon Paugh Ferris. *Information on Music: A Handbook of Reference Sources in European Languages, Volume II, The Americas.* Littleton, Colo.: Libraries Unlimited, 1977. ISBN 0-87287-141-X. The section devoted to the United States is arranged thus:
1. Direct information sources (pp. 35–76) further divided as introductions and general surveys, folk music and folksong (subdivided by Indian music, Anglo-American folk music, country-and-western music, other folk music), popular music (subdivided by general, theater music, including film, songs, jazz, ragtime and blues, rock to soul), opera and vocal music, church and religious music, music theory and musicology, historical studies, chronologies, contemporary narratives, regional and local histories, music printing and publishing, directories, periodicals, instruments, performing groups, black American music.
2. Biographical sources (pp. 76–80).
3. Guides to other sources (pp. 81–82).
4. Lists of music (pp. 83–90), subdivided as bibliographies of lists of music, selective and critical lists, popular music, instrumental music, opera and vocal music, lists of music by black composers, lists of early music, lists of nineteenth- and twentieth-century music, annual and periodic lists.
5. Discographies (pp. 90–93), subdivided as folk music and folksong and popular music.

The subject index is a useful complement to this perspective, the conceptual features of which can be best grasped through a careful reading of p. 274.   [757.

Bertrun Delli. "Music." Section R. in Bernard Karpel, *Arts in America:*

232

A Bibliography (Washington: Smithsonian Institution Press, 1979), 84 unpaginated pp. in vol. 3. A rather miscellaneous assortment of titles, covered by a detailed index in vol. 4.   [758.

Resources of American Music History (1981; see 443 above). Major reference sources are cited in the "Bibliography," pp. 11–13.

The New Grove Dictionary of American Music. Edited by H. Wiley Hitchcock and Stanley Sadie. London: Macmillan; New York: Grove's Dictionaries of Music, 1986. Includes citations under "Bibliographies" (vol. 1, pp. 206–13) and "Dictionaries" (vol. 1, pp. 612–22; by Diane O. Ota), each with about 250 titles, as well as under particular name and subject entries.   [759.

Jack Salzman. *American Studies: An Annotated Bibliography.* Cambridge: Cambridge University Press, 1986. ISBN 0-521-32555-2. Limited to books and annotated for general readers. The "Music" section (pp. 965–83 in vol. 2) has 445 entries (classified, with 36 "General Music," 94 "Classical and Concert," 71 "Folk and Country," 43 "Blues," 121 "Jazz," and 80 "Popular and Rock"), and is preceded by a brief essay by Barbara L. Tischler.   [760.

Name and Subject Index

Our American Music (Howard), 751, p. 189
Outdoor amusements, 300
Owens, William A., p. 60
Ozark Folksongs (Randolph), 90

Paine, Silas K., pp. 161, 163
Pan American Union, 191
Pan Pipes of Sigma Alpha Iota, 189, p. 51
Pantomime, p. 27
Panzeri, Louis, 84
Parker, James, 702
Parlor music, 661
Pastoral Music, p. 51
Patriotic songs, pp. 142–44
Patterson, Daniel W., 619
Pavlakis, Christopher, 684
Pazdirek, Franz, p. 41
Pebworth, James R., 85
Peck, Mariol R., 103
Pennsylvania, early German music, 695
A Penny from Heaven (Winkler), 715
Perabo, Johann Ernst, p. 163
Percussion music, 263, p. 52
Percussive Notes, p. 52
Performance, history of, pp. 110–11
Performing Arts Research (Whalen), 555
Periodicals, pp. 19–21, 36–41, 50–53, 170–75
Periodization of American music, p. 9
Perkins, Charles Callahan, p. 65
Perlis, Vivian, 736
Perry, Edward D., 290
Perspectives of New Music (Basart index), 485
Peters, Harry T., 633
Peters, William Cumming, 744
Peterson, Caralyn Sue, 375
Pfatteicher, Helen E., 410
Phemister, William, 282
Philadelphia, 714, 734

Phillips, Linda Nell, 272
Phonolog, 577
Photographs, 121, 467. *See also* Iconography
The Pianist's Resource Guide (Rezits and Deatsman), 52
Piano concertos, 282
"A Piano in Every Parlor" (Pray), 106
Piano music, 269, pp. 50, 52, 106–8 passim
"Piano Music by Black Composers" (Phillips), 272
Piano Quarterly, p. 52
Piano sonatas, 265
The Piano Trio in the Twentieth Century (Ping-Robbins), 281
A Pictorial Bibliography of . . . Stephen C. Foster (Fuld), 203
Picture the Songs (Levy), 662
Pierce, Deborah, p. 52
Pierpont Morgan Library, p. 164
Piersol, Jon L., 486
Ping-Robbins, Nancy R., 281
Pioneer Discography Series, p. 202
Pitts, Lilla Belle, 543
"A Pittsburgh Collection of Nineteenth Century Household Music" (Thomas), 740
Pittsburgh Theological Seminary, pp. 160–61
Ploski, Harry A., 151
Poe, Edgar Allan, 221
Poetry, p. 91
Polish music, 176
Pollock, Bruce, 344
Pond, William A., 712
Poole, William F., 23
Poole's Index to Periodical Literature, 23
Popular culture, 298–99
Popular Music: An Annotated Guide to Recordings (Tudor and Tudor), 612
Popular Music: An Annotated Index (Shapiro and Pollock), 343

Books in the Series Music in American Life